Chi's Sweet Home

チーズ スイートホーム

11

Konami Kanata

D0026991

contents
homemade 183~200+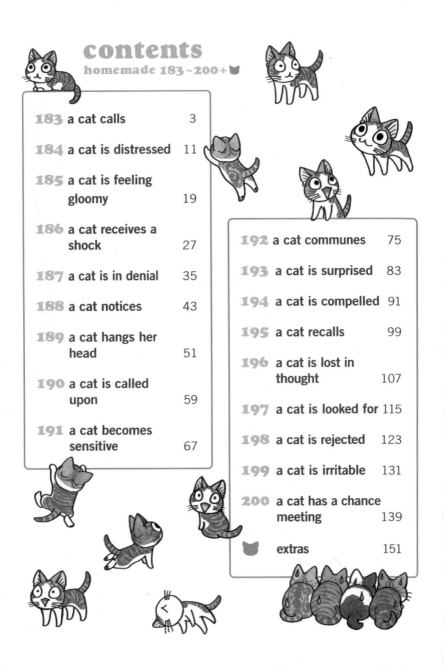

homemade 183: a cat calls

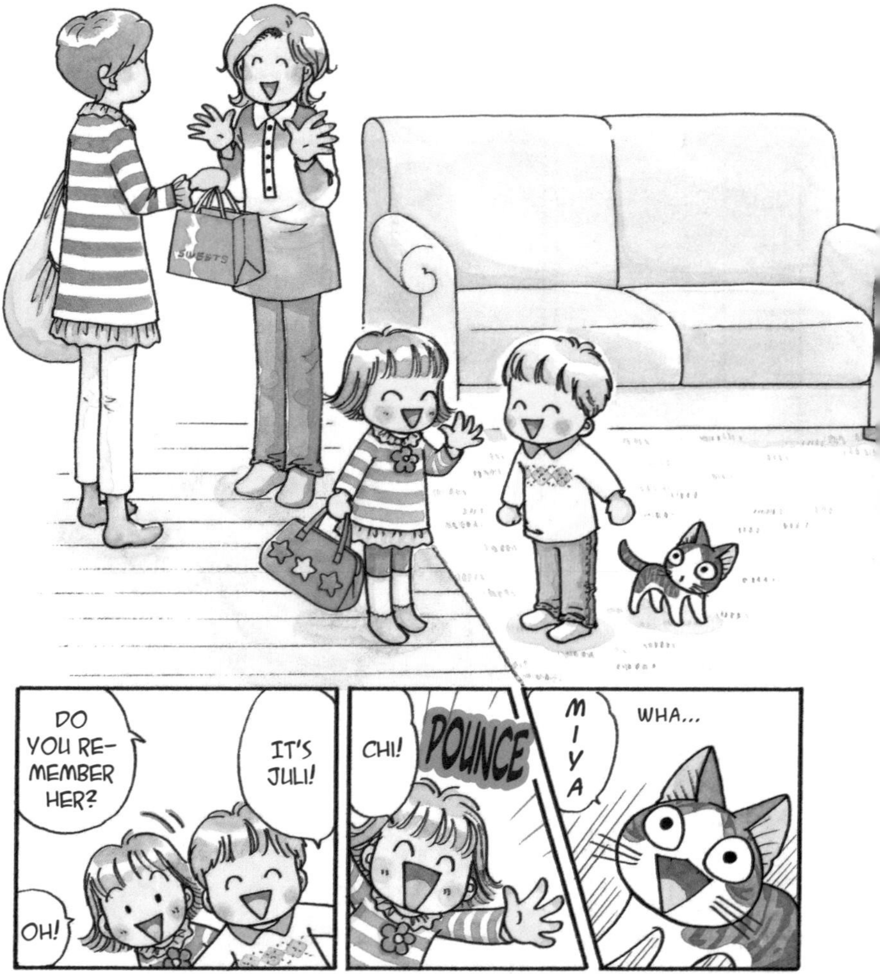

DO YOU RE-MEMBER HER?
IT'S JULI!
OH!
CHI!
POUNCE
MIYA
WHA...

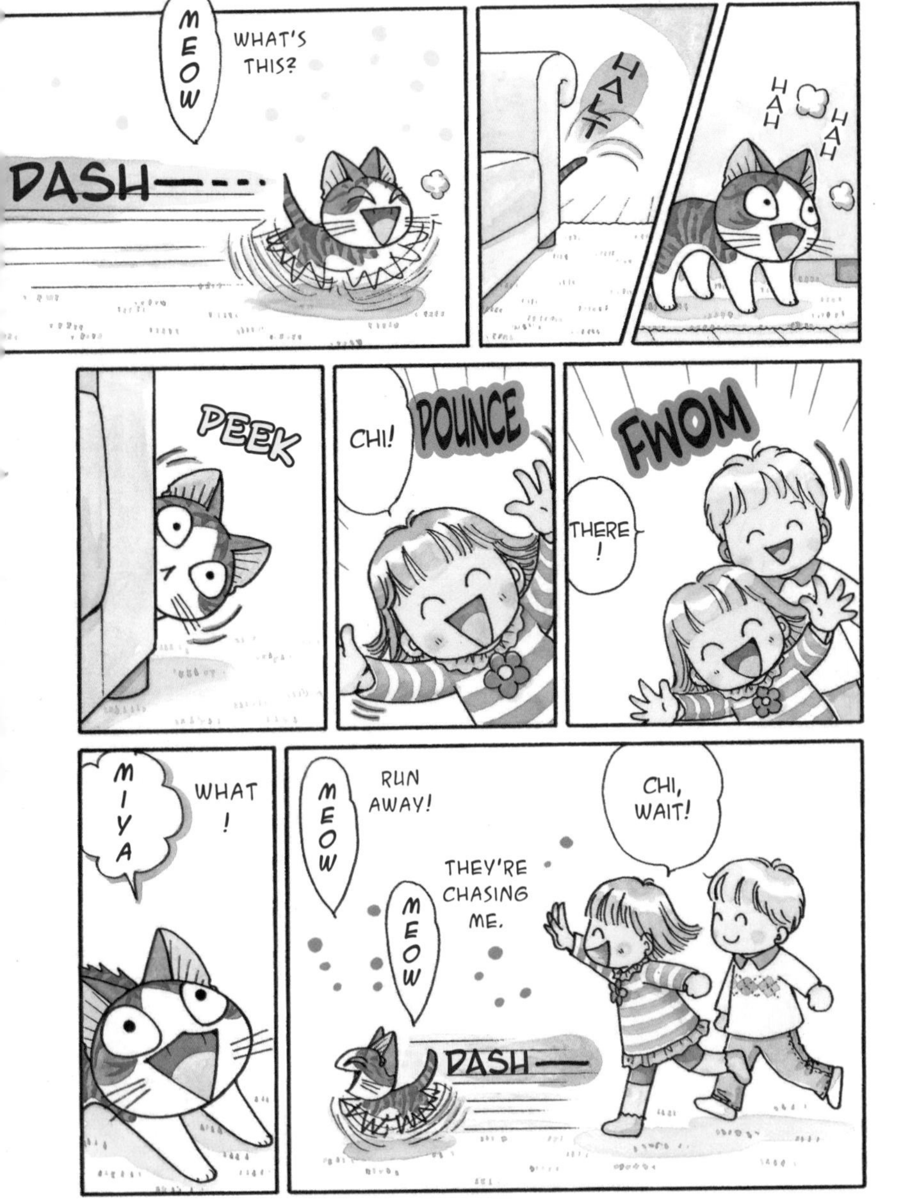
MEOW
WHAT'S THIS?
DASH—
HALT
HAH HAH
PEEK
CHI!
POUNCE
FWOM
THERE!
MIYA
WHAT!
MEOW
RUN AWAY!
CHI, WAIT!
THEY'RE CHASING ME.
MEOW
DASH—

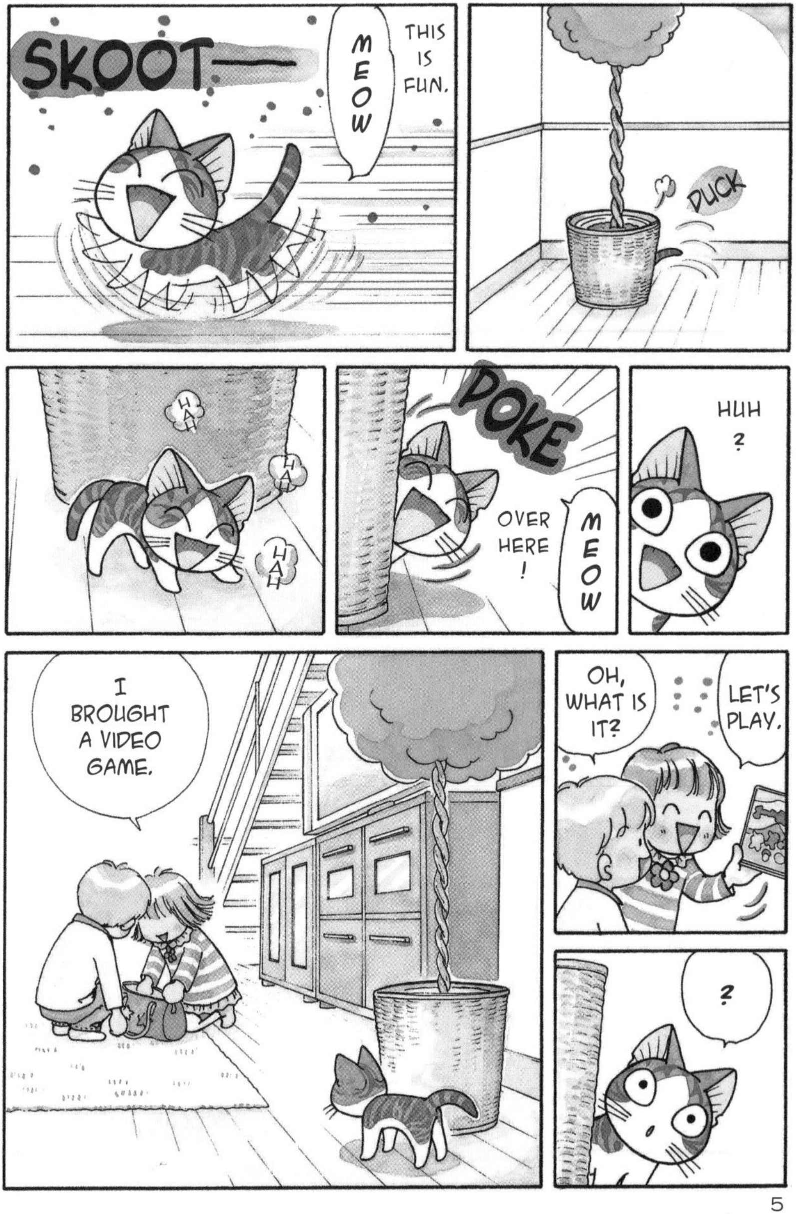
SKOOT——
MEOW
THIS IS FUN.
DUCK
HAH
HAH
HAH
DOKE
OVER HERE!
MEOW
HUH?
I BROUGHT A VIDEO GAME.
OH, WHAT IS IT?
LET'S PLAY.
?

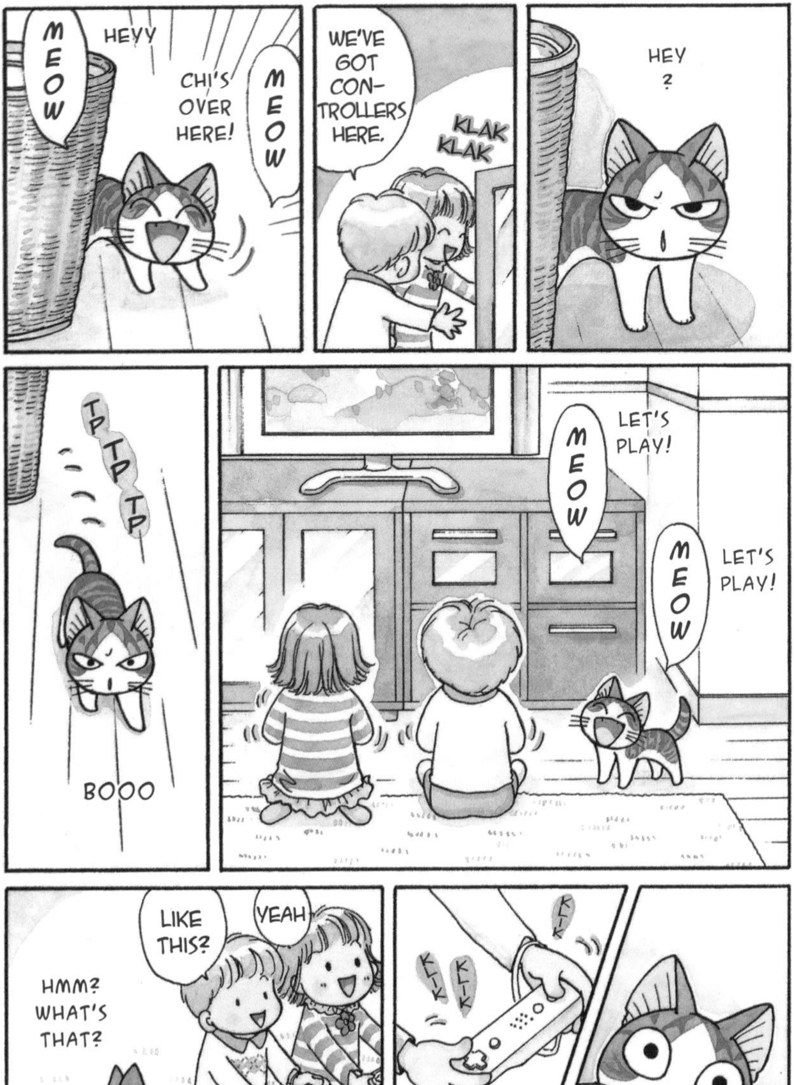
MEOW
HEYY
CHI'S OVER HERE!
MEOW
WE'VE GOT CON-TROLLERS HERE.
KLAK KLAK
HEY ?
TP TP TP
BOOO
MEOW
LET'S PLAY!
MEOW
LET'S PLAY!
LIKE THIS?
YEAH
HMM? WHAT'S THAT?
KLIK
KLIK
KLIK
KLIK

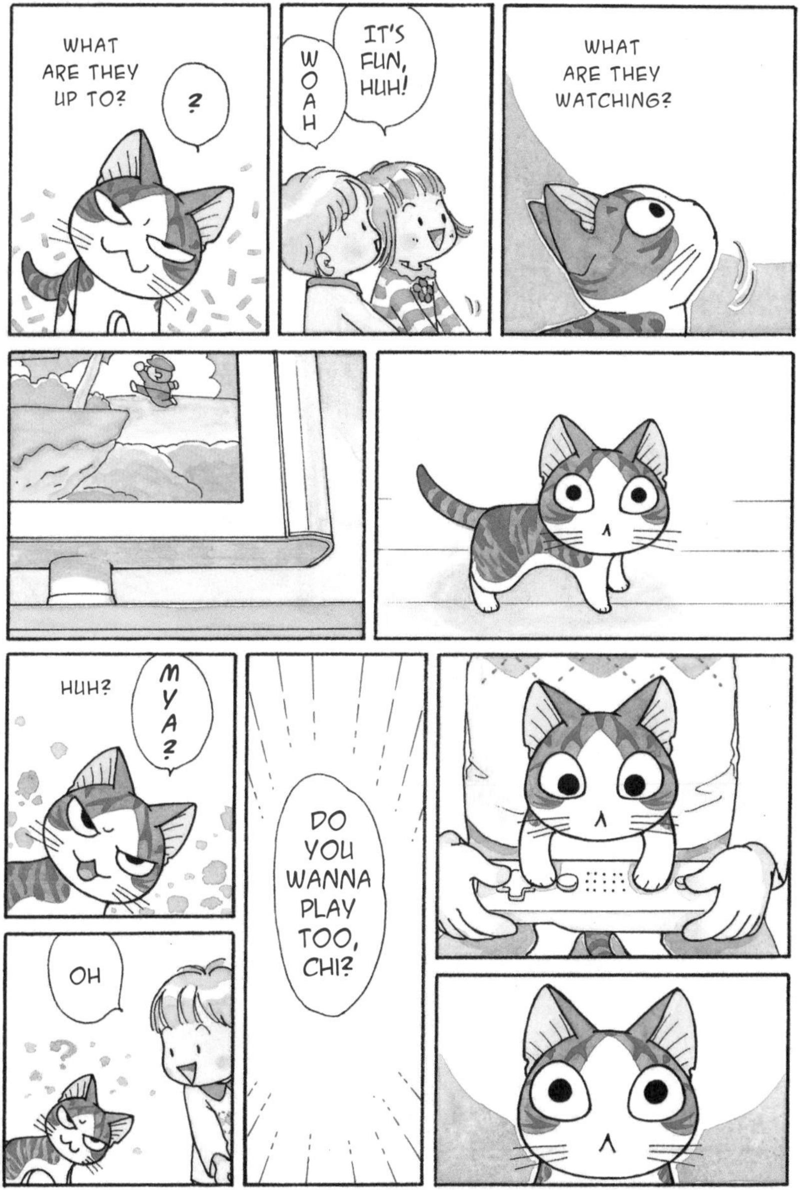
WHAT ARE THEY UP TO?
?
WOAH
IT'S FUN, HUH!
WHAT ARE THEY WATCHING?
HUH?
MYA?
OH
DO YOU WANNA PLAY TOO, CHI?

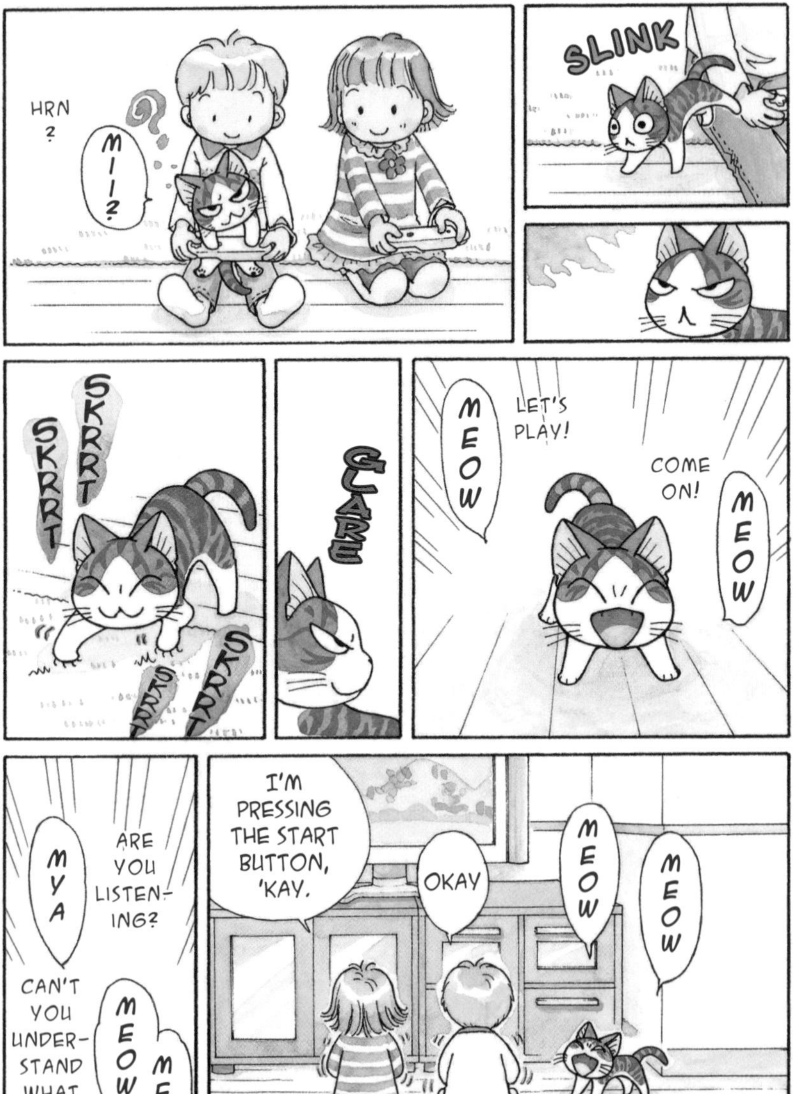
HRN ?
MII ?
SLINK
SKRRT SKRRT
SKRRT SKRRT
GLARE
MEOW
LET'S PLAY!
COME ON!
MEOW
ARE YOU LISTENING?
MYA
CAN'T YOU UNDERSTAND WHAT CHI'S SAYING ?
MEOW
MEOW
I'M PRESSING THE START BUTTON, 'KAY.
OKAY
MEOW
MEOW

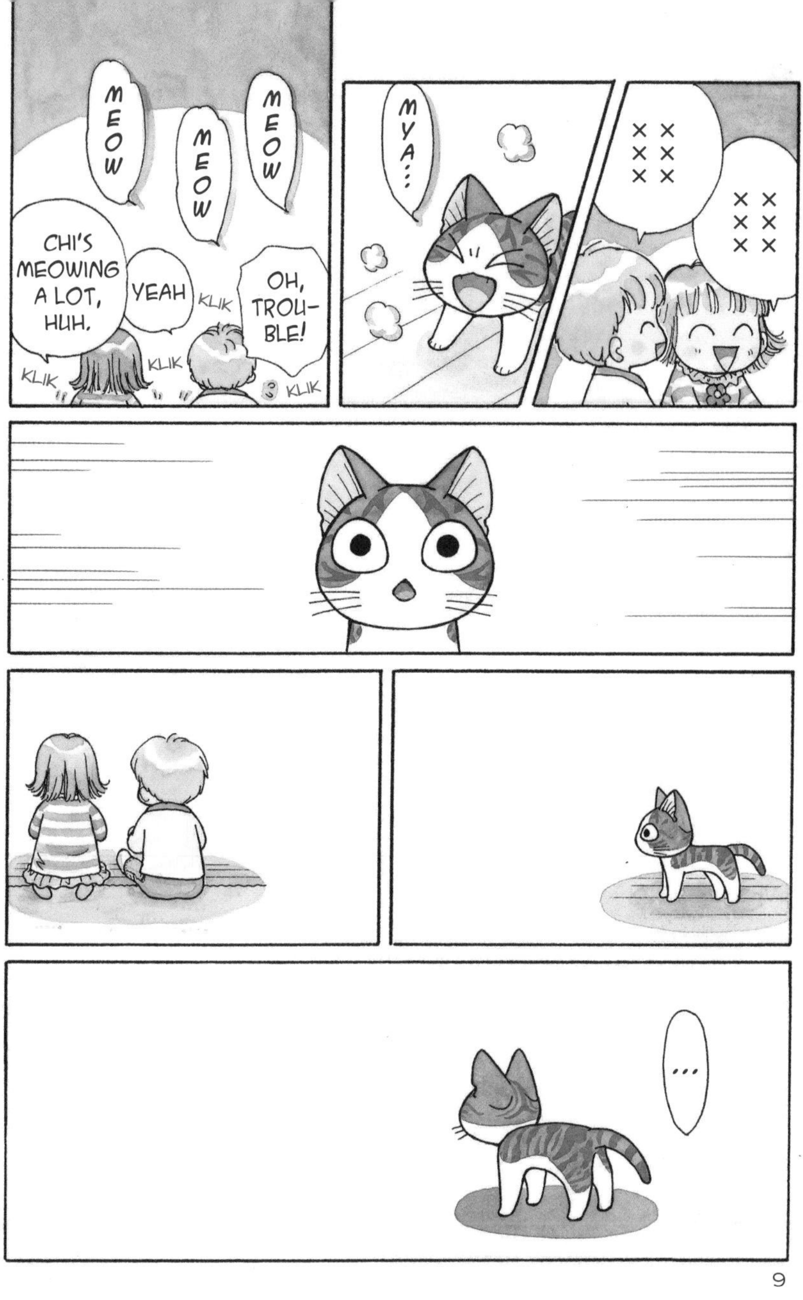
MEOW
MEOW
MEOW
CHI'S MEOWING A LOT, HUH.
YEAH
KLIK
OH, TROUBLE!
KLIK
KLIK
KLIK
MYA...
...

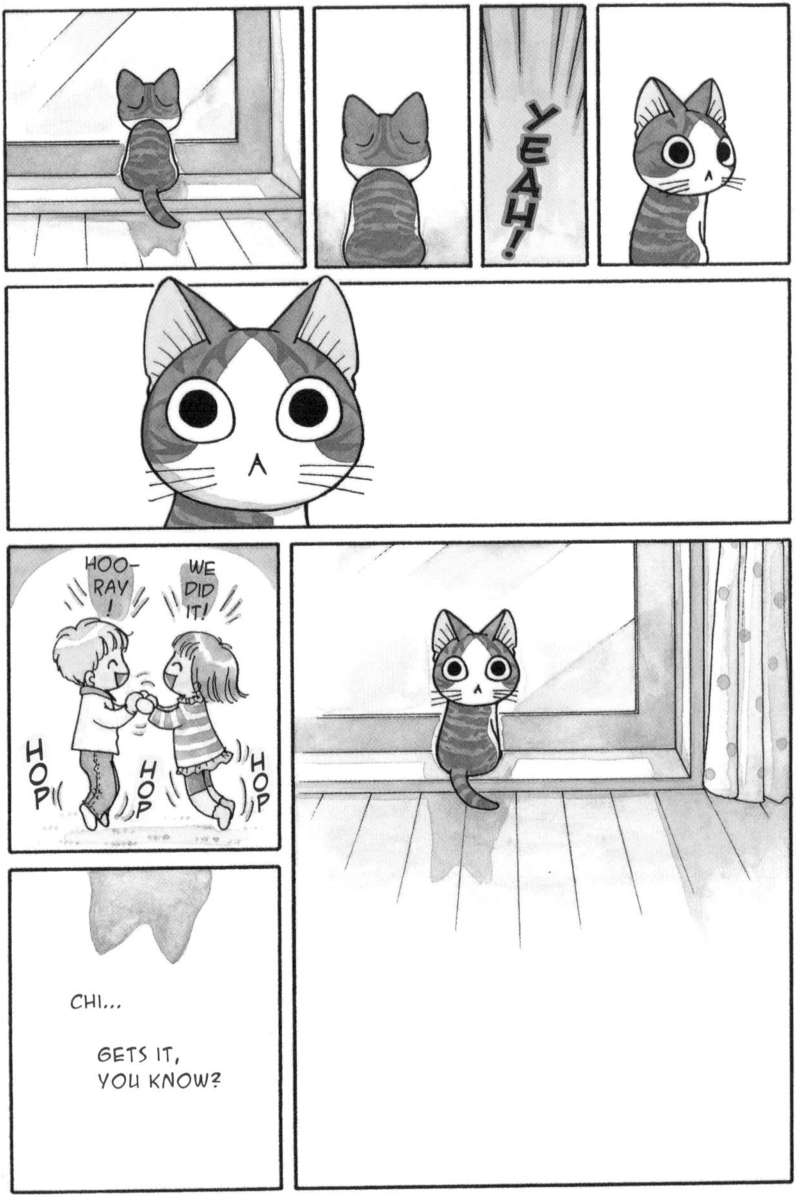
YEAH!
HOO-RAY!
WE DID IT!
HOP
HOP
HOP
CHI...
GETS IT, YOU KNOW?

the end

homemade 184: a cat is distressed

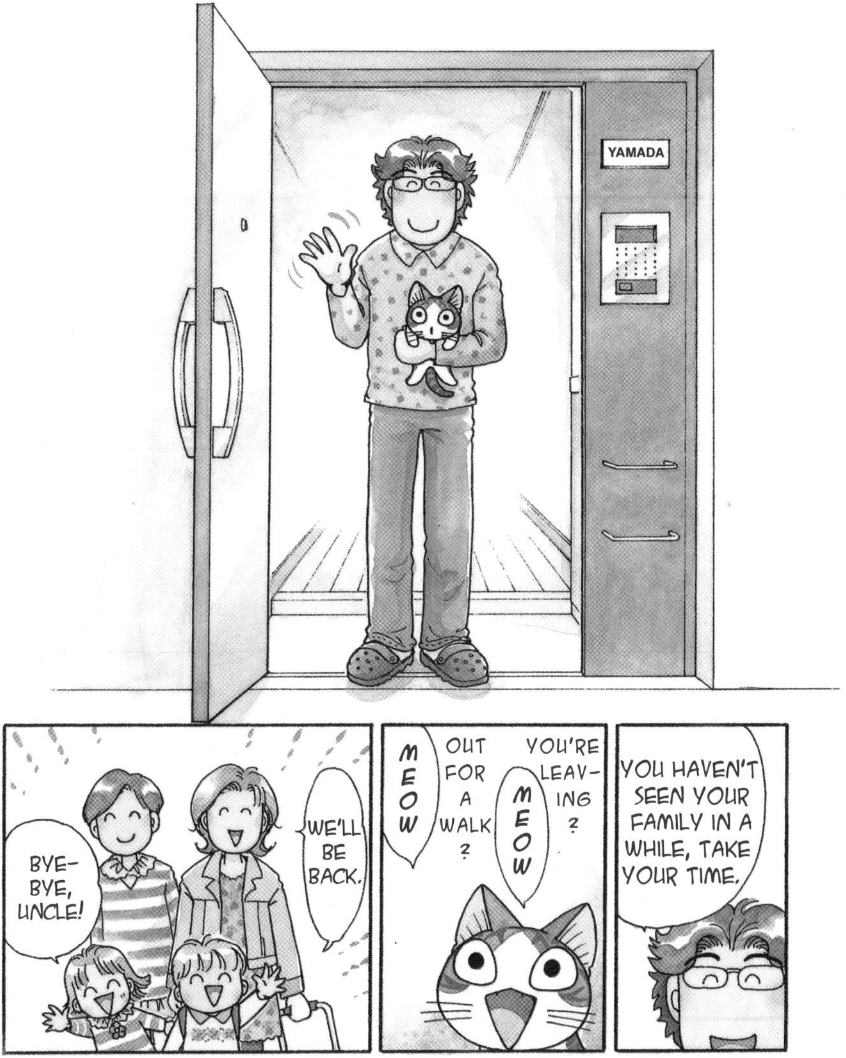
YAMADA
BYE-BYE, UNCLE!
WE'LL BE BACK.
MEOW
OUT FOR A WALK?
MEOW
YOU'RE LEAVING?
YOU HAVEN'T SEEN YOUR FAMILY IN A WHILE, TAKE YOUR TIME.

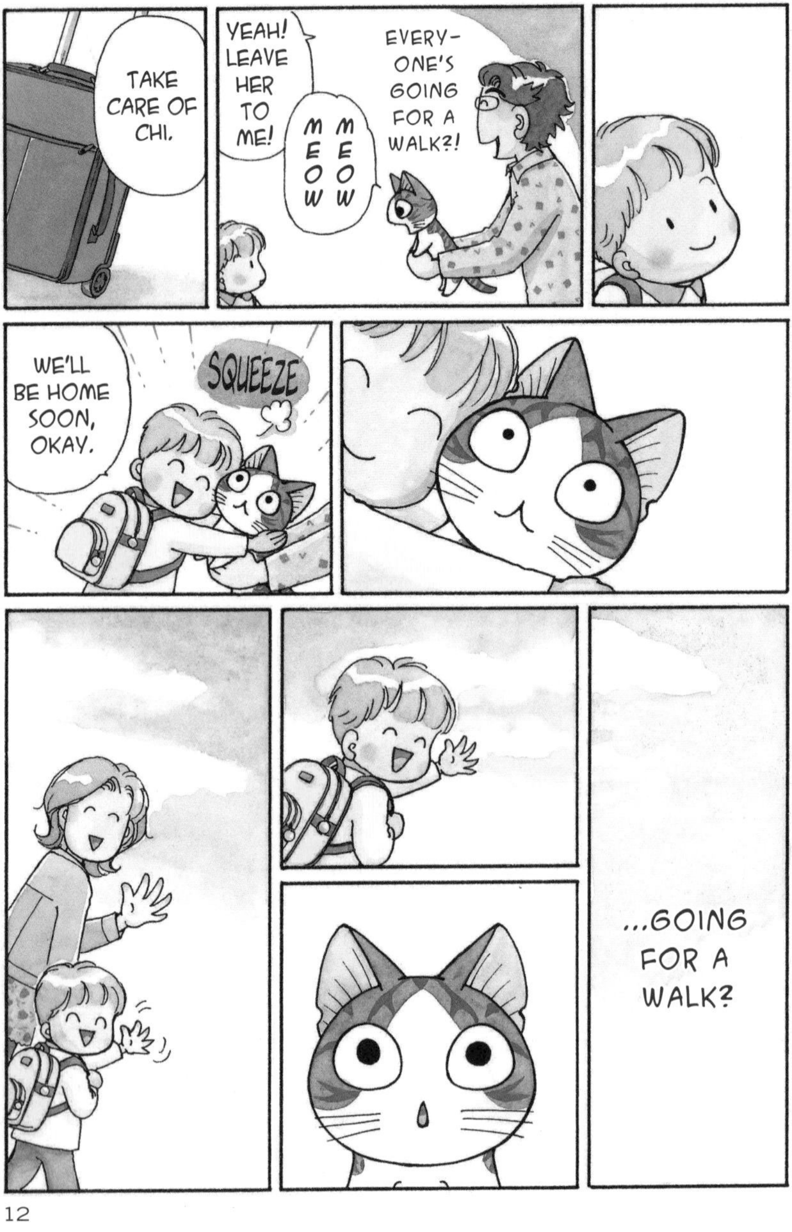
TAKE CARE OF CHI.
YEAH! LEAVE HER TO ME!
EVERYONE'S GOING FOR A WALK?!
MEOW MEOW
WE'LL BE HOME SOON, OKAY.
SQUEEZE
...GOING FOR A WALK?

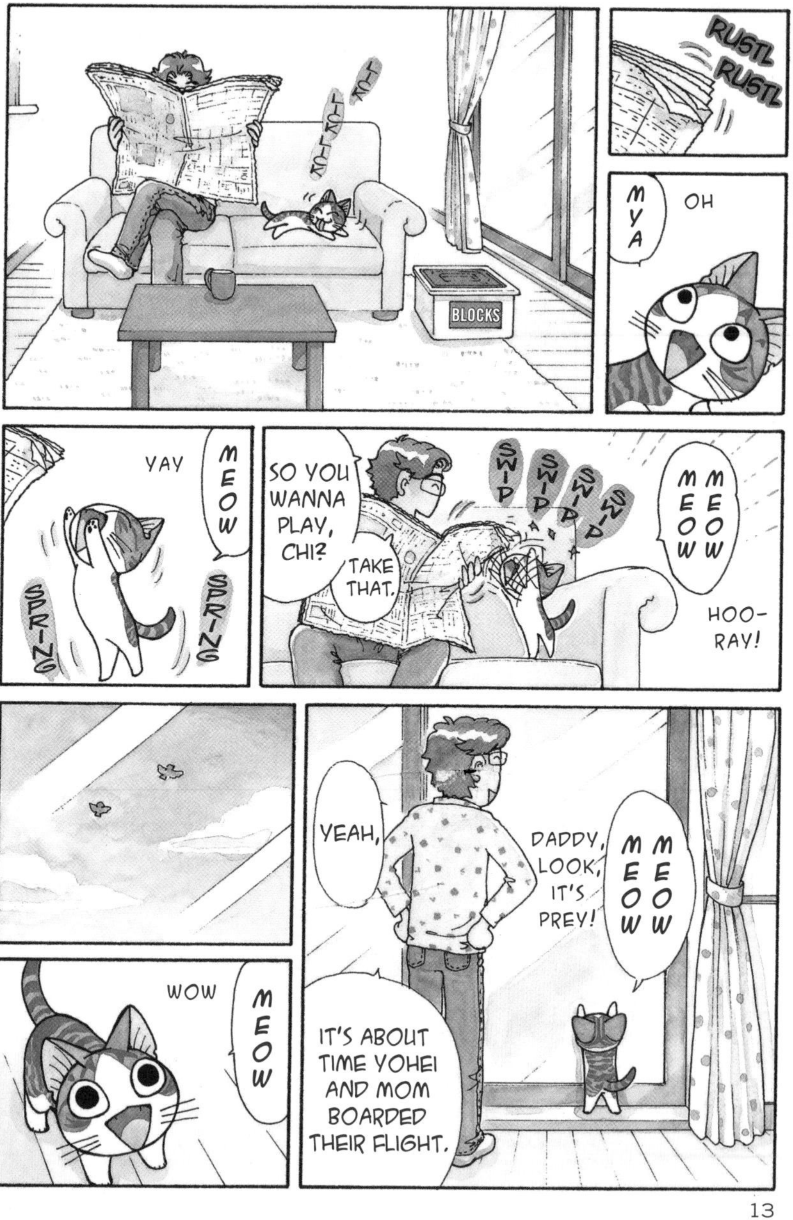
LICK LICK LICK
RUSTL RUSTL
MYA
OH
YAY
MEOW
SPRING SPRING
SO YOU WANNA PLAY, CHI?
TAKE THAT.
SWIP SWIP SWIP SWIP
MEOW MEOW
HOO-RAY!
WOW
MEOW
MEOW MEOW
DADDY, LOOK, IT'S PREY!
YEAH,
IT'S ABOUT TIME YOHEI AND MOM BOARDED THEIR FLIGHT.

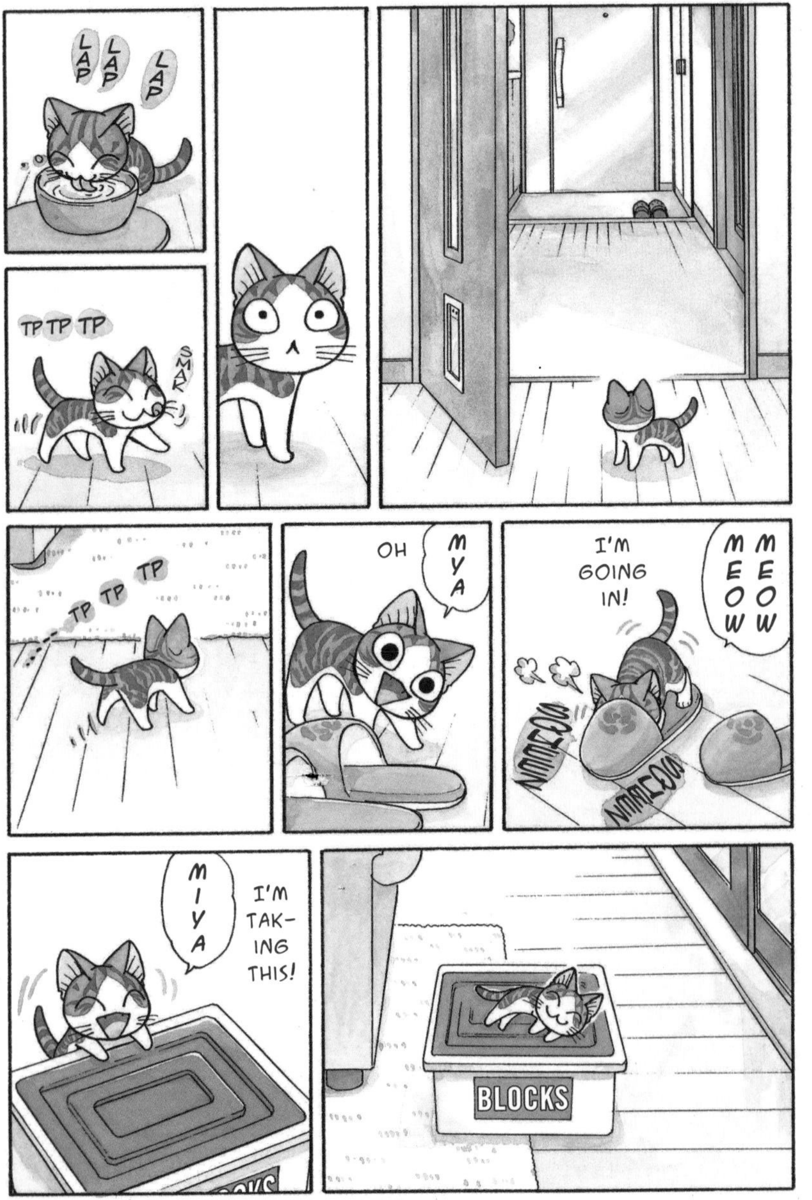
LAP LAP LAP
TP TP TP
SMAK
TP TP TP
OH
MYA
I'M GOING IN!
MEOW MEOW
NMMEOW
NMMEOW
MIYA
I'M TAK-ING THIS!
BLOCKS

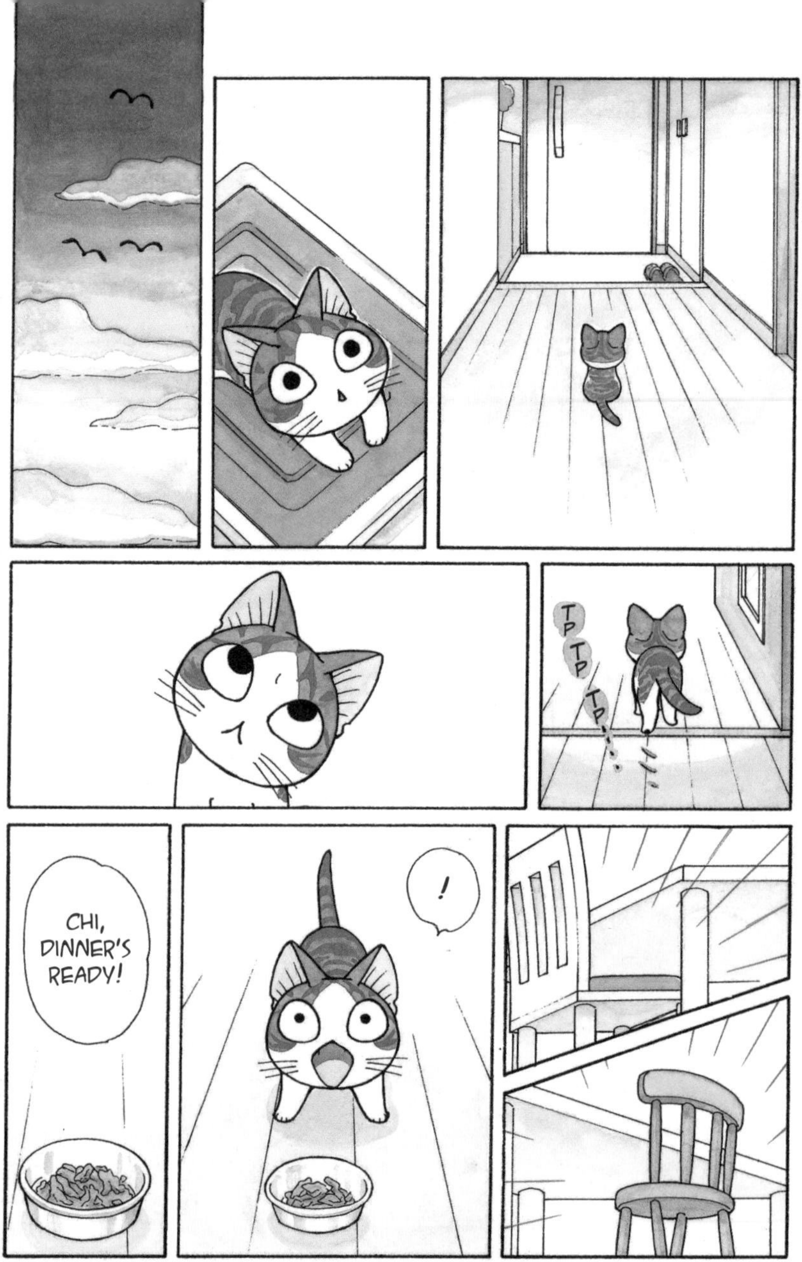
TP TP TP TP...
CHI, DINNER'S READY!
!

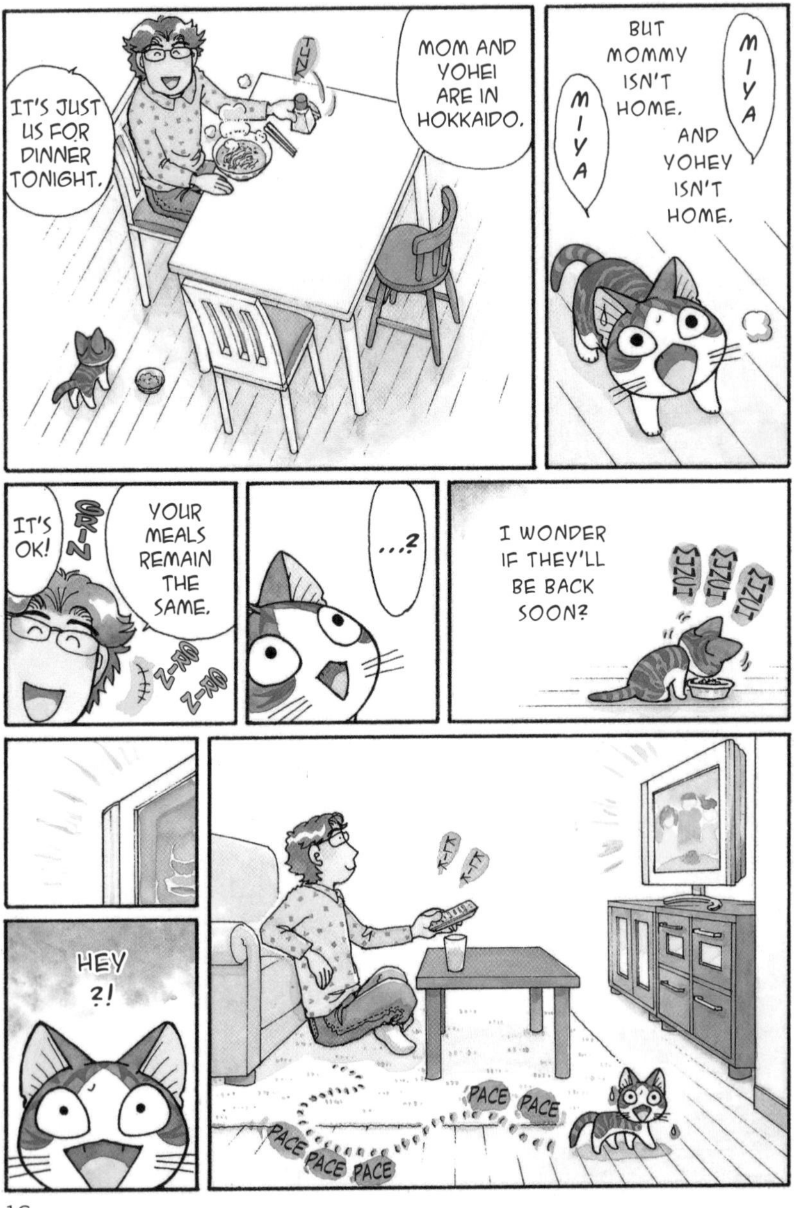
IT'S JUST US FOR DINNER TONIGHT.
MOM AND YOHEI ARE IN HOKKAIDO.
BUT MOMMY ISN'T HOME.
MIYA
AND YOHEY ISN'T HOME.
MIYA
IT'S OK!
GRIN
YOUR MEALS REMAIN THE SAME.
...?
I WONDER IF THEY'LL BE BACK SOON?
HEY ?!
PACE PACE
PACE PACE PACE

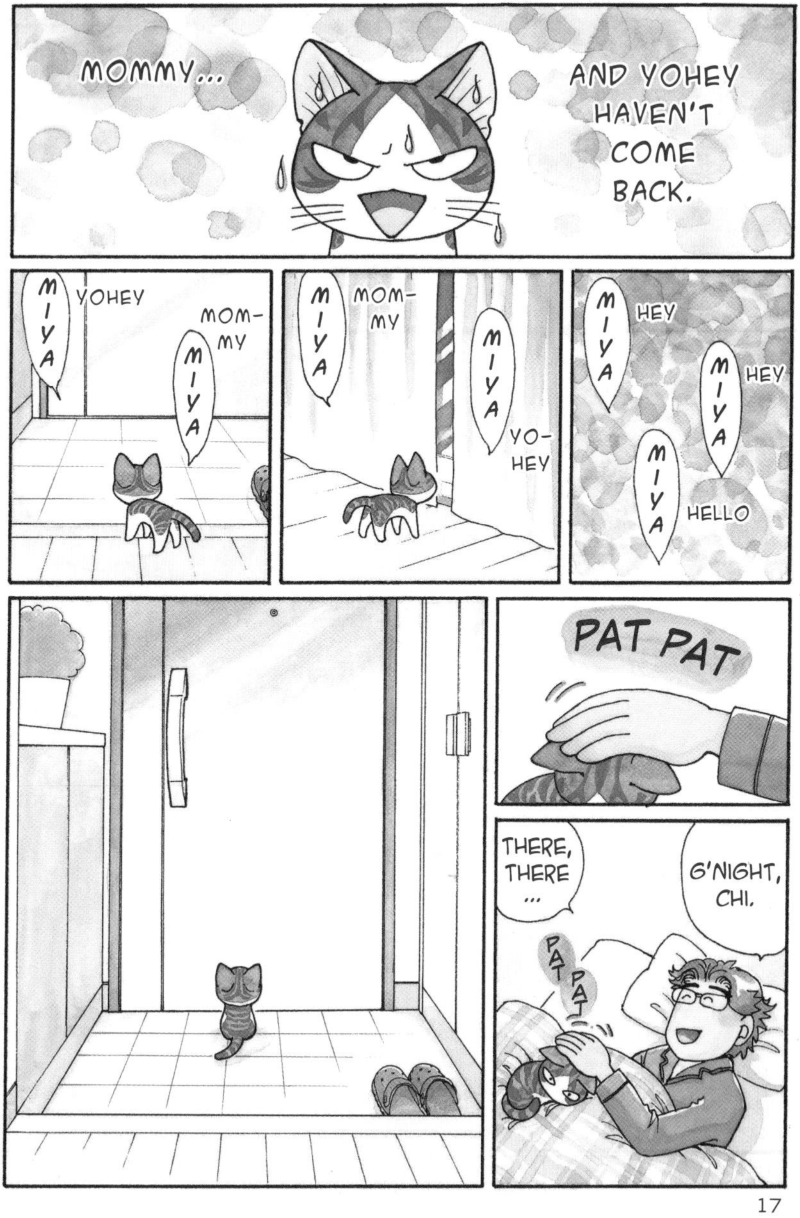
MOMMY...
AND YOHEY HAVEN'T COME BACK.
MIYA
YOHEY
MOM-MY
MIYA
MIYA
MOM-MY
MIYA
YO-HEY
MIYA
HEY
MIYA
HEY
MIYA
HELLO
PAT PAT
THERE, THERE ...
G'NIGHT, CHI.
PAT PAT

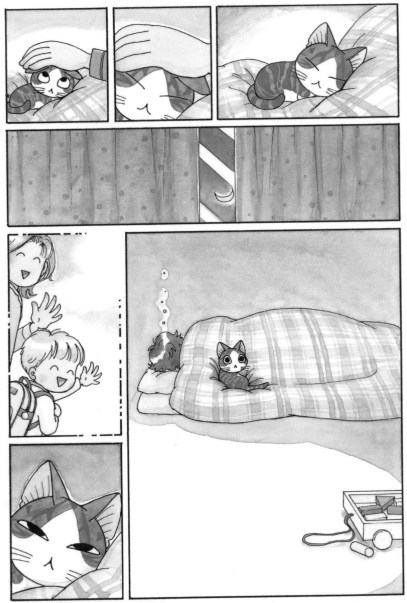

the end

homemade 185: a cat is feeling gloomy

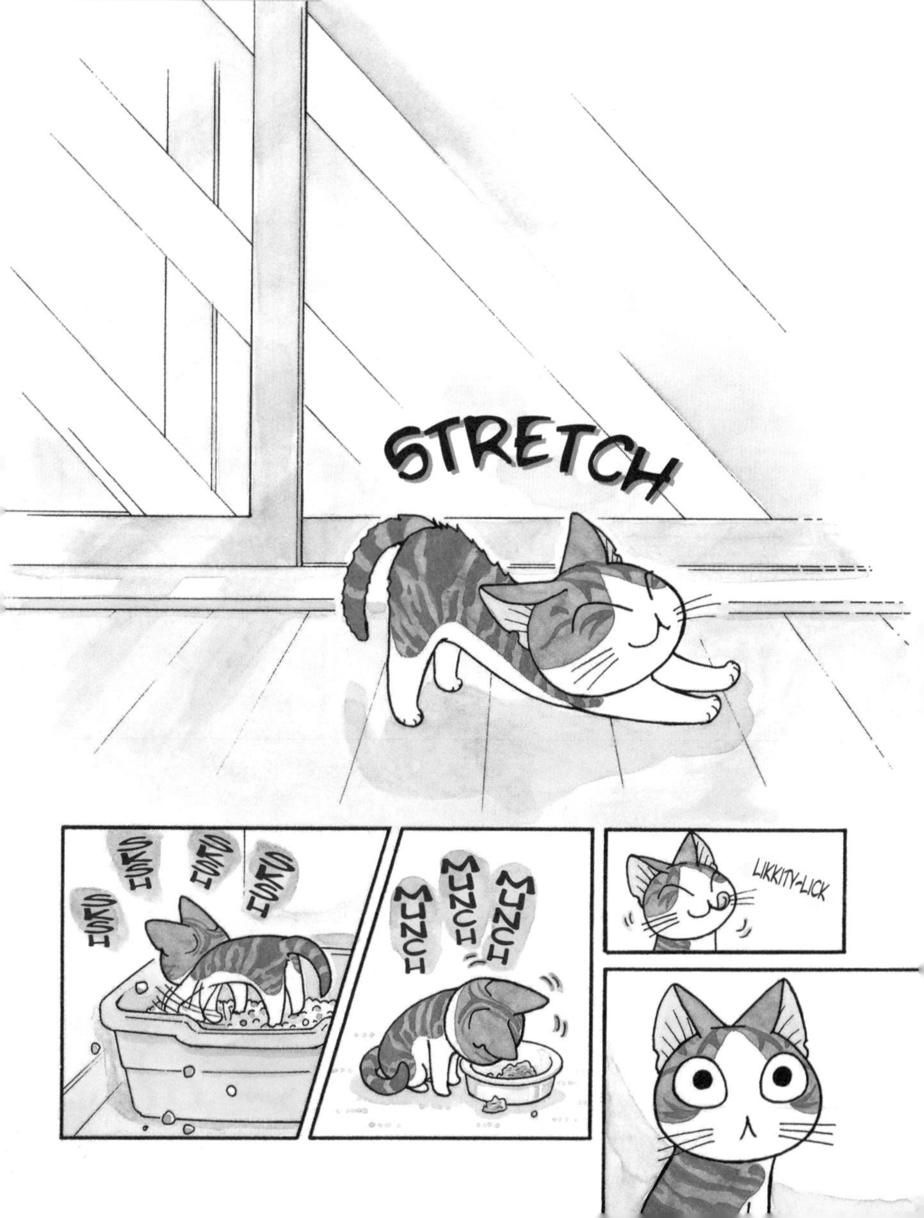
STRETCH
SKRSH
SKRSH
SKRSH
SKRSH
MUNCH
MUNCH
MUNCH
LIKKITY-LICK

MIYA DADDY MEOW YOHEY'S NOT HERE.

NEITHER IS MOMMY. MEOW

WHAT'S UP, CHI?

WAS BREAKFAST GOOD?

RUB RUB

GREAT.

?

ALL RIGHT...

I'VE GOTTA DO SOME WORK,

SO I'LL BE UPSTAIRS.

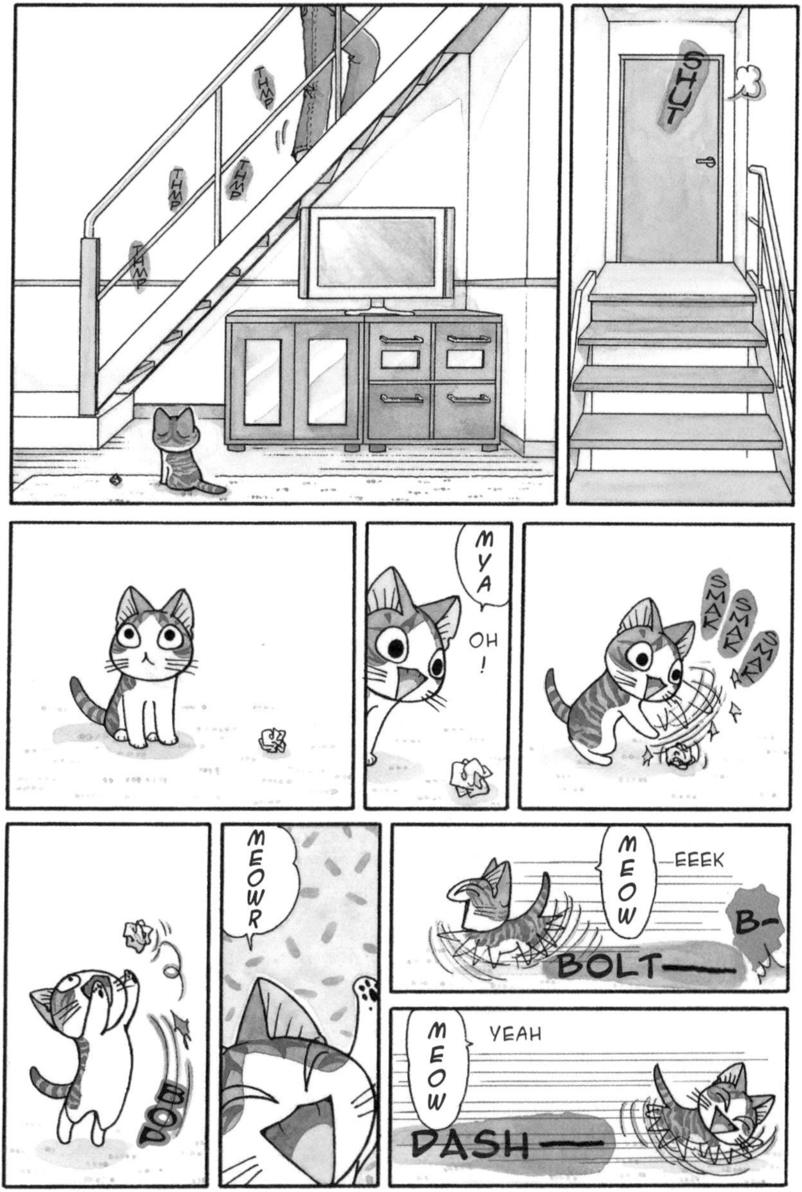
THMP
THMP
THMP
THMP
SHUT
MYA
OH!
SMAK
SMAK
SMAK
BOP
MEOWR
MEOW
EEEK
B-
BOLT——
MEOW
YEAH
DASH——

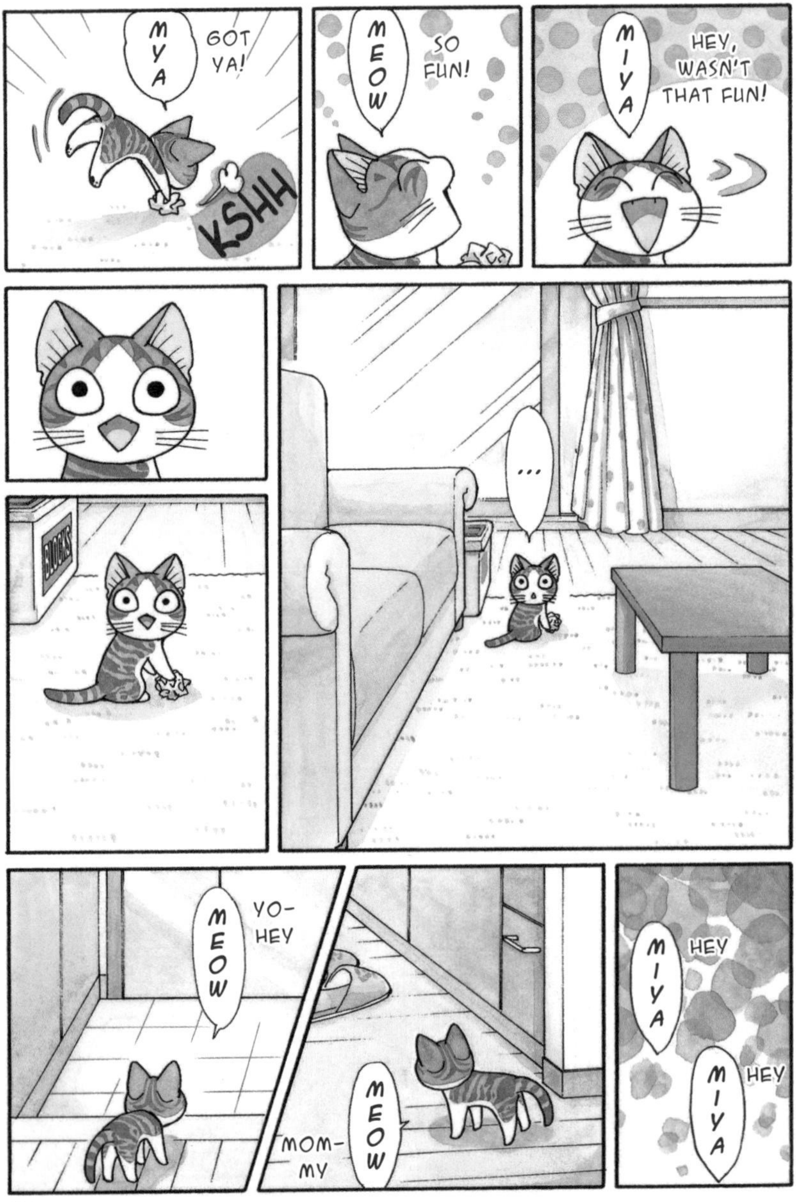
MYA
GOT YA!
KSHH
MEOW
SO FUN!
MIYA
HEY, WASN'T THAT FUN!
...
BLOCKS
MEOW
YO-HEY
MEOW
MOM-MY
MIYA
HEY
MIYA
HEY

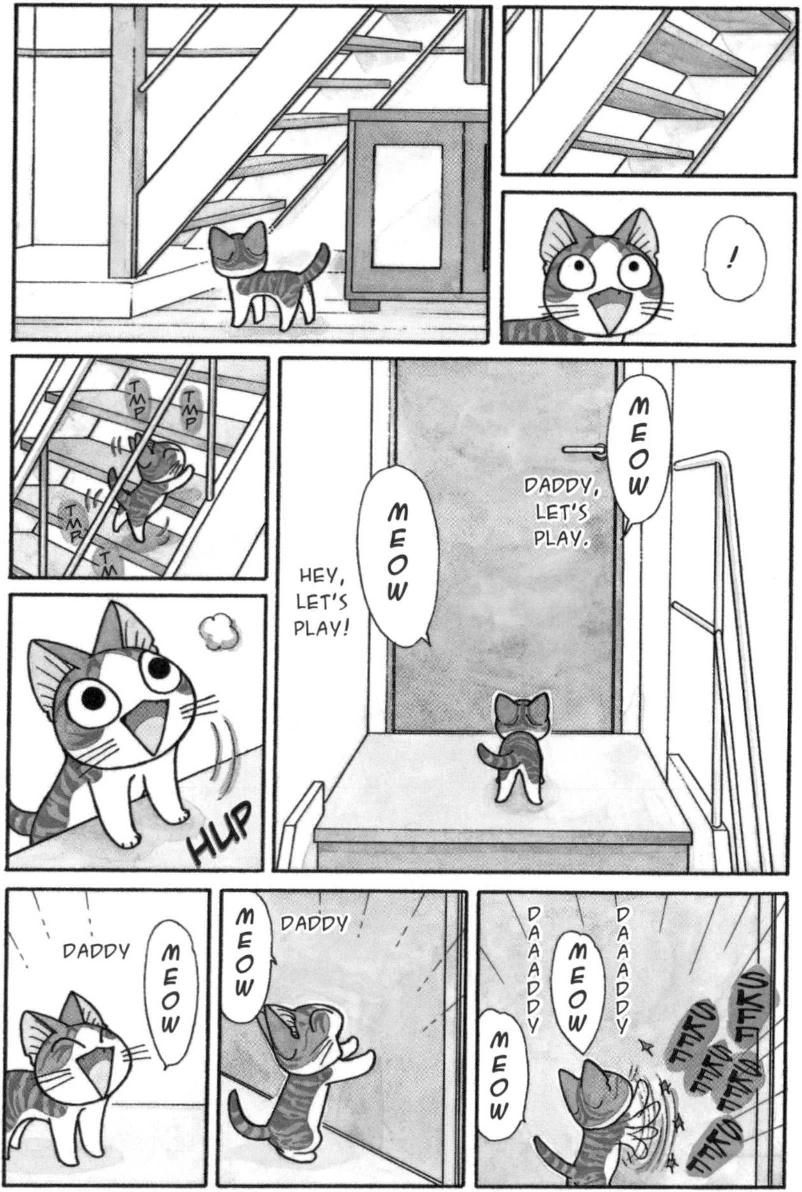
!
TMP
TMP
TMP
TM
HUP
MEOW
DADDY, LET'S PLAY.
MEOW
HEY, LET'S PLAY!
DADDY
MEOW
MEOW
DADDY
DAAAADDY
MEOW
DAAAADDY
MEOW

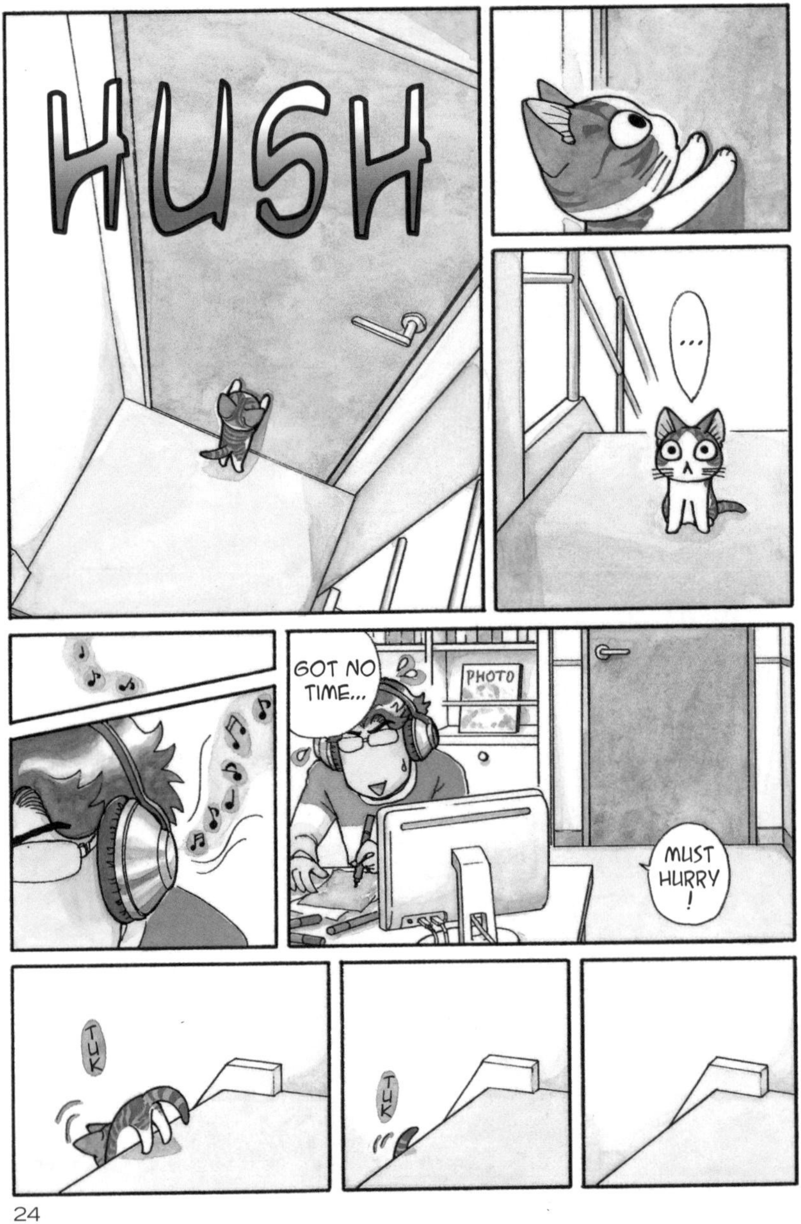
HUSH
...
GOT NO TIME...
MUST HURRY!
TUK
TUK

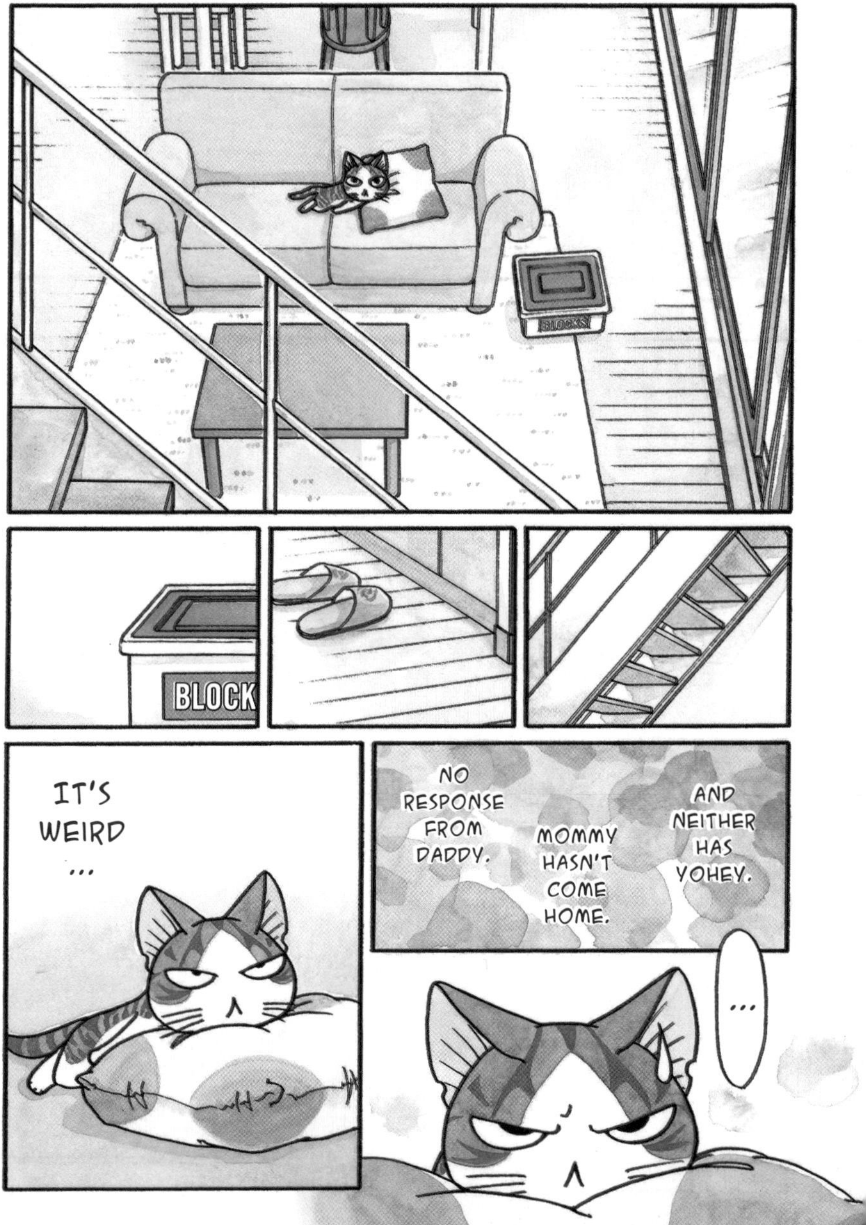
BLOCKS
BLOCK
IT'S WEIRD ...
NO RESPONSE FROM DADDY.
MOMMY HASN'T COME HOME.
AND NEITHER HAS YOHEY.
...

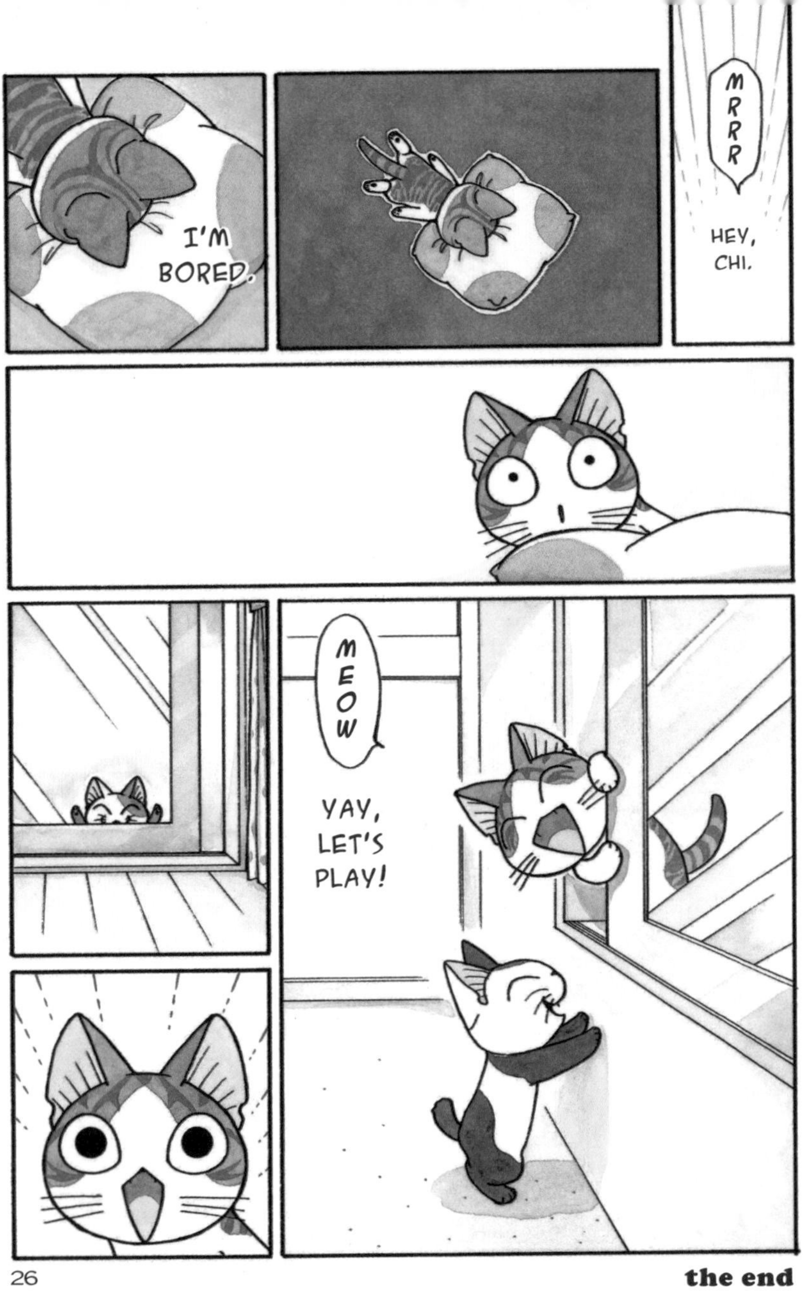
I'M BORED.
MRRR
HEY, CHI.
MEOW
YAY, LET'S PLAY!

the end

homemade 186: a cat receives a shock

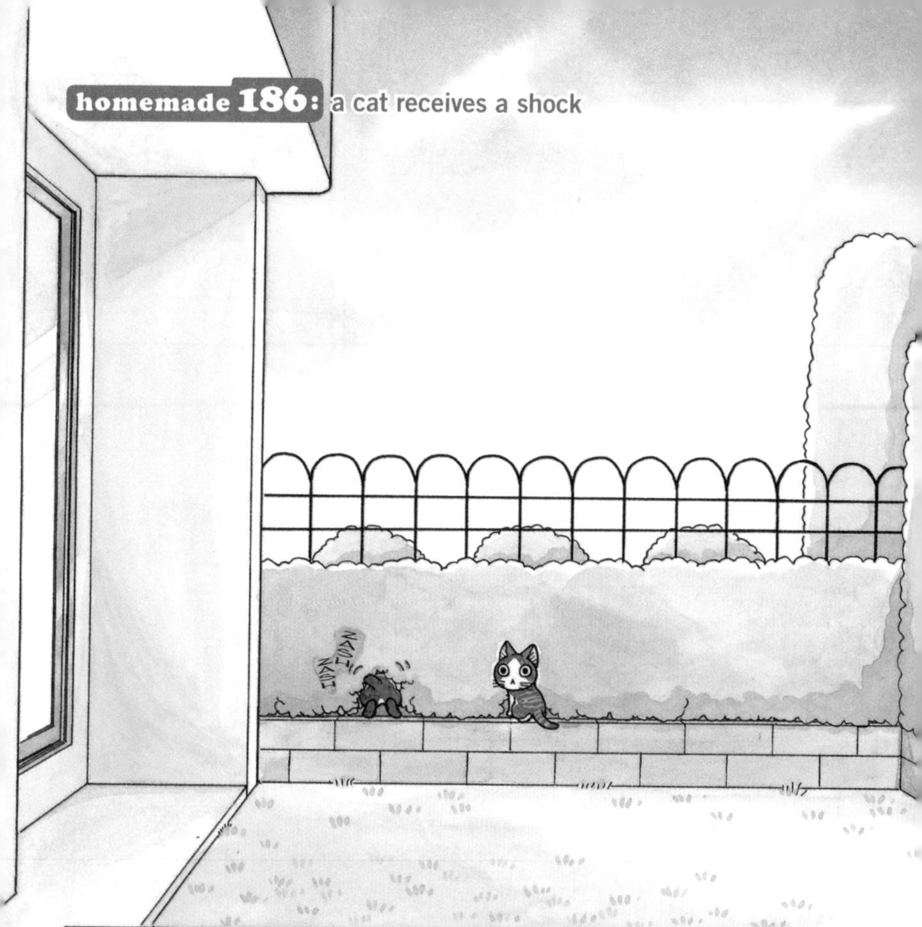
ZASH
ZASH

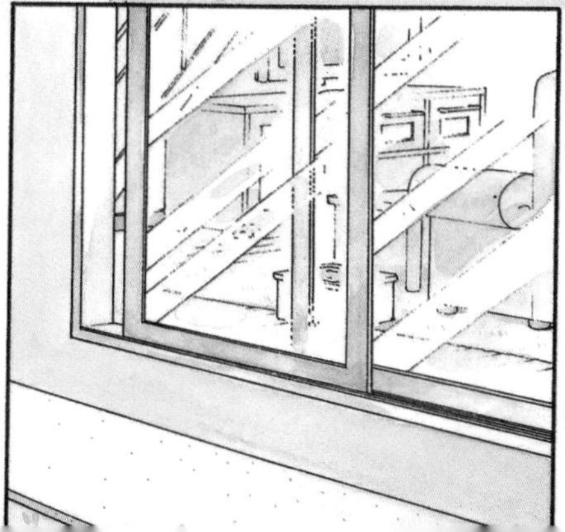

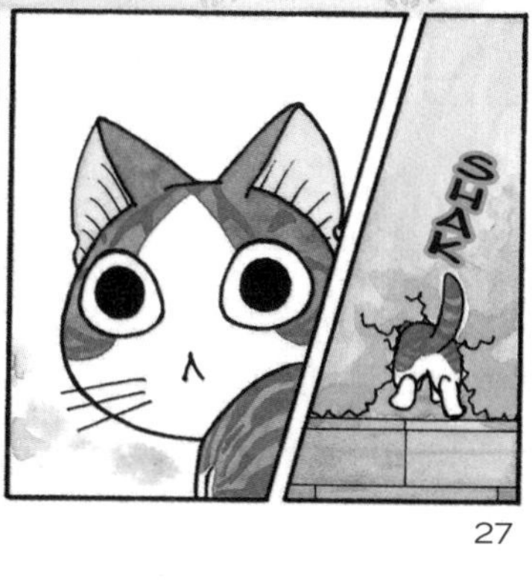
SHAK

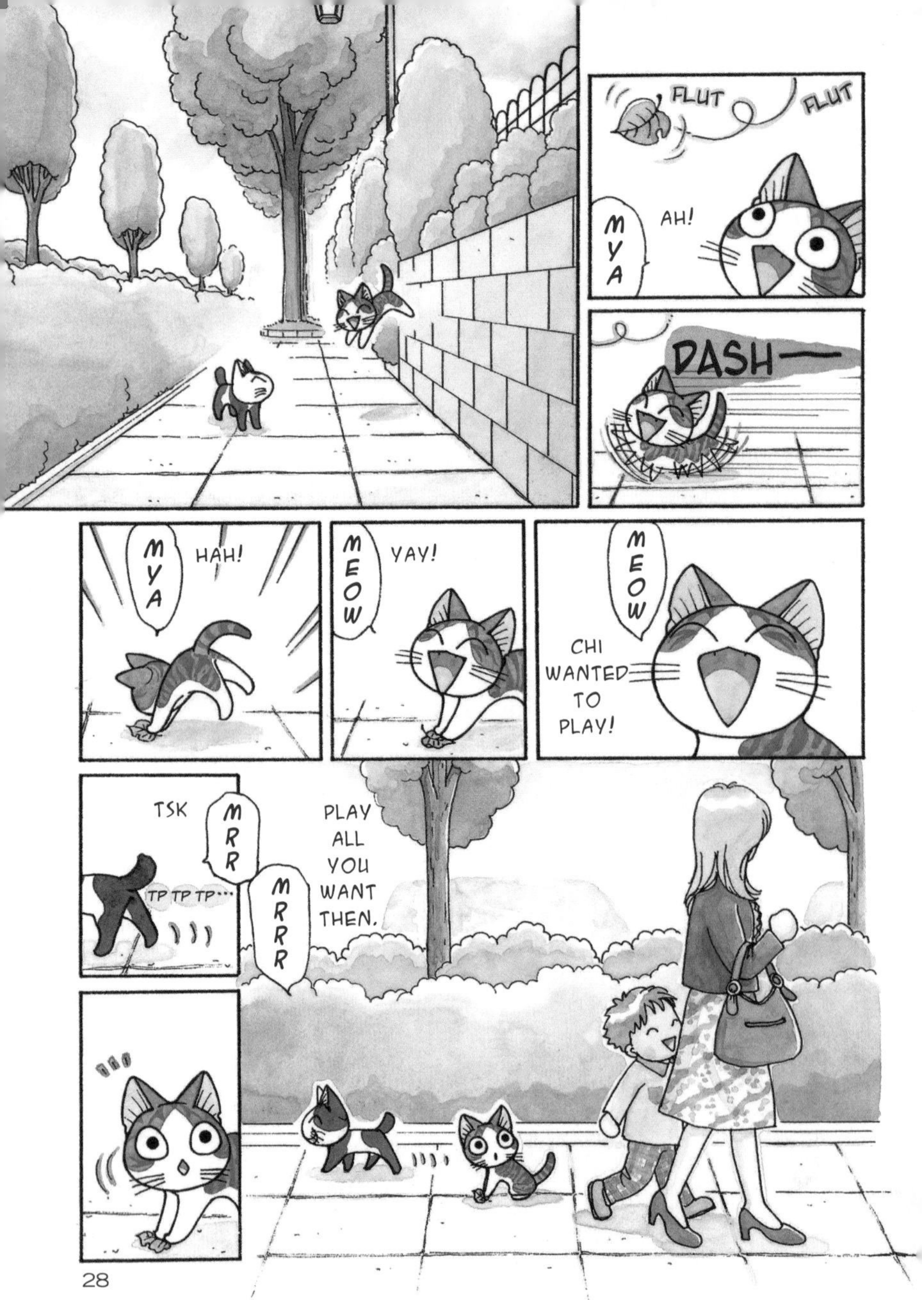
FLUT
FLUT
MYA
AH!
DASH—
MYA
HAH!
MEOW
YAY!
MEOW
CHI WANTED TO PLAY!
TSK
MRR
TP TP TP···
MRRR
PLAY ALL YOU WANT THEN.

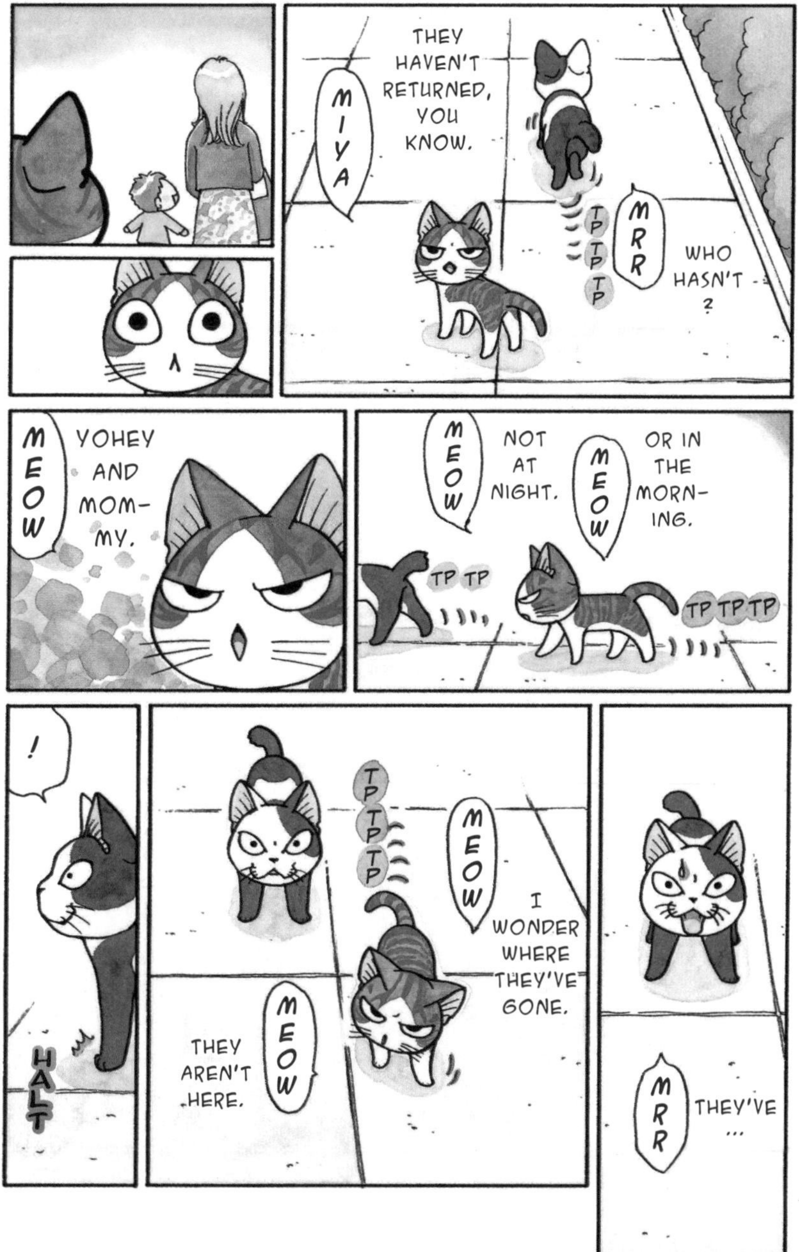
MIYA
THEY HAVEN'T RETURNED, YOU KNOW.
MRR
TP TP TP TP
WHO HASN'T?
MEOW
YOHEY AND MOM-MY.
MEOW
NOT AT NIGHT.
MEOW
OR IN THE MORN-ING.
TP TP
TP TP TP
!
HALT
TP TP TP TP
MEOW
I WONDER WHERE THEY'VE GONE.
MEOW
THEY AREN'T HERE.
MRR
THEY'VE ...

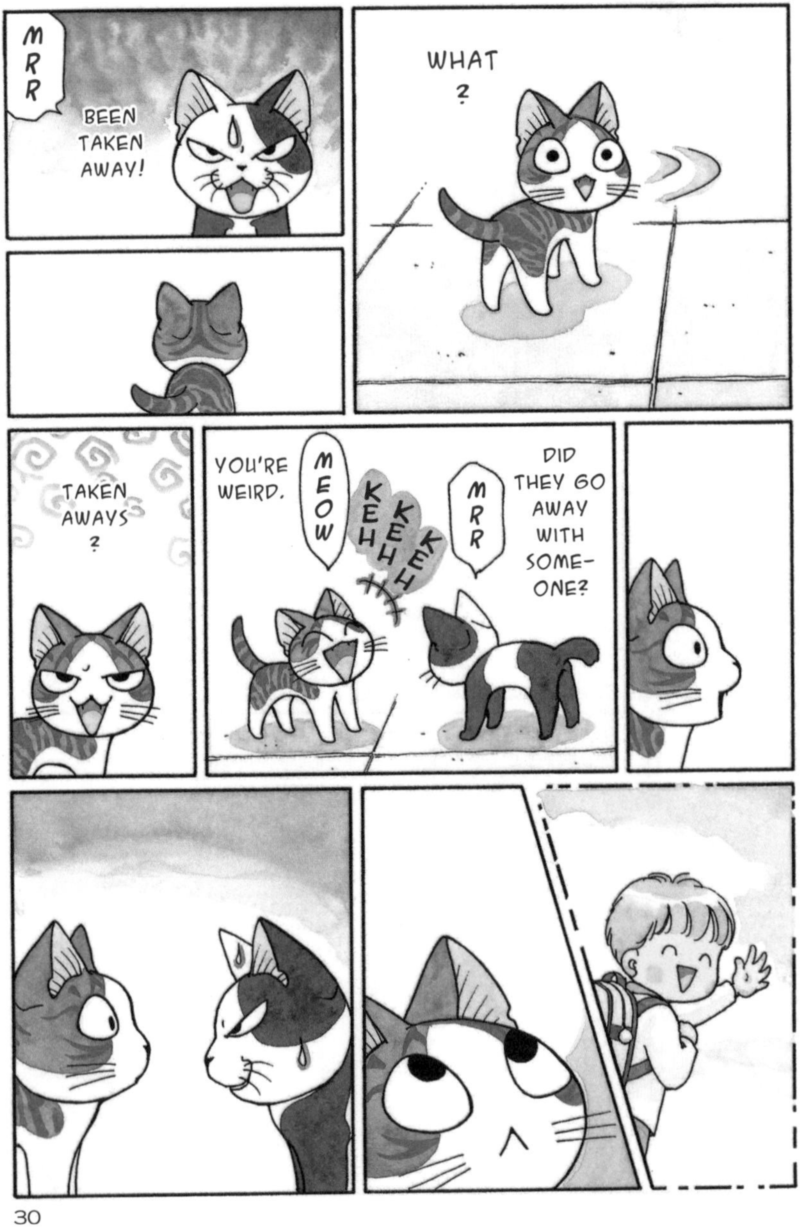
MRR
BEEN TAKEN AWAY!
WHAT?
TAKEN AWAYS?
YOU'RE WEIRD.
MEOW
KEH KEH KEH
MRR
DID THEY GO AWAY WITH SOME-ONE?

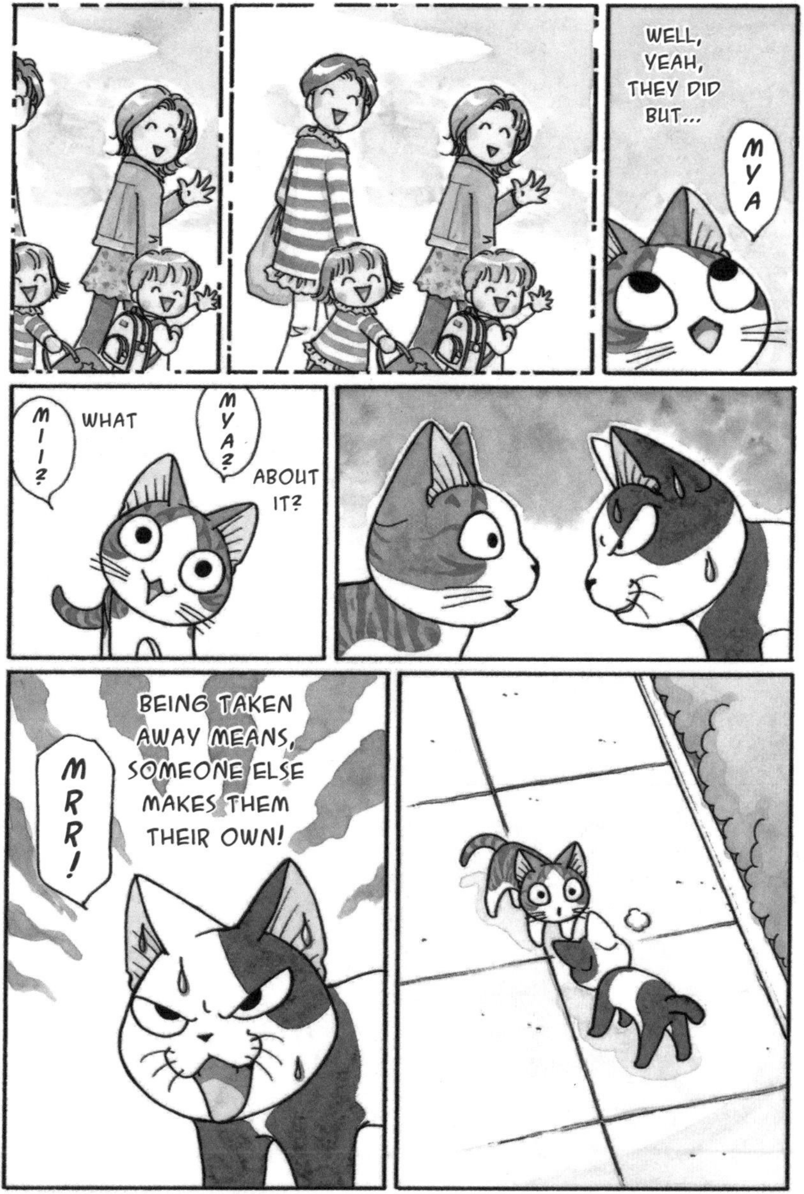

WELL, YEAH, THEY DID BUT...
MYA
MII?
WHAT
MYA?
ABOUT IT?
BEING TAKEN AWAY MEANS, SOMEONE ELSE MAKES THEM THEIR OWN!
MRR!

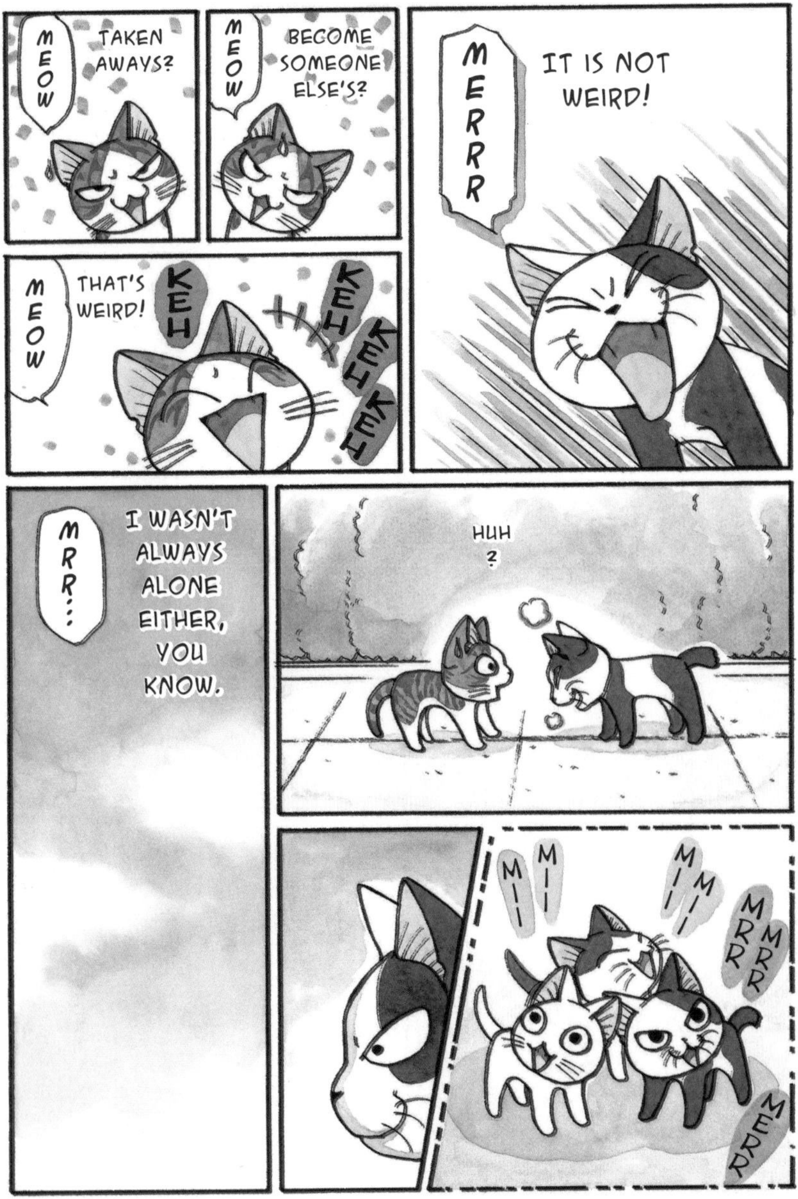
MEOW
TAKEN AWAYS?
MEOW
BECOME SOMEONE ELSE'S?
MEOW
THAT'S WEIRD!
KEH KEH KEH KEH
MERRR
IT IS NOT WEIRD!
MRR...
I WASN'T ALWAYS ALONE EITHER, YOU KNOW.
HUH?
MI MI MI MI
MRR MRR
MERR

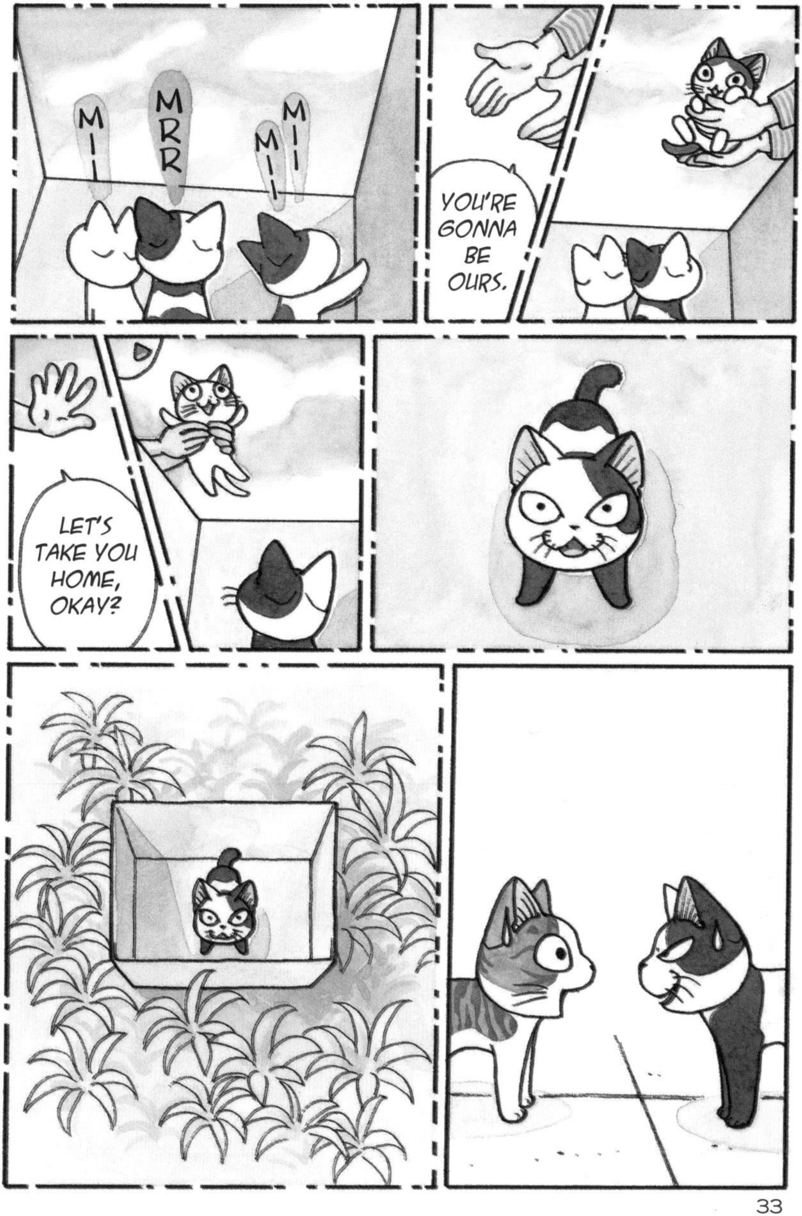
MI
MRR
MI
MI
YOU'RE GONNA BE OURS.
LET'S TAKE YOU HOME, OKAY?

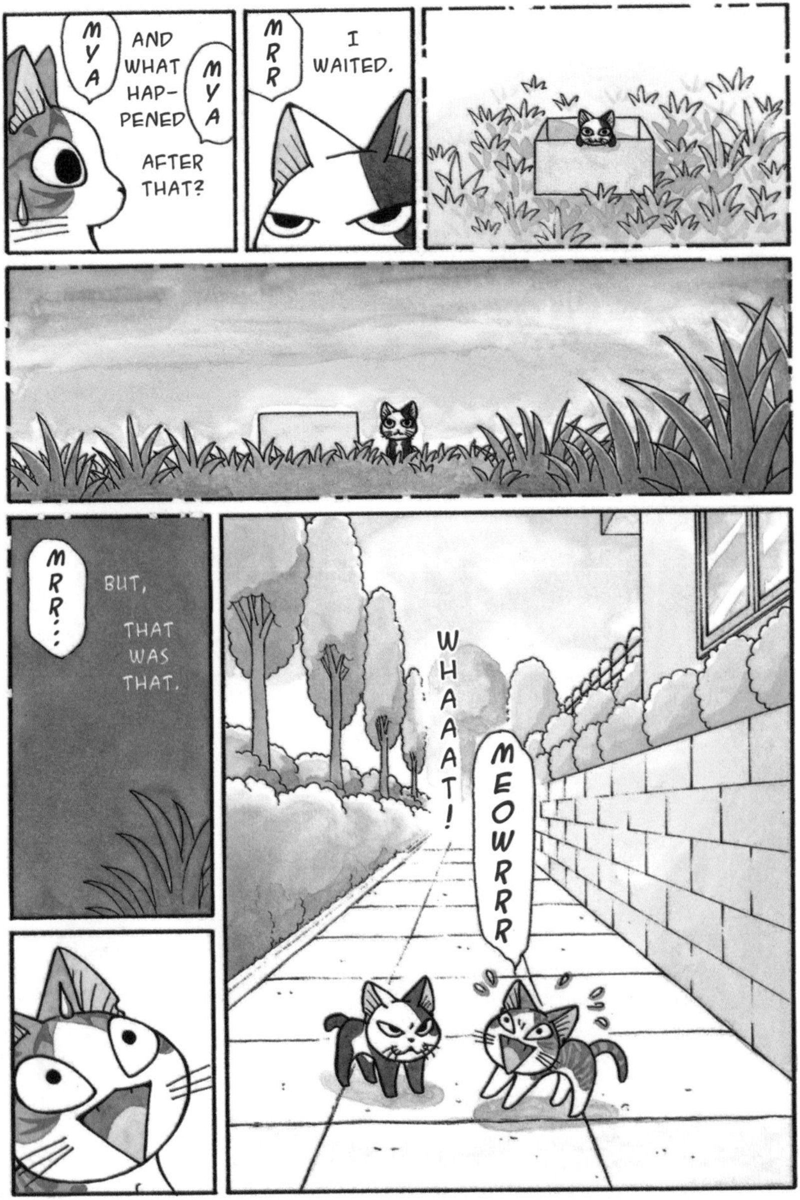
MYA
AND WHAT HAP-PENED AFTER THAT?
MYA
MRR
I WAITED.
MRR...
BUT, THAT WAS THAT.
WHAAAT!
MEOWRRR

the end

homemade 187: a cat is in denial

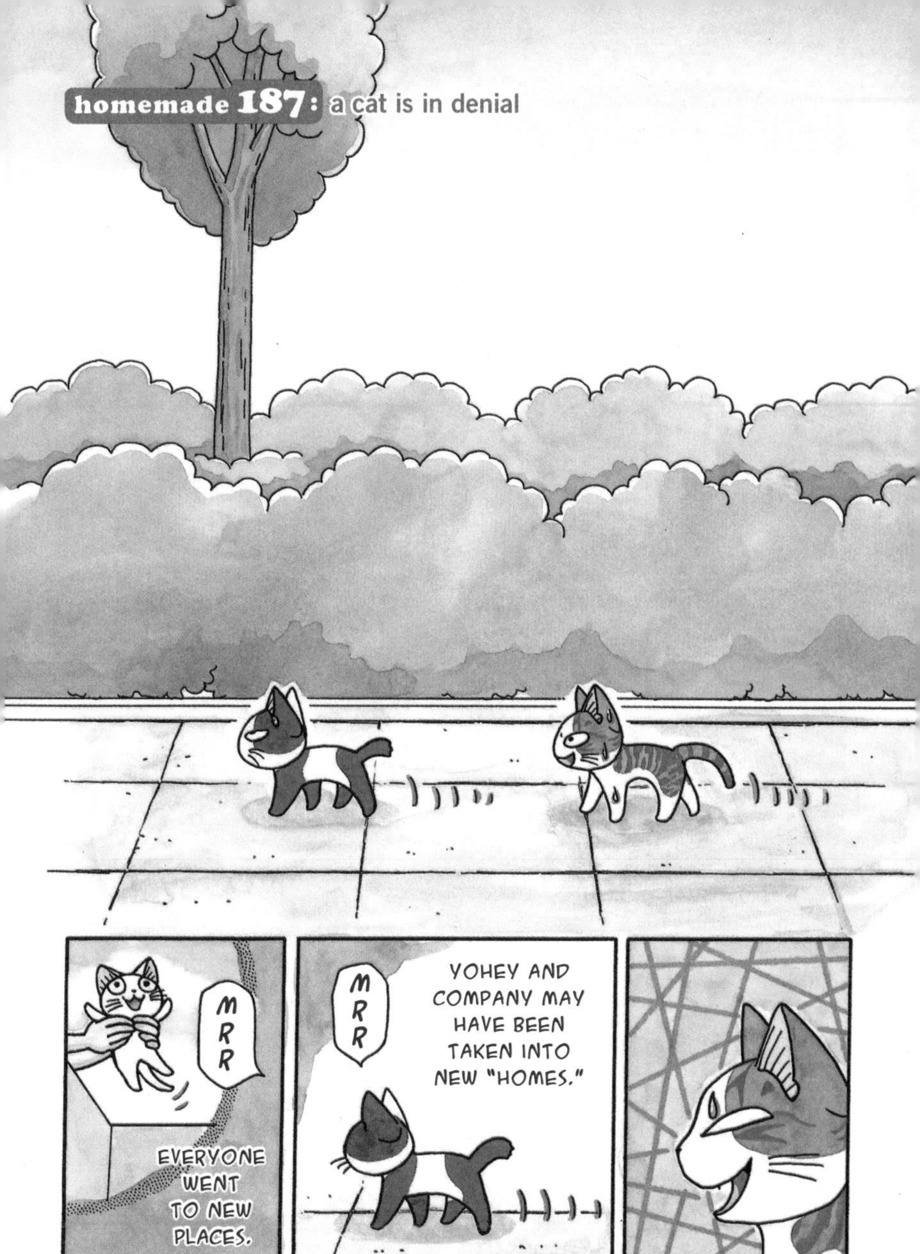
MRR
EVERYONE WENT TO NEW PLACES.
MRR
YOHEY AND COMPANY MAY HAVE BEEN TAKEN INTO NEW "HOMES."

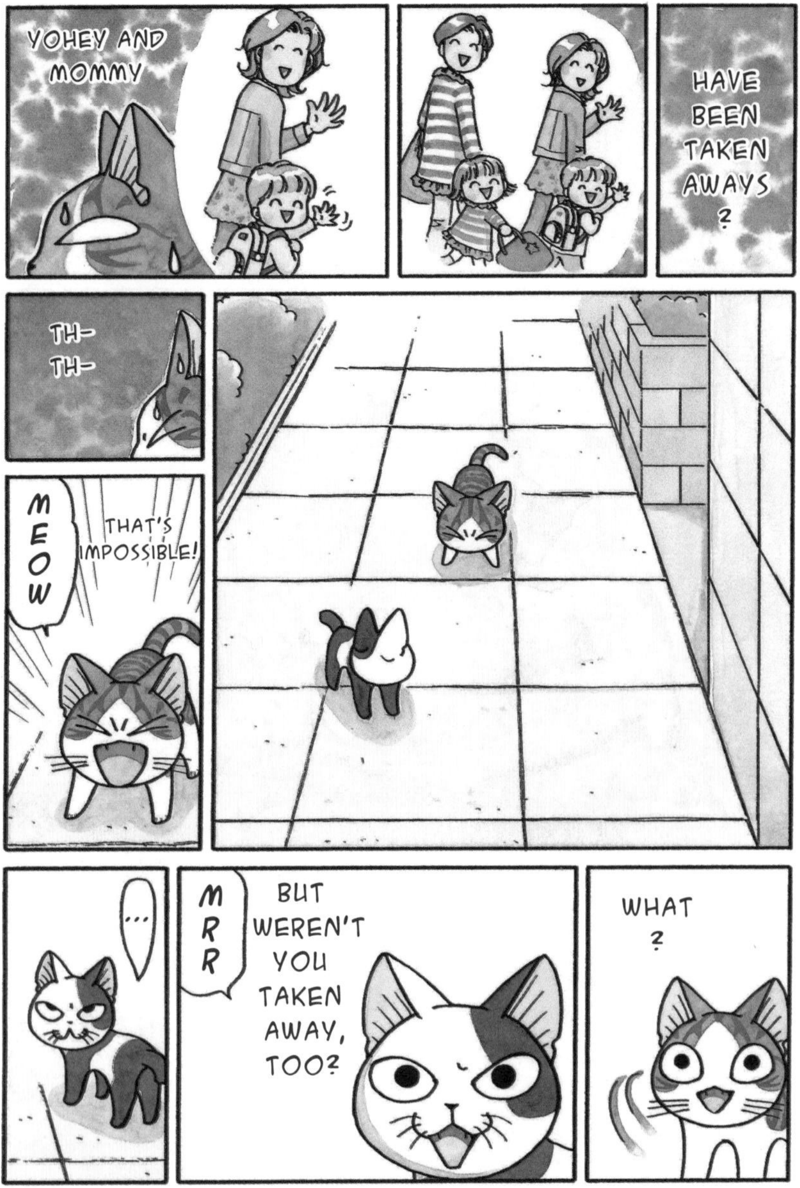
YOHEY AND MOMMY
HAVE BEEN TAKEN AWAYS ?
TH- TH-
MEOW
THAT'S IMPOSSIBLE!
...
MRR
BUT WEREN'T YOU TAKEN AWAY, TOO?
WHAT ?

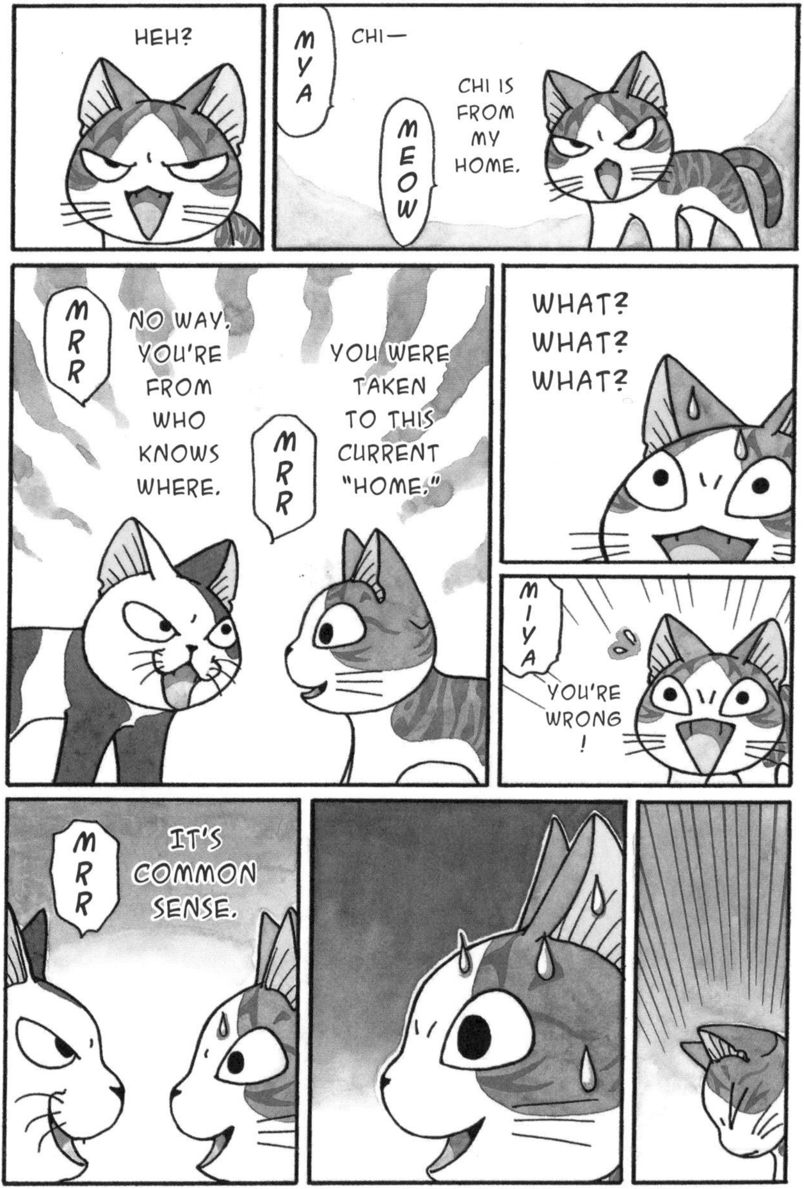
HEH?
MYA
CHI—
MEOW
CHI IS FROM MY HOME.
MRR
NO WAY. YOU'RE FROM WHO KNOWS WHERE.
MRR
YOU WERE TAKEN TO THIS CURRENT "HOME."
WHAT? WHAT? WHAT?
MIYA
YOU'RE WRONG!
MRR
IT'S COMMON SENSE.

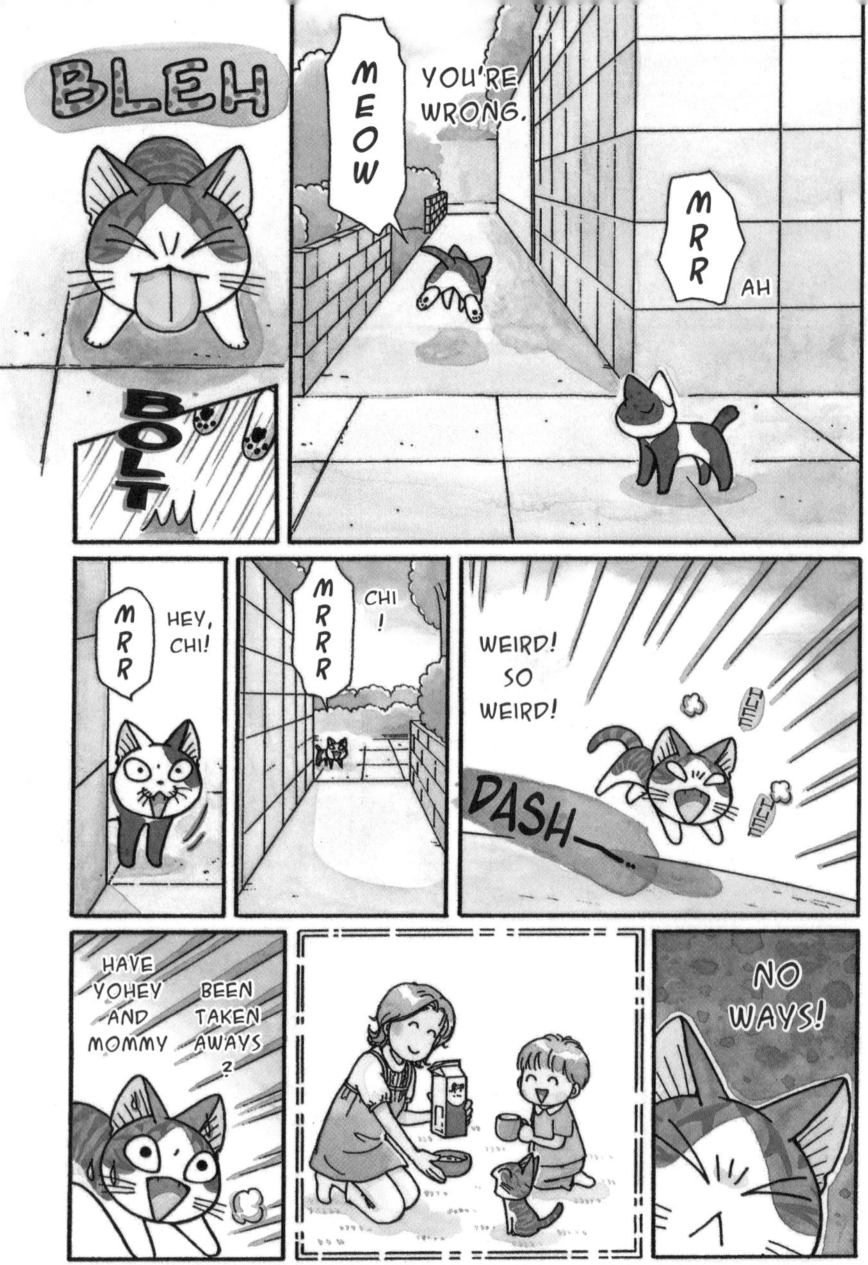
BLEH
BOLT
MEOW
YOU'RE WRONG.
MRR
AH
MRR
HEY, CHI!
MRRR
CHI!
WEIRD! SO WEIRD!
DASH—
HAVE YOHEY AND MOMMY BEEN TAKEN AWAYS?
NO WAYS!

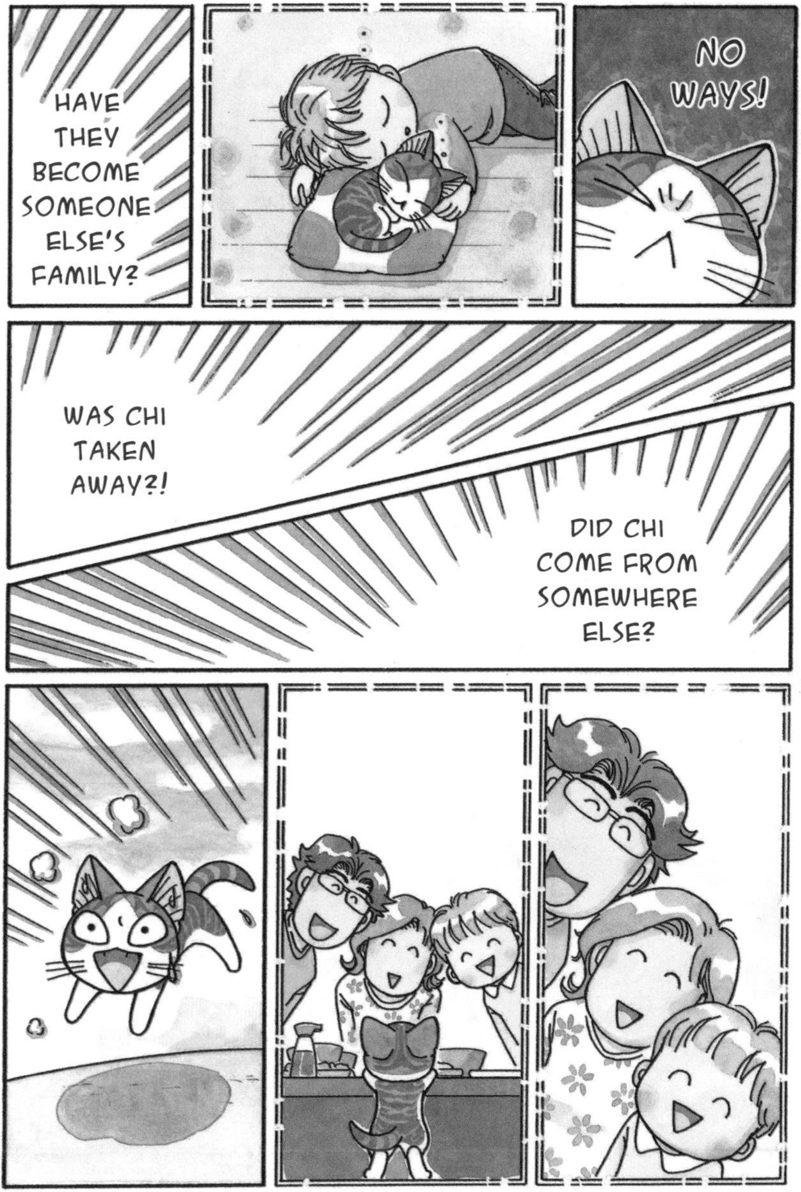
HAVE THEY BECOME SOMEONE ELSE'S FAMILY?
NO WAYS!
WAS CHI TAKEN AWAY?!
DID CHI COME FROM SOMEWHERE ELSE?

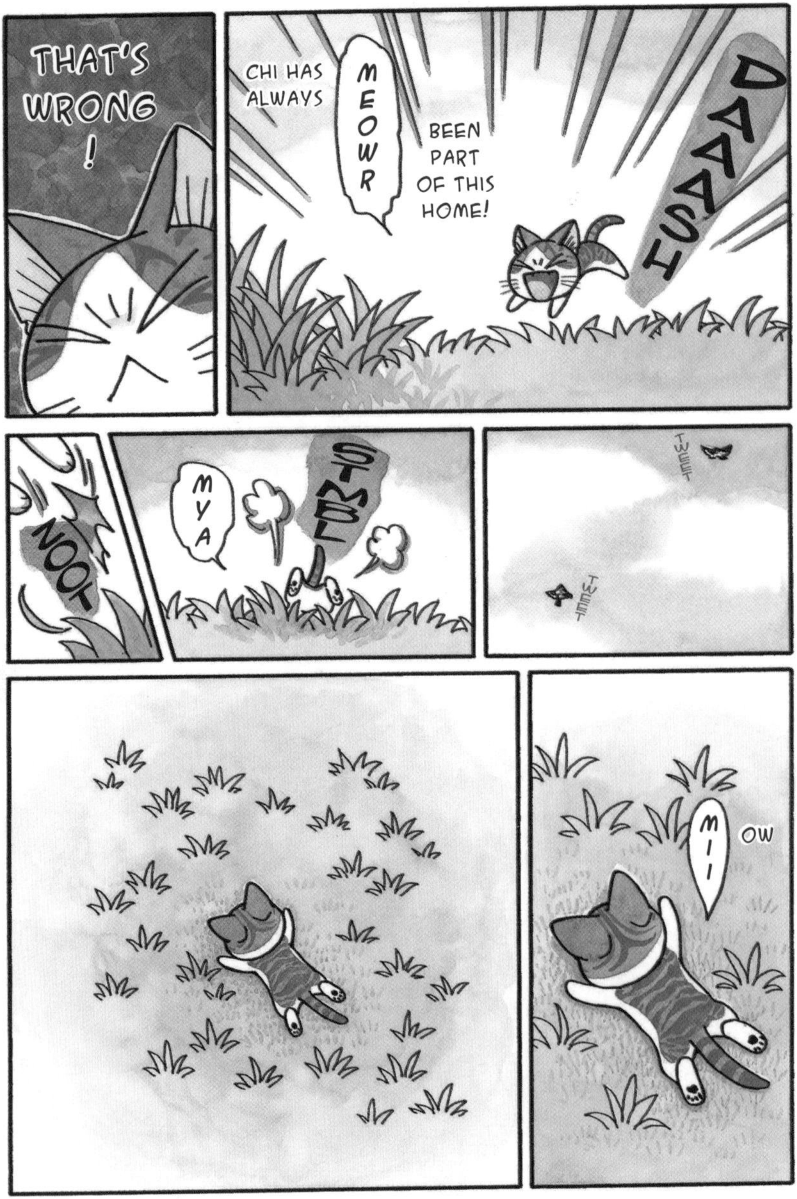
THAT'S WRONG!
CHI HAS ALWAYS BEEN PART OF THIS HOME!
MEOWR
DAAASH
NOOT
MYA
STMBL
TWEET
TWEET
MII
OW

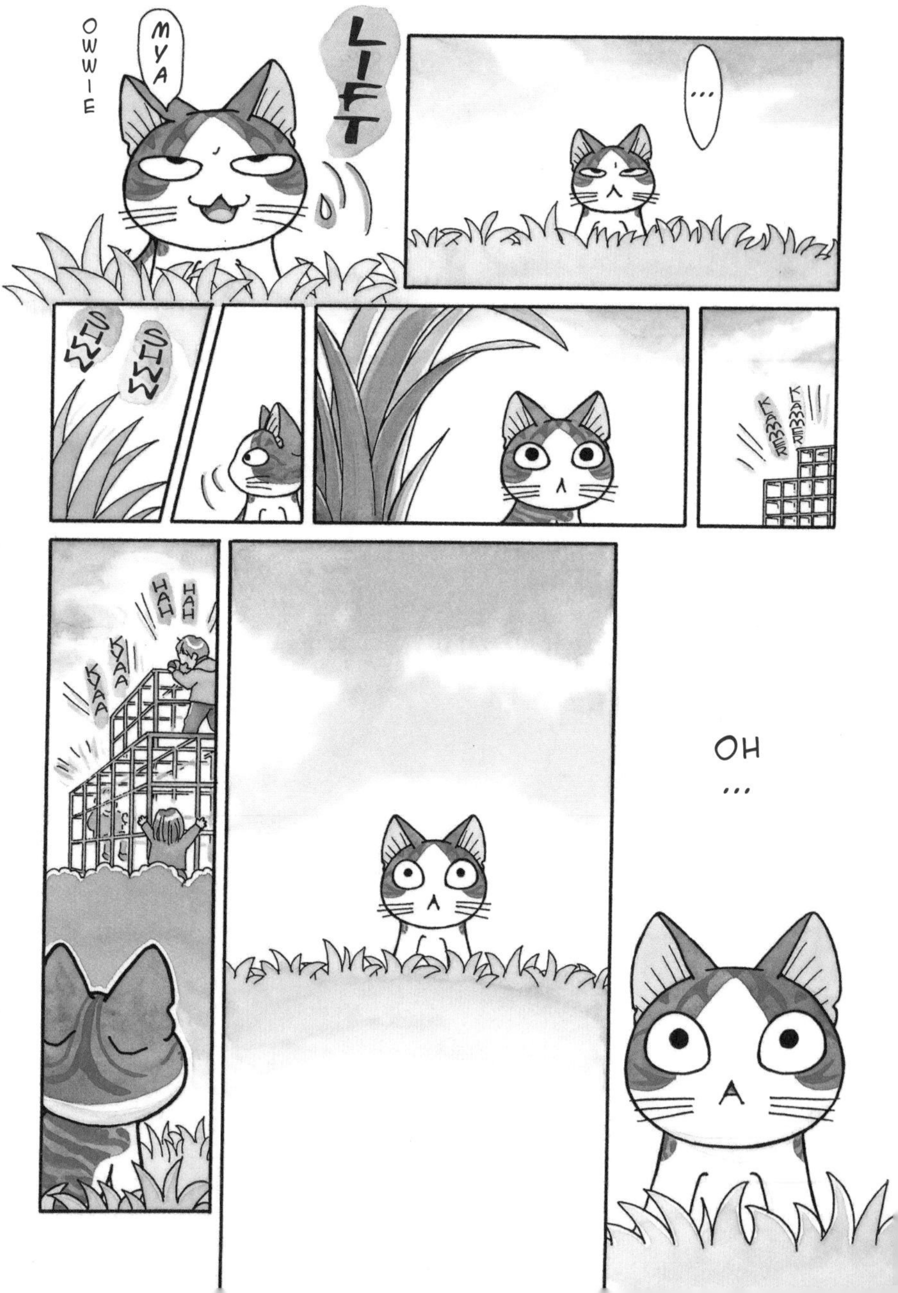
OWWIE
MYA
LIFT
...
SHWW
SHWW
KLAMMER
KLAMMER
HAH
HAH
KYAA
KYAA
OH
...

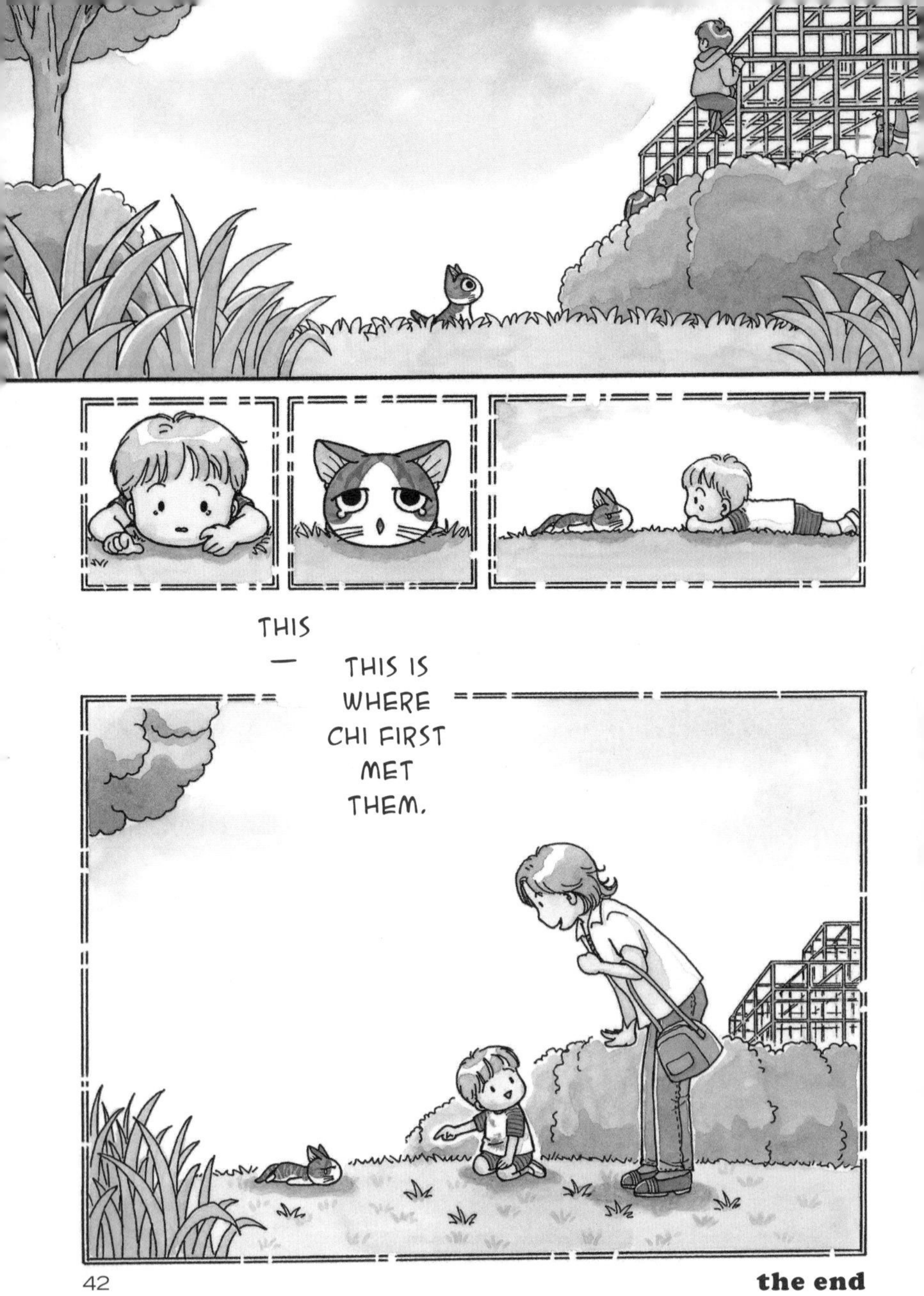
THIS —
THIS IS WHERE CHI FIRST MET THEM.

the end

homemade 188: a cat notices

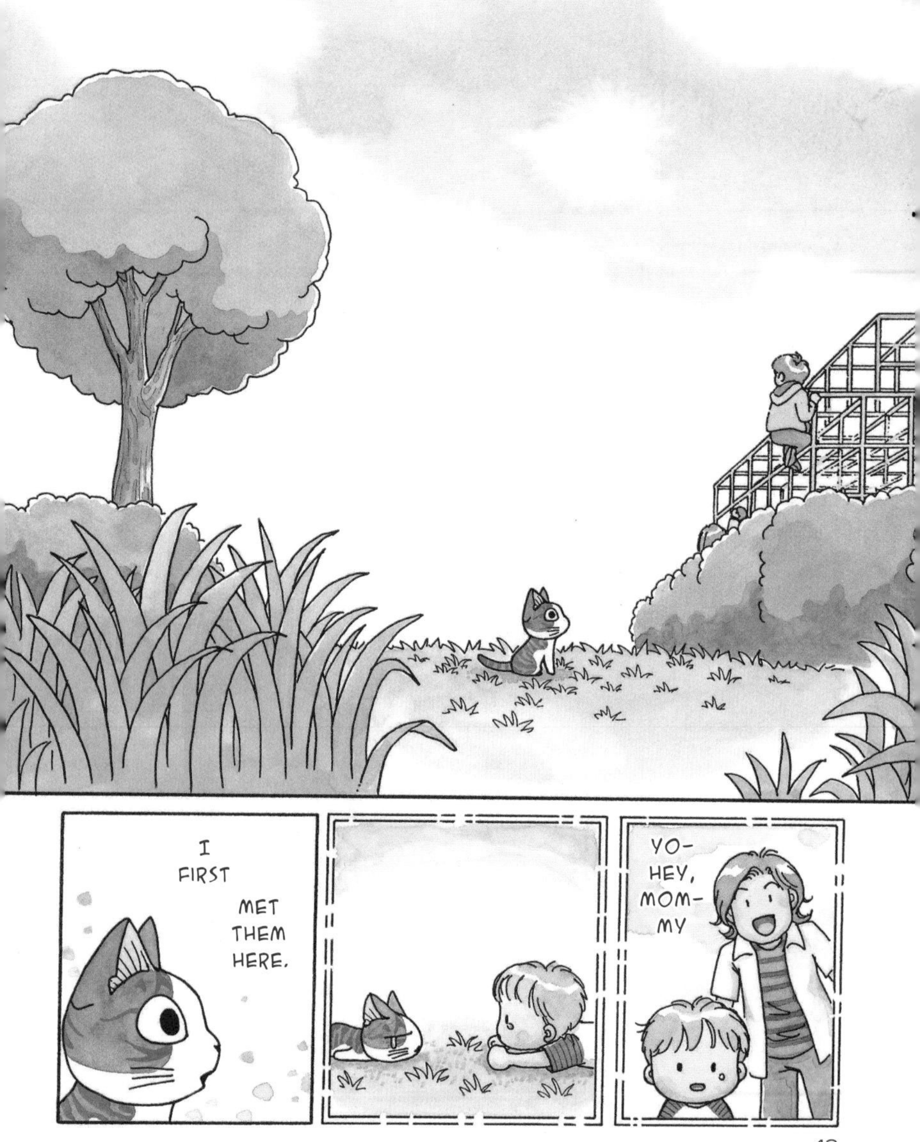
I FIRST MET THEM HERE.
YO-HEY, MOMMY

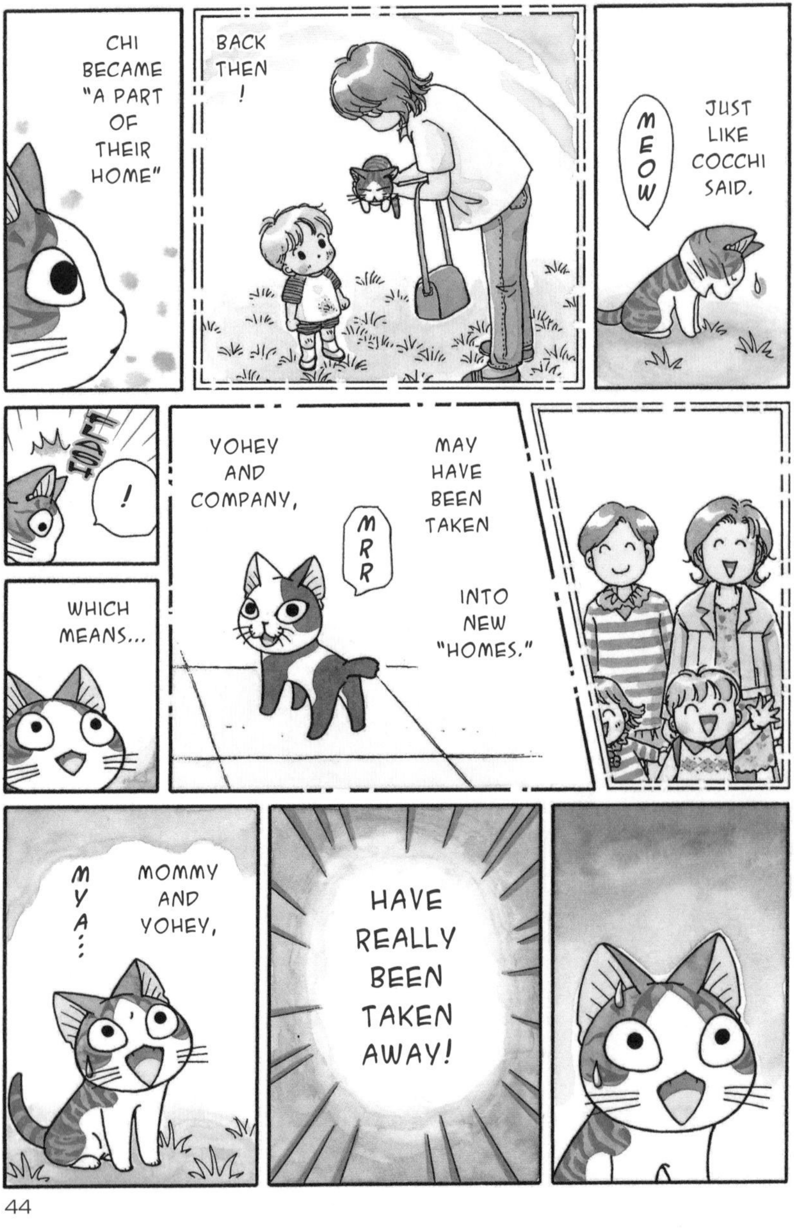
CHI BECAME "A PART OF THEIR HOME"
BACK THEN!
JUST LIKE COCCHI SAID.
MEOW
!
WHICH MEANS...
YOHEY AND COMPANY,
MRR
MAY HAVE BEEN TAKEN
INTO NEW "HOMES."
MYA...
MOMMY AND YOHEY,
HAVE REALLY BEEN TAKEN AWAY!

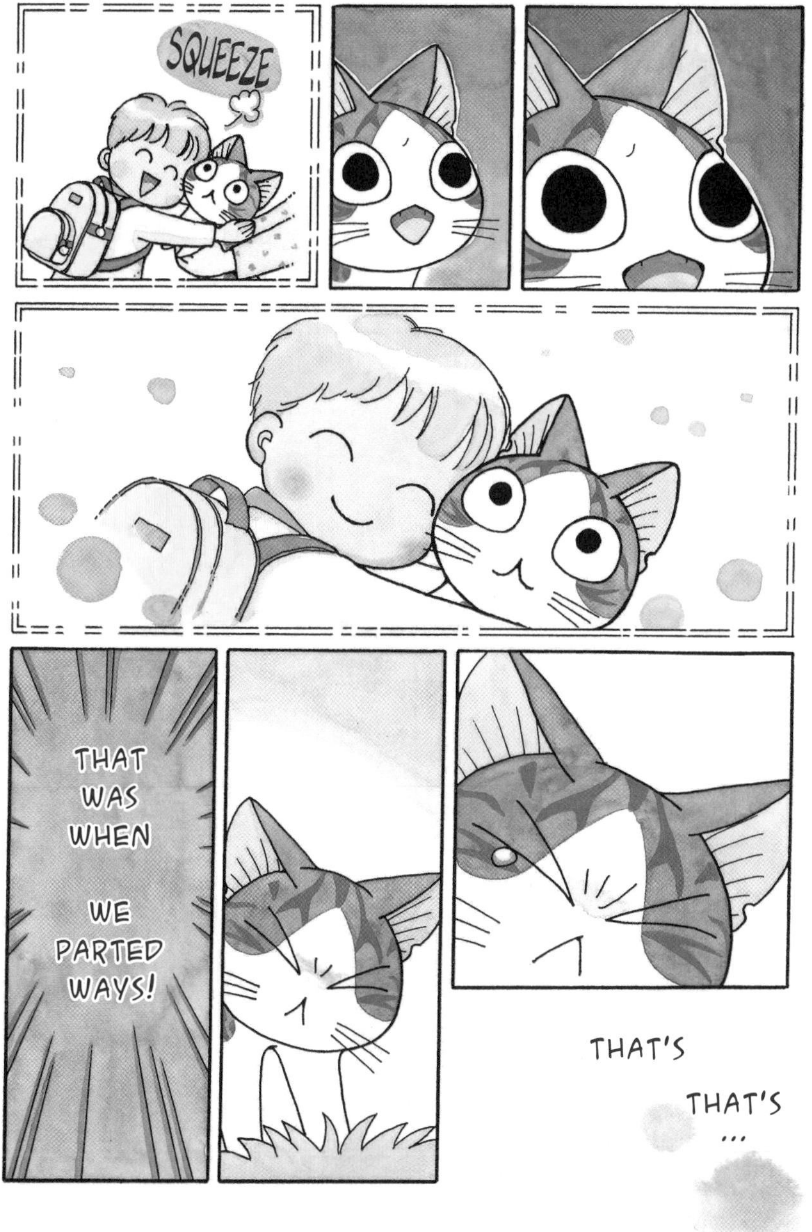
SQUEEZE
THAT WAS WHEN
WE PARTED WAYS!
THAT'S
THAT'S
...

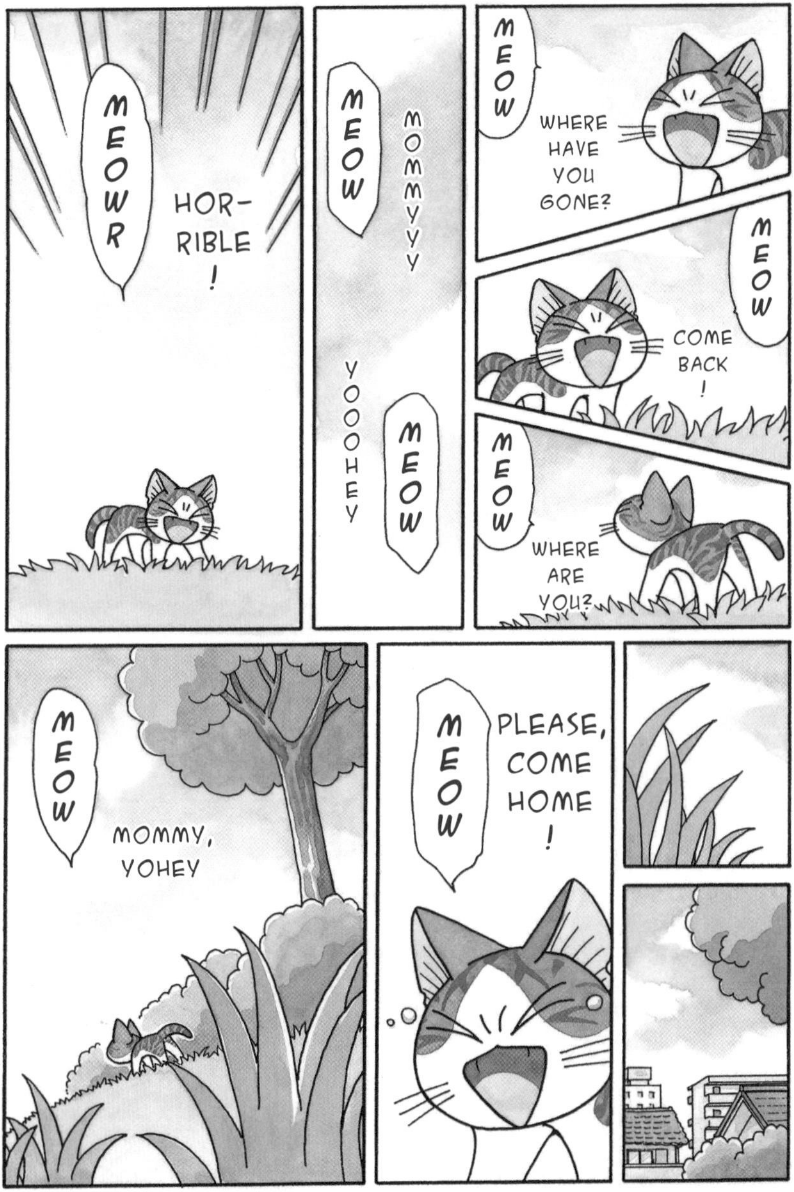
MEOWR
HOR-RIBLE!
MEOW
MOMMYYY
YOOOOHEY
MEOW
MEOW
WHERE HAVE YOU GONE?
MEOW
COME BACK!
MEOW
WHERE ARE YOU?
MEOW
MOMMY, YOHEY
MEOW
PLEASE, COME HOME!

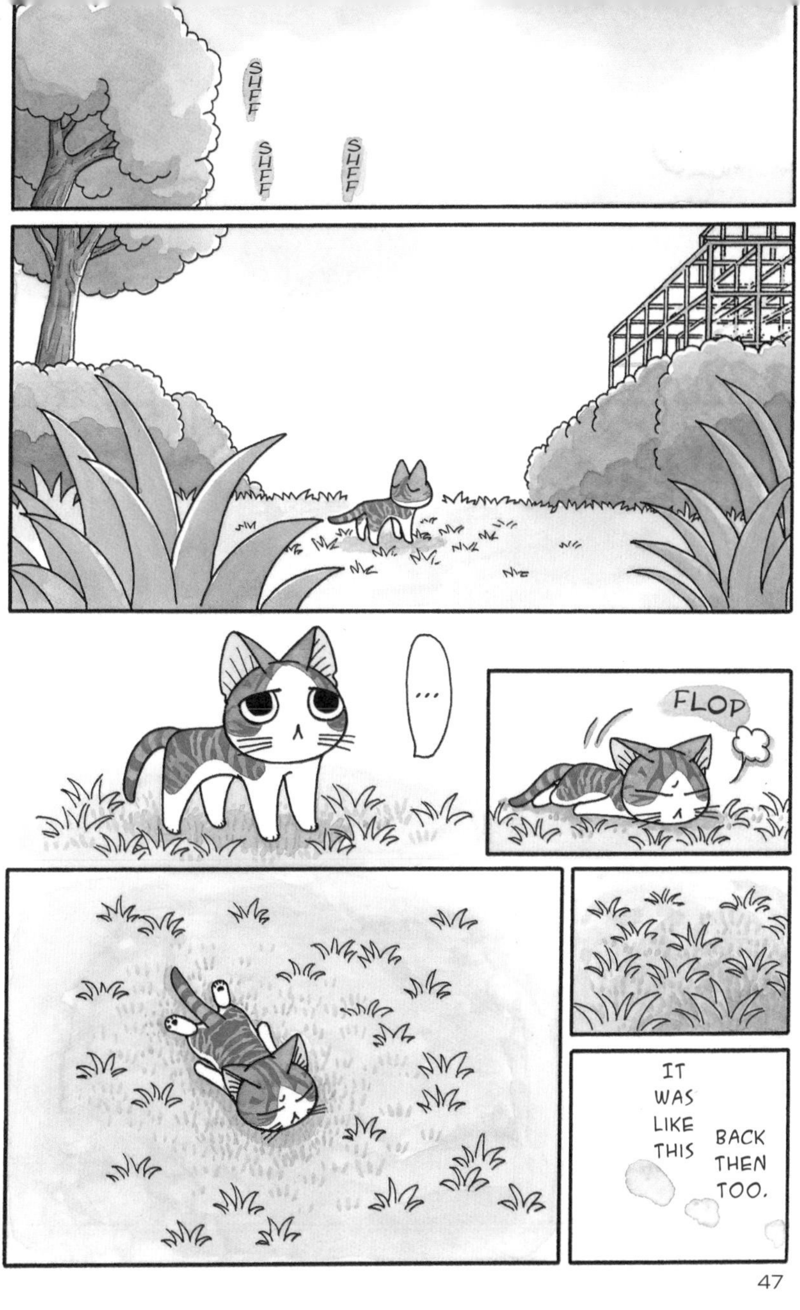
SHFF
SHFF
SHFF
...
FLOP
IT WAS LIKE THIS BACK THEN TOO.

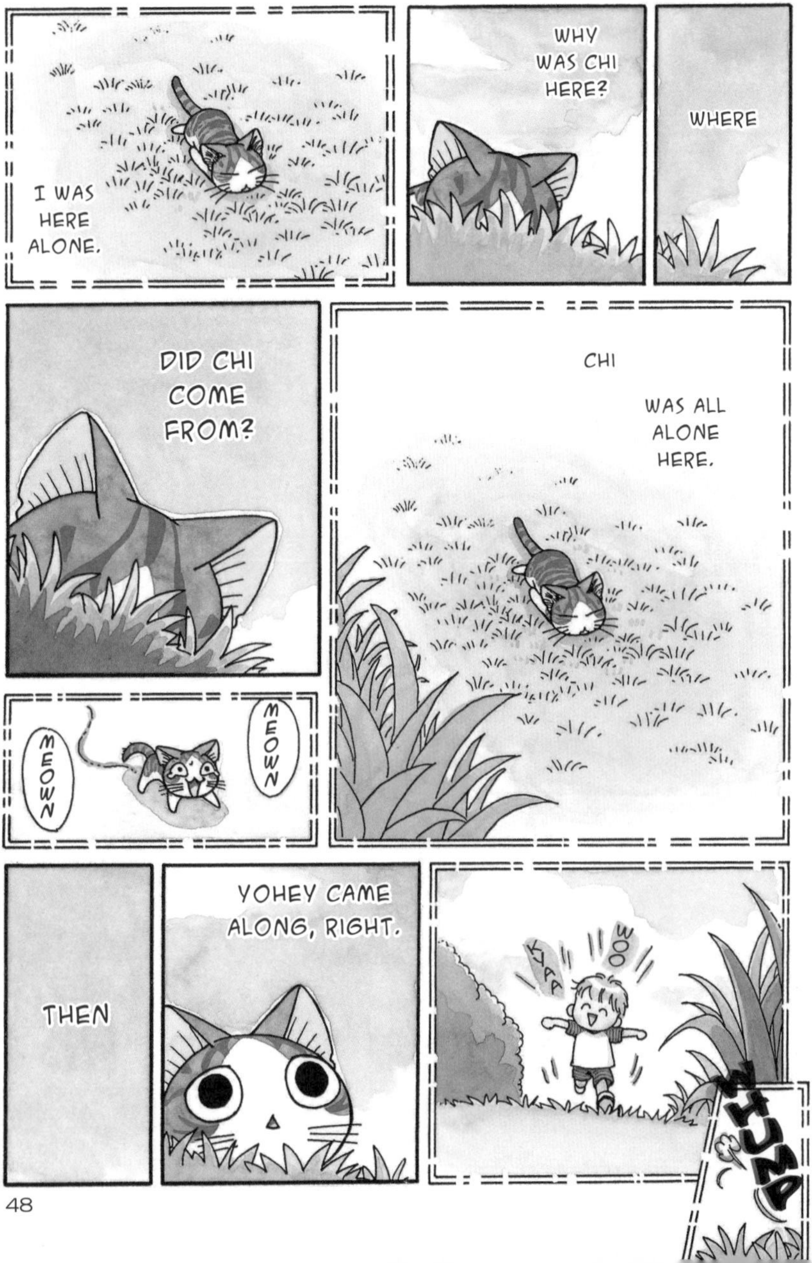
I WAS HERE ALONE.
WHY WAS CHI HERE?
WHERE
DID CHI COME FROM?
MEOWN
MEOWN
CHI
WAS ALL ALONE HERE.
THEN
YOHEY CAME ALONG, RIGHT.
KYAA
WOO
WHUMP

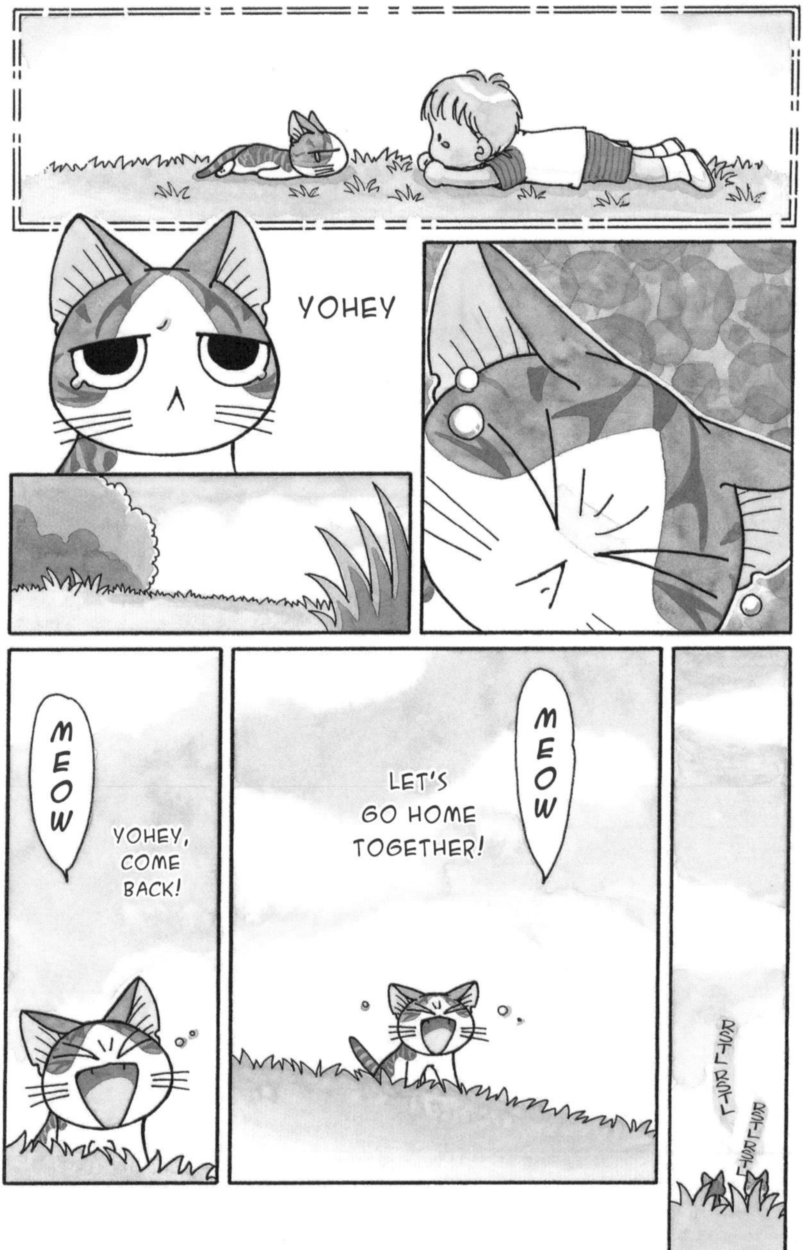
YOHEY
MEOW
YOHEY, COME BACK!
LET'S GO HOME TOGETHER!
MEOW
RSTL RSTL
RSTL RSTL

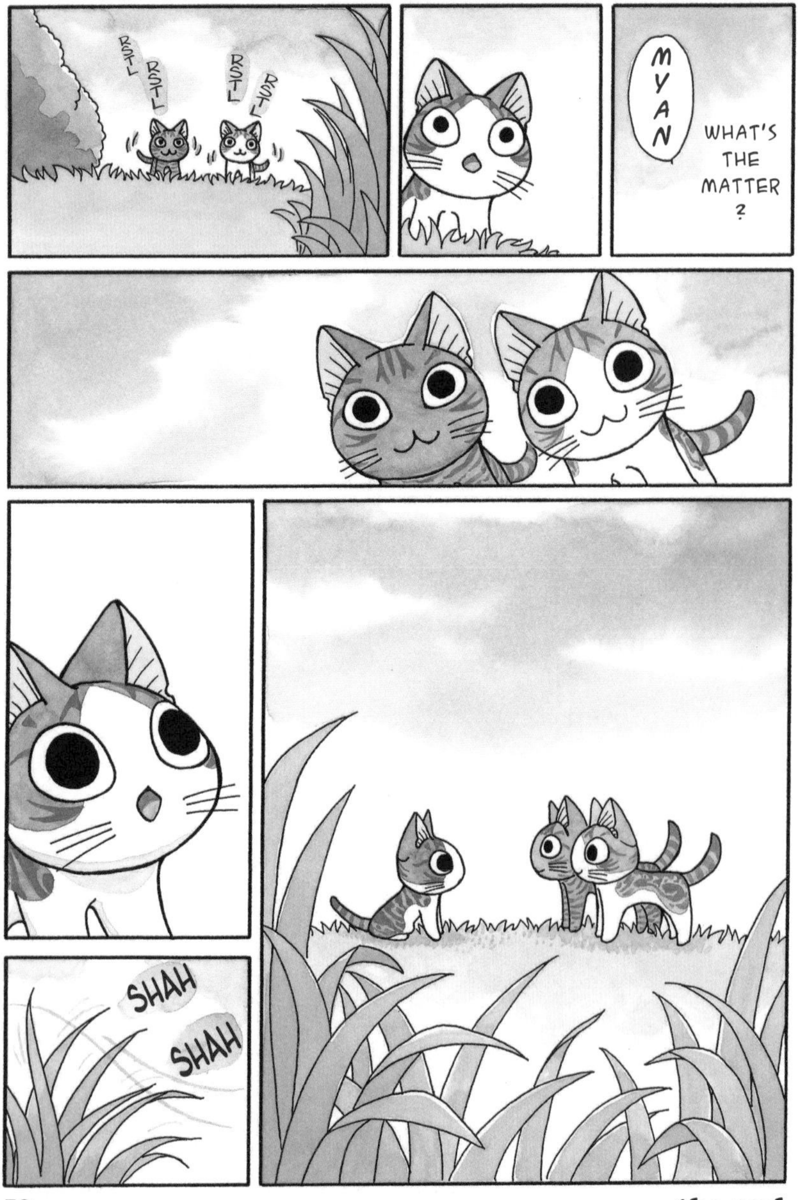
RSTL
RSTL
RSTL
RSTL
MYAN
WHAT'S THE MATTER ?
SHAH
SHAH

the end

homemade 189: a cat hangs her head

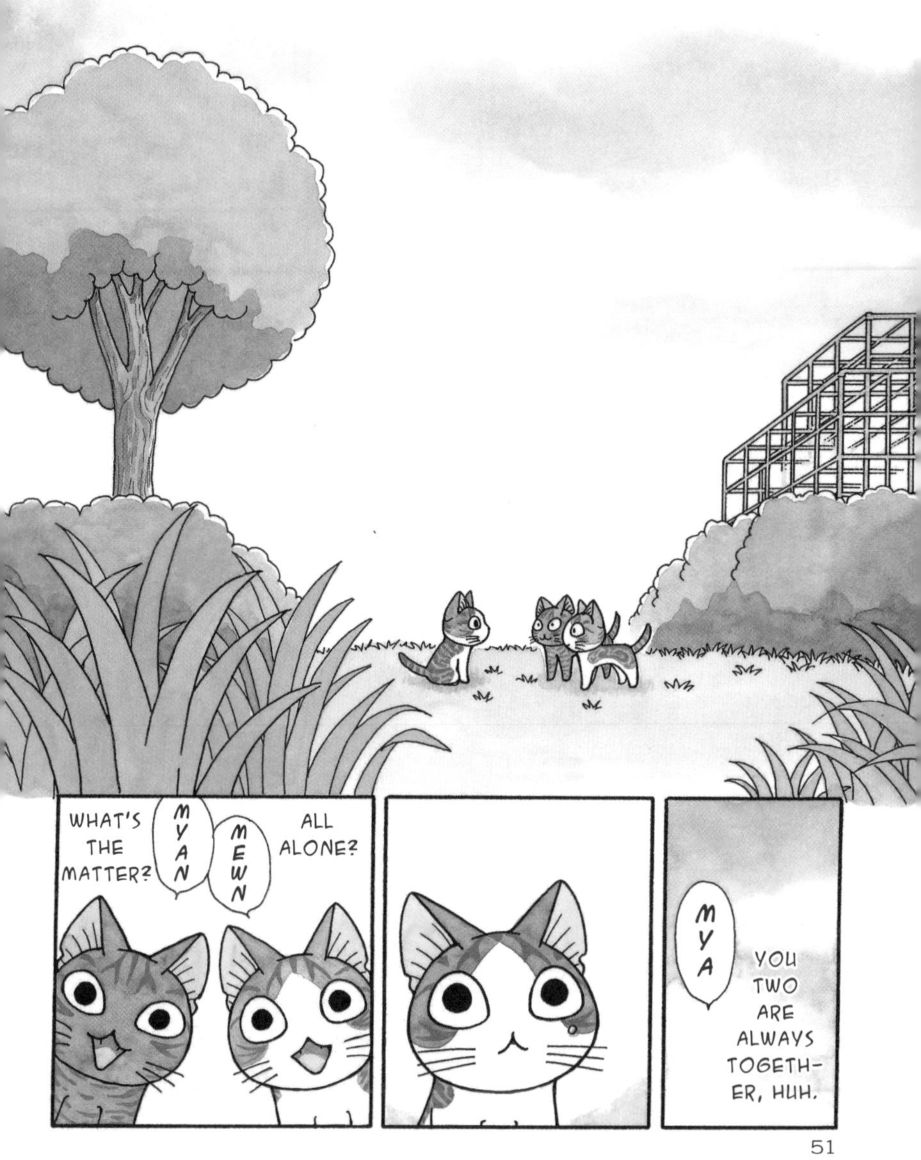
WHAT'S THE MATTER?
MYAN
MEWN
ALL ALONE?
MYA
YOU TWO ARE ALWAYS TOGETH- ER, HUH.

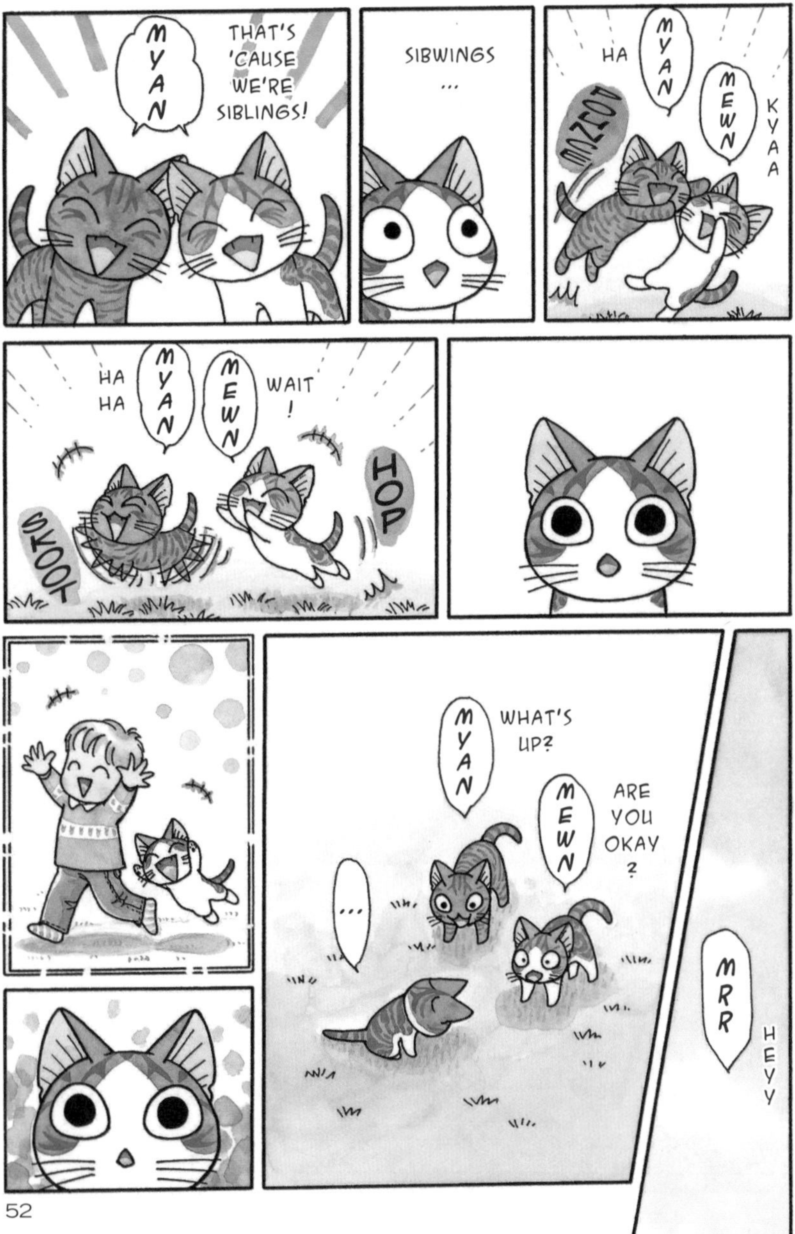
MYAN
THAT'S 'CAUSE WE'RE SIBLINGS!
SIBWINGS ...
HA
MYAN
MEWN
KYAA
POUNCE
HA HA
MYAN
MEWN
WAIT!
SKOOT
HOP
MYAN
WHAT'S UP?
MEWN
ARE YOU OKAY?
...
MRR
HEYY

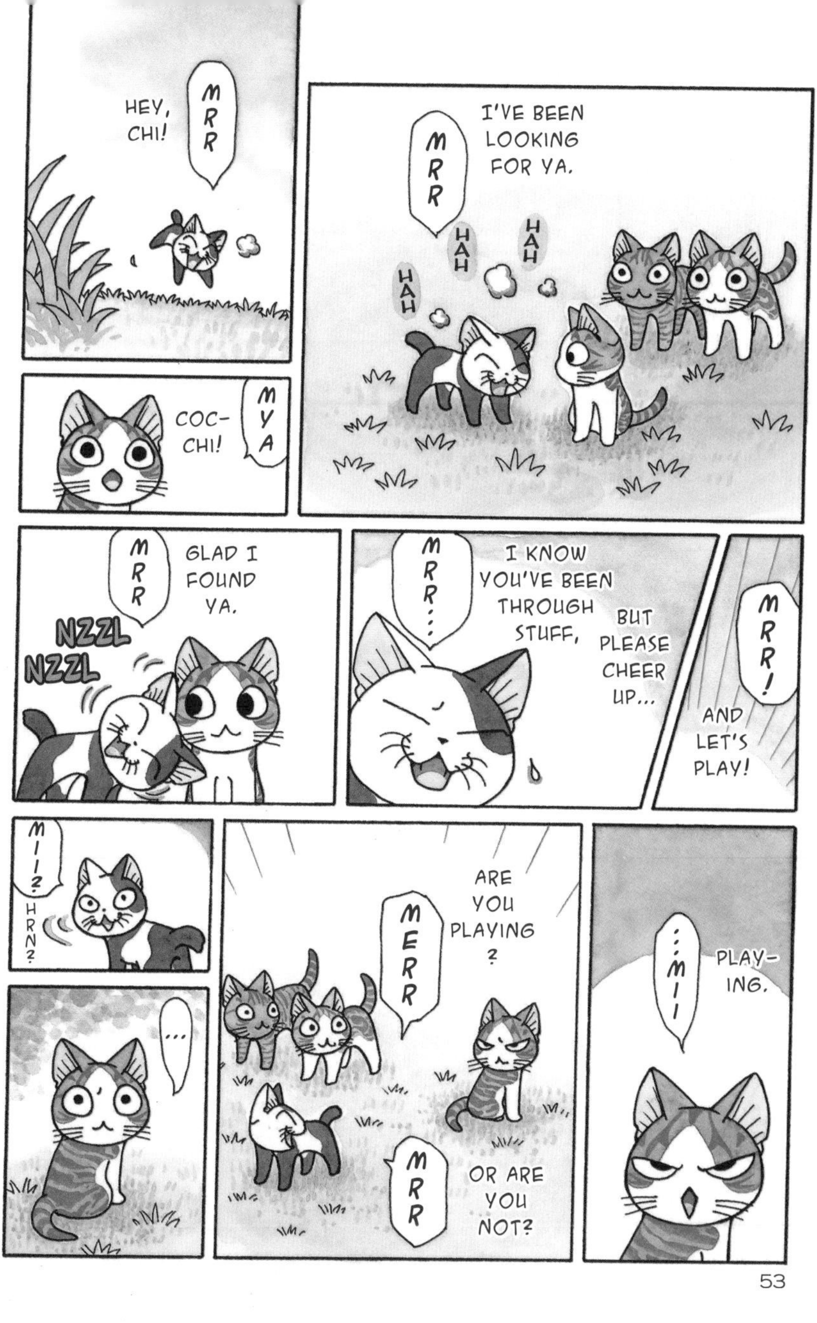

HEY, CHI!
MRR
COC-CHI!
MYA
I'VE BEEN LOOKING FOR YA.
MRR
HAH
HAH
HAH
GLAD I FOUND YA.
MRR
NZZL NZZL
I KNOW YOU'VE BEEN THROUGH STUFF,
BUT PLEASE CHEER UP...
MRR...
MRR!
AND LET'S PLAY!
MII?
HRN?
...
ARE YOU PLAYING?
MERR
OR ARE YOU NOT?
MRR
...MII
PLAY-ING.

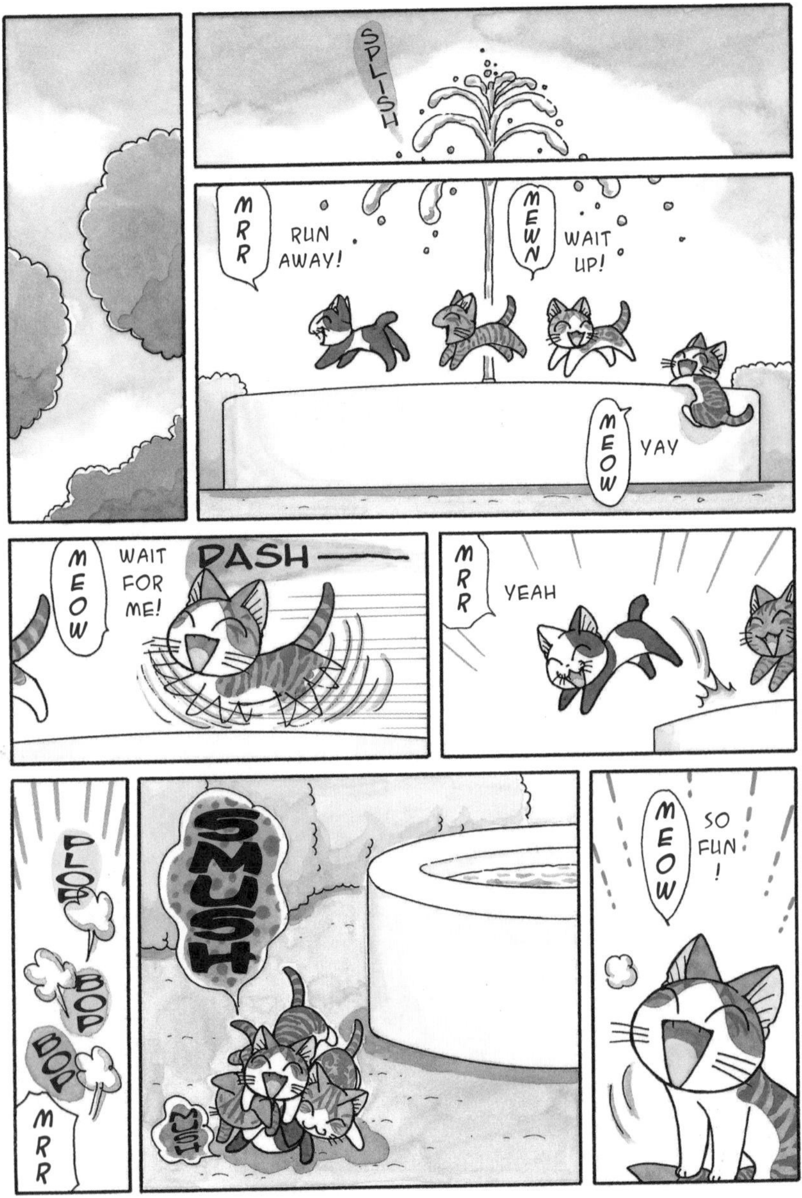
SPLISH
MRR
RUN AWAY!
MEWN
WAIT UP!
MEOW
YAY
MEOW
WAIT FOR ME!
DASH
MRR
YEAH
PLOP
BOP
BOP
MRR
SMUSH
MUSH
MEOW
SO FUN!

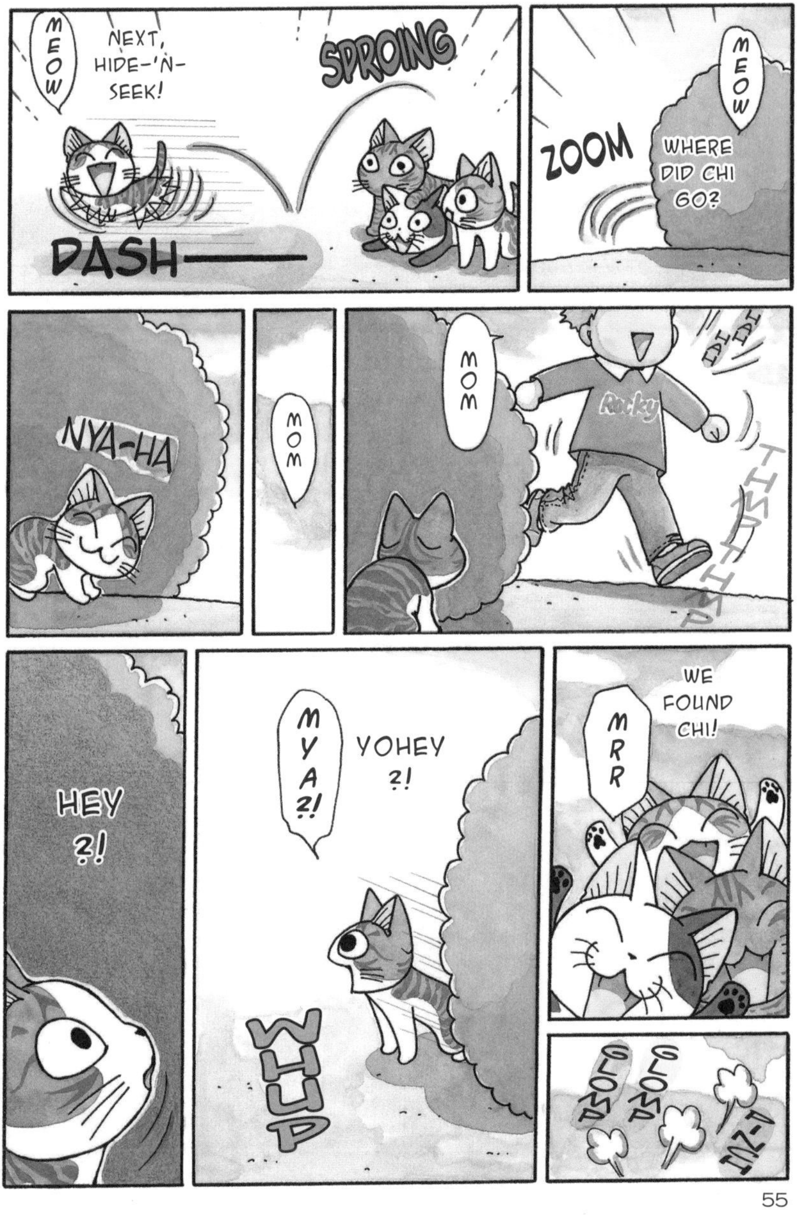
MEOW
NEXT, HIDE-'N-SEEK!
SPROING
DASH——
MEOW
ZOOM
WHERE DID CHI GO?
NYA-HA
MOM
MOM
THMP THMP
HEY ?!
MYA?!
YOHEY ?!
WHUP
MRR
WE FOUND CHI!
GLOMP
GLOMP

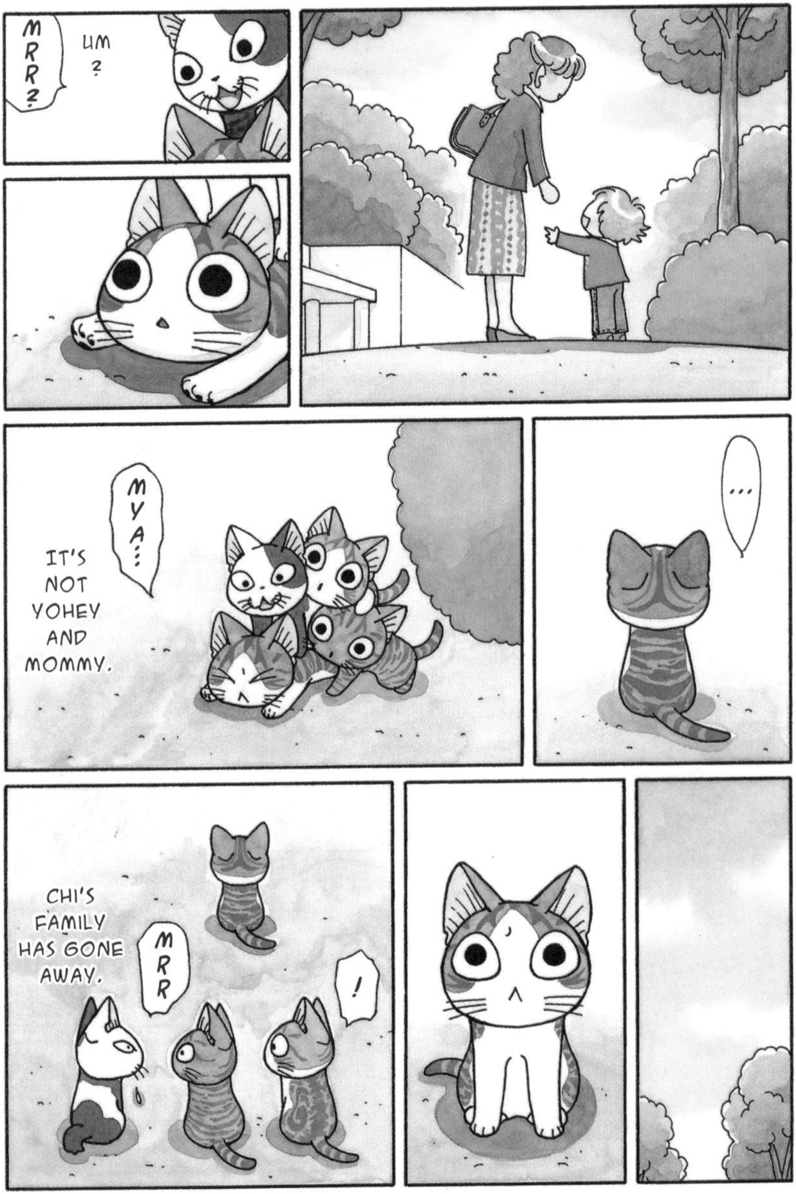
MRR?
UM?
MYA...
IT'S NOT YOHEY AND MOMMY.
...
CHI'S FAMILY HAS GONE AWAY.
MRR
!

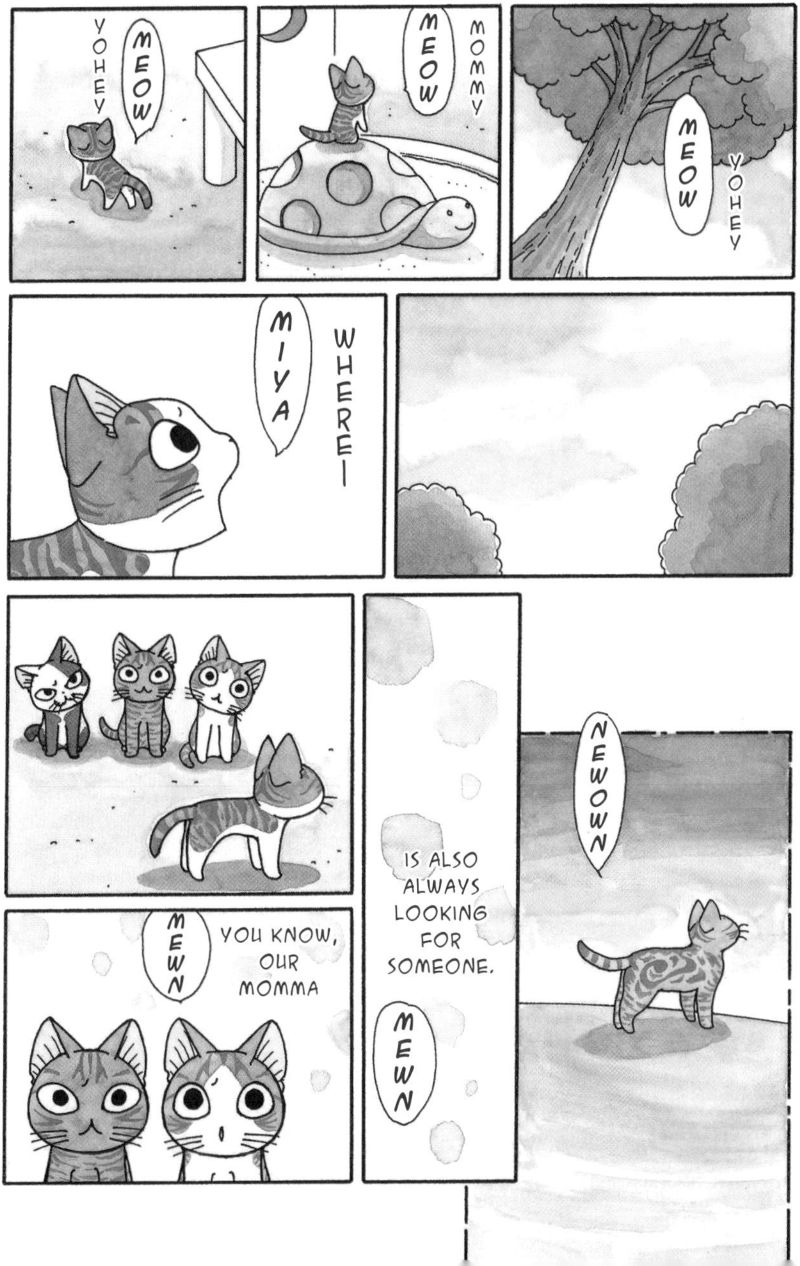
YOHEY
MEOW
MEOW
MOMMY
MEOW
YOHEY
MIYA
WHERE!
MEWN
YOU KNOW, OUR MOMMA
IS ALSO ALWAYS LOOKING FOR SOMEONE.
MEWN
NEWOWN

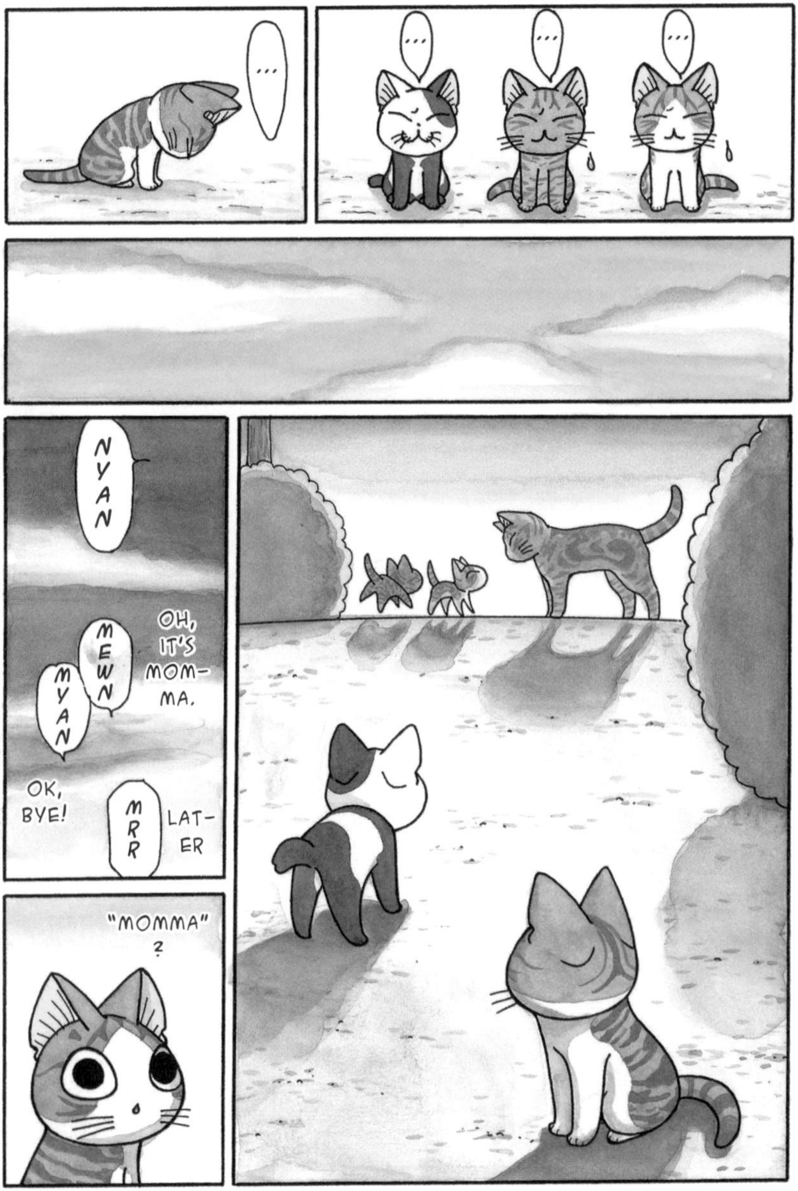
...
...
...
...
NYAN
OH, IT'S MOMMA.
MEWN
MYAN
LATER
MRR
OK, BYE!
"MOMMA"?

the end

homemade 190: a cat is called upon

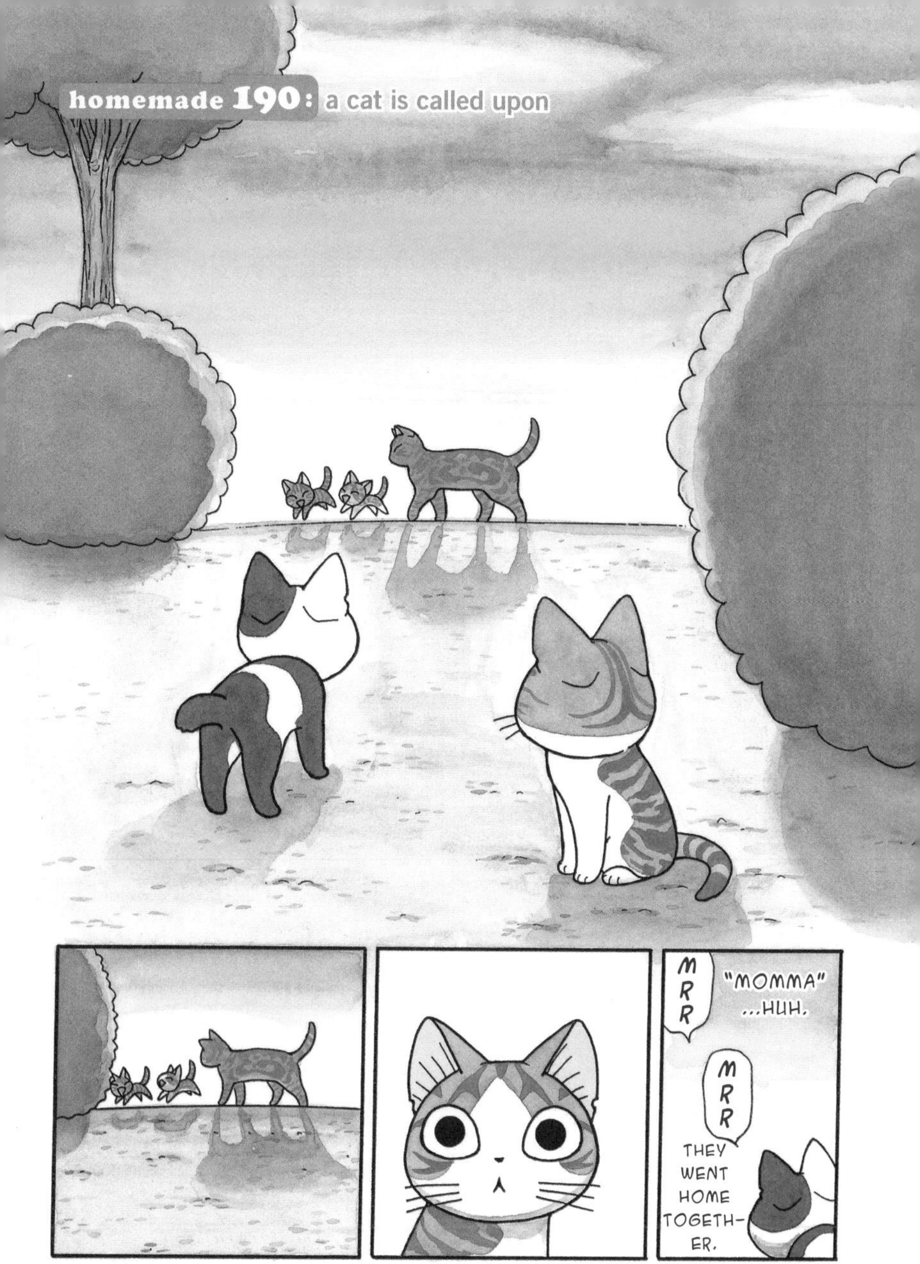
MRR
"MOMMA" ...HUH.
MRR
THEY WENT HOME TOGETH-ER.

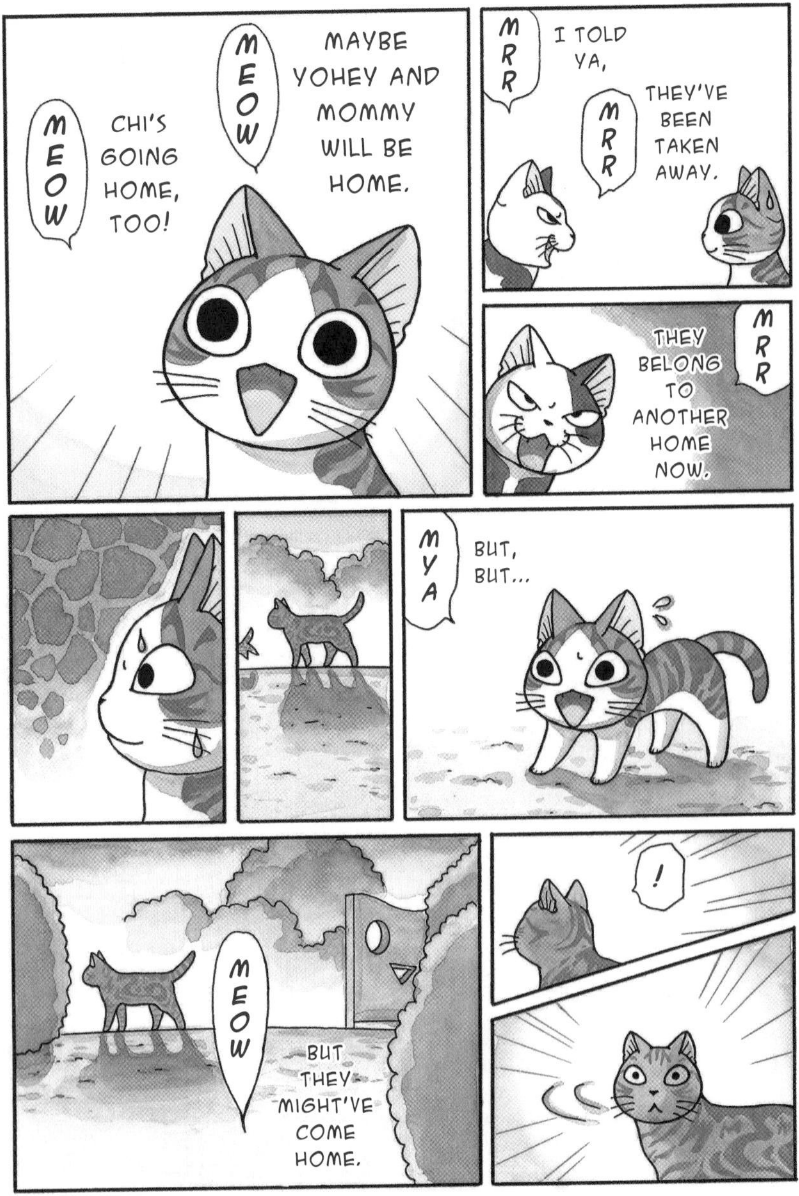
MEOW
CHI'S GOING HOME, TOO!
MEOW
MAYBE YOHEY AND MOMMY WILL BE HOME.
MRR
I TOLD YA,
MRR
THEY'VE BEEN TAKEN AWAY.
THEY BELONG TO ANOTHER HOME NOW.
MRR
MYA
BUT, BUT...
MEOW
BUT THEY MIGHT'VE COME HOME.
!

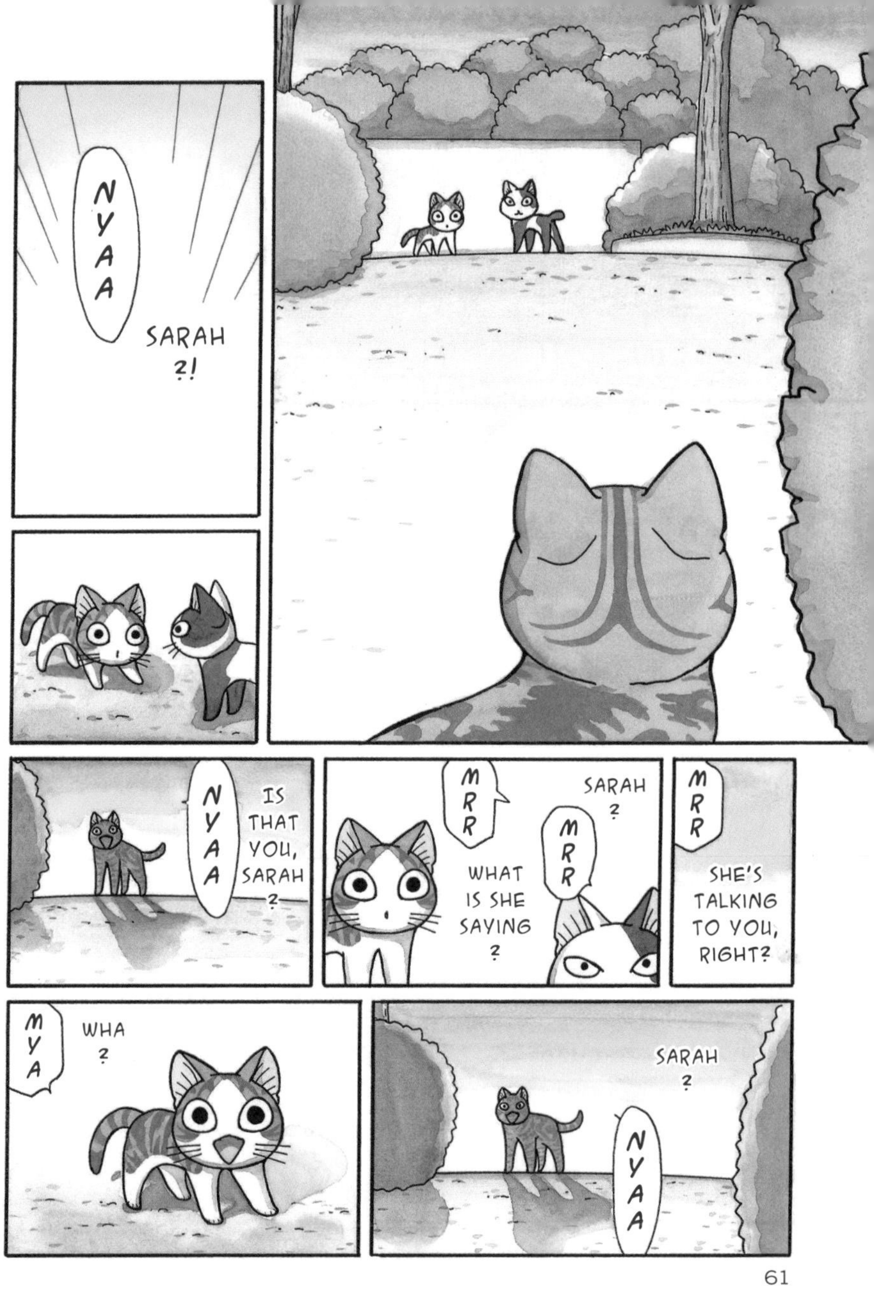
NYAA
SARAH?!
NYAA
IS THAT YOU, SARAH?
MRR
SARAH?
MRR
WHAT IS SHE SAYING?
MRR
SHE'S TALKING TO YOU, RIGHT?
MYA
WHA?
SARAH?
NYAA

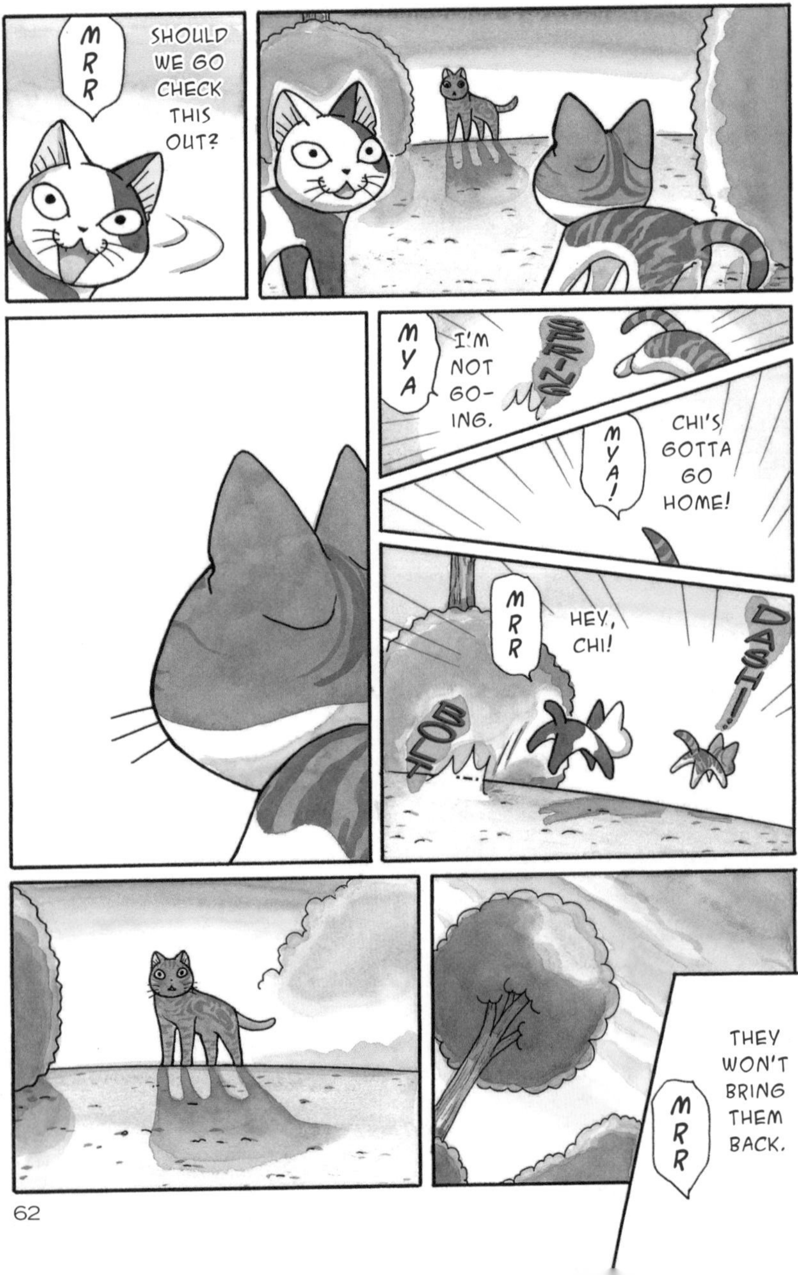
MRR
SHOULD WE GO CHECK THIS OUT?
MYA
I'M NOT GO-ING.
SPRING
MYA!
CHI'S GOTTA GO HOME!
MRR
HEY, CHI!
BOLT
DASH!
MRR
THEY WON'T BRING THEM BACK.

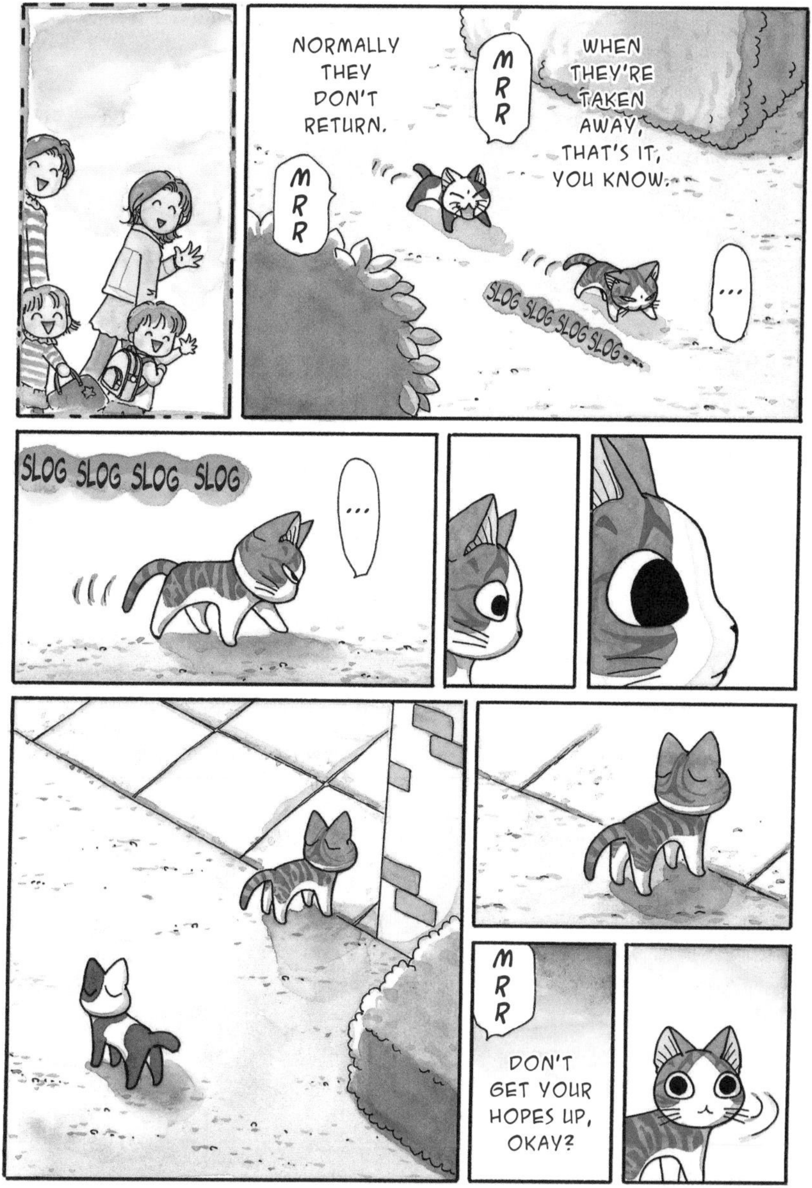
NORMALLY THEY DON'T RETURN.
MRR
WHEN THEY'RE TAKEN AWAY, THAT'S IT, YOU KNOW.
MRR
SLOG SLOG SLOG SLOG...
...
SLOG SLOG SLOG SLOG
...
MRR
DON'T GET YOUR HOPES UP, OKAY?

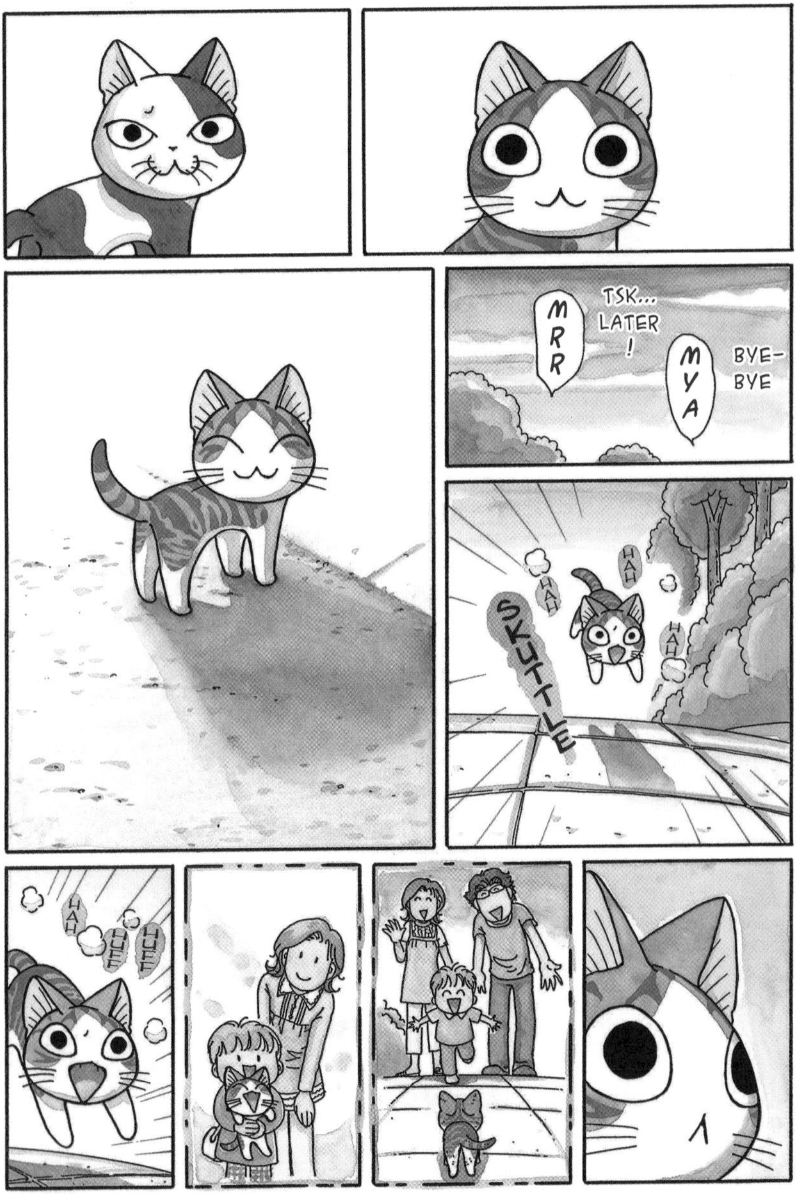
MRR
TSK... LATER!
MYA
BYE-BYE
HAH
SKUTTLE
HAH
HAH
HAH
HUFF
HUFF

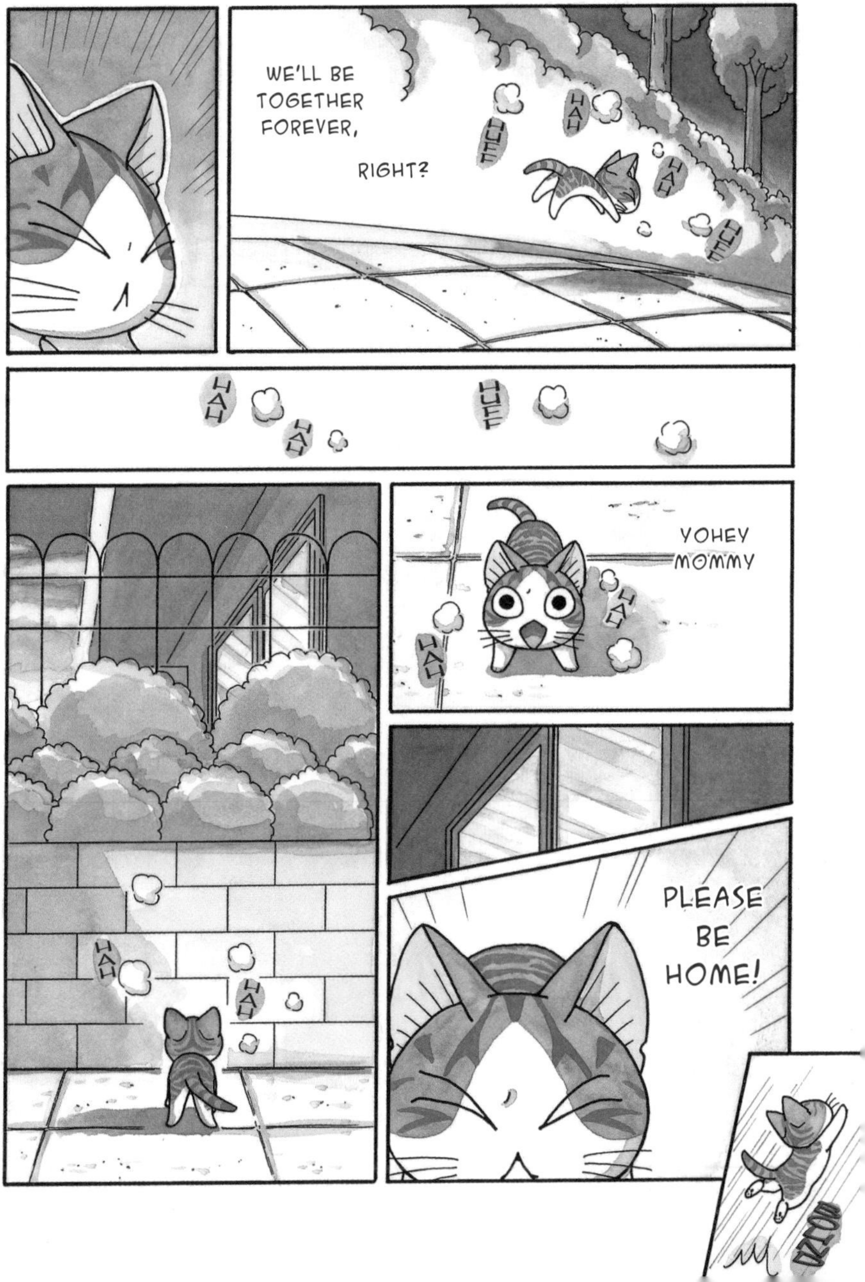
WE'LL BE TOGETHER FOREVER,
RIGHT?
HUFF
HAH
HAH
HUFF
HAH
HAH
HUFF
HAH
HAH
YOHEY MOMMY
HAH
HAH
PLEASE BE HOME!
ZOOM

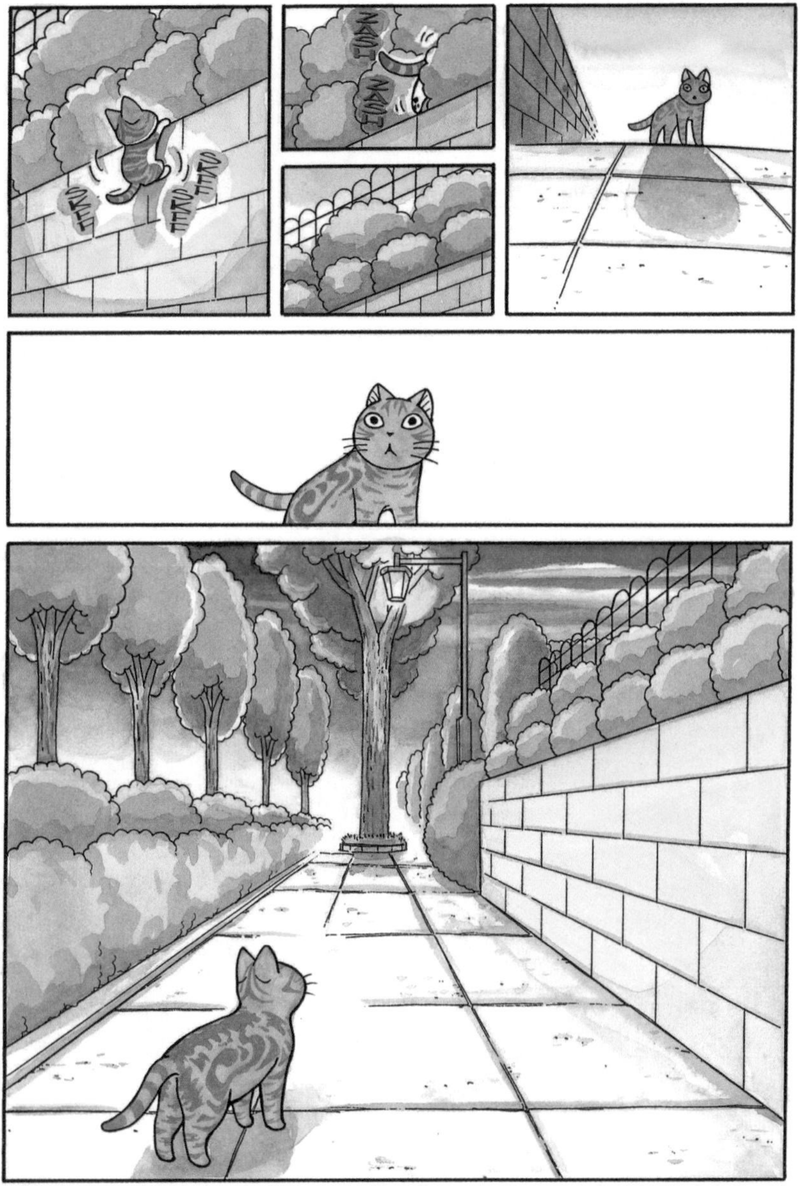
SKRFF
SKRFF
SKRFF
ZASH
ZASH

the end

homemade 191: a cat becomes sensitive

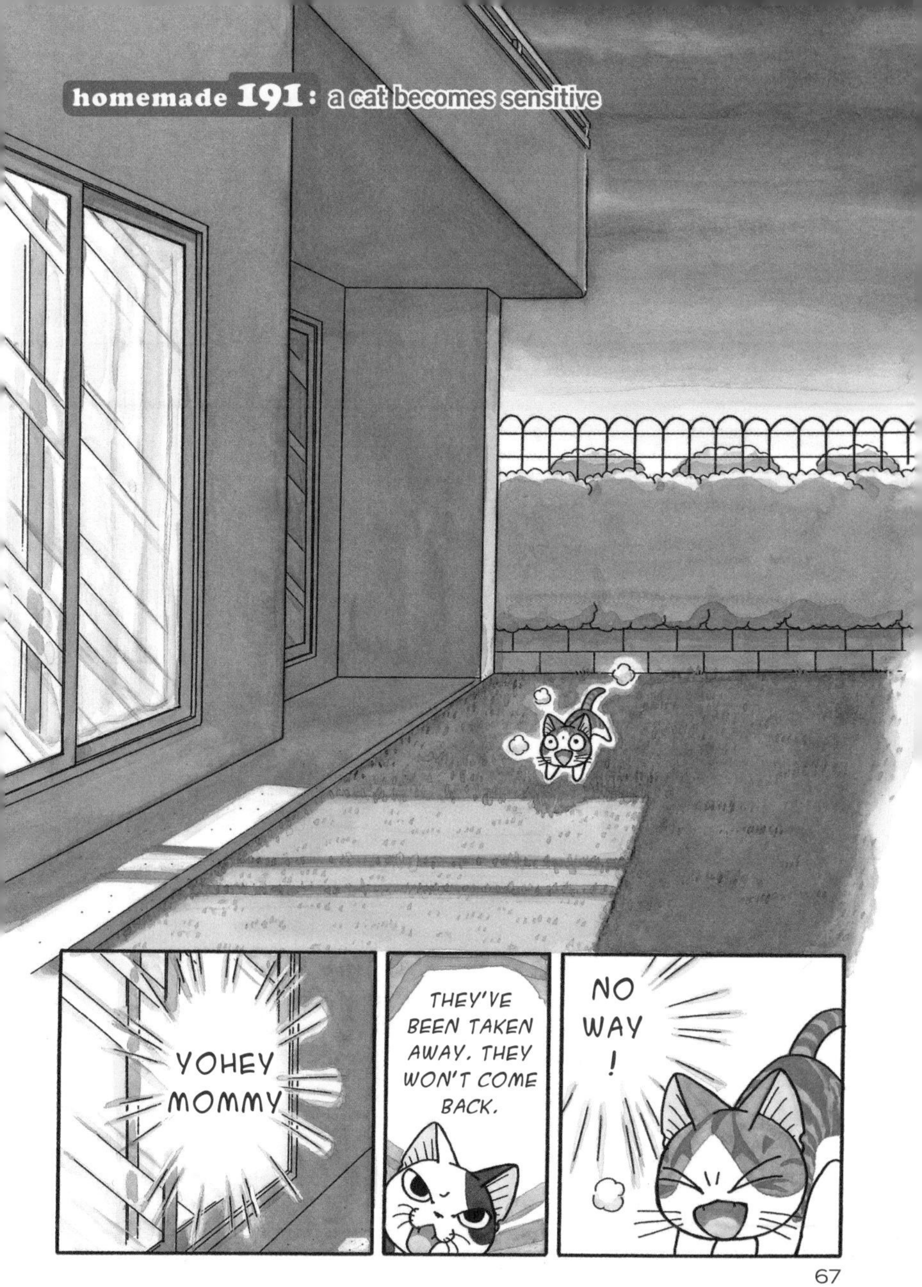
YOHEY MOMMY
THEY'VE BEEN TAKEN AWAY. THEY WON'T COME BACK.
NO WAY!

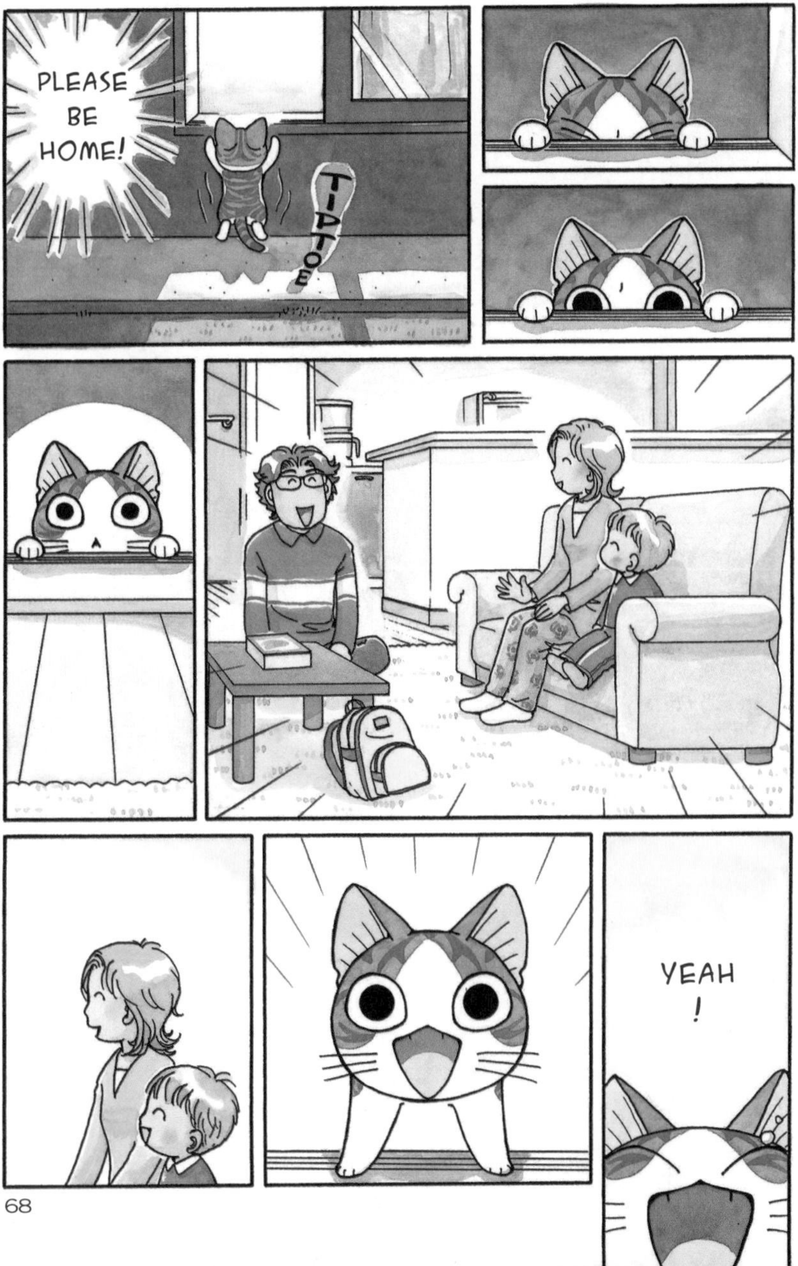
PLEASE BE HOME!
TIPTOE
YEAH!

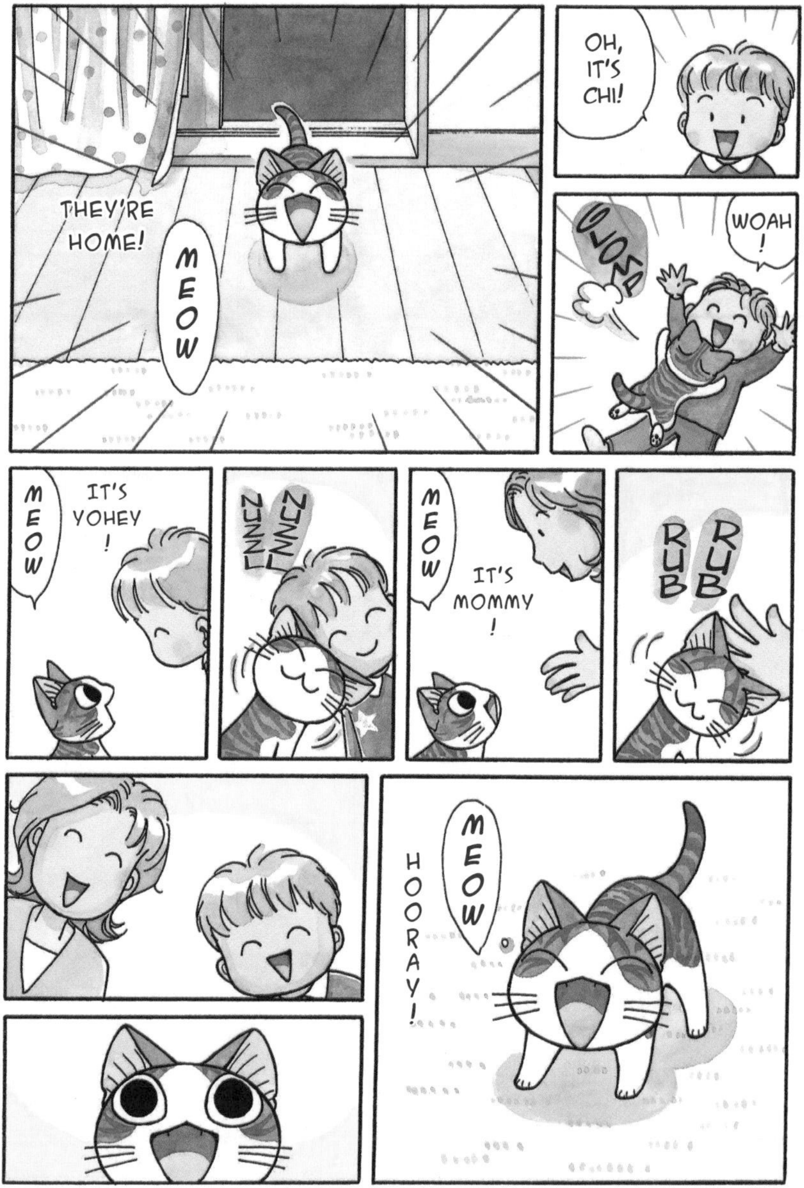
THEY'RE HOME!
MEOW
OH, IT'S CHI!
GLOMP
WOAH!
MEOW
IT'S YOHEY!
NUZZLE NUZZLE
MEOW
IT'S MOMMY!
RUB RUB
MEOW
HOORAY!

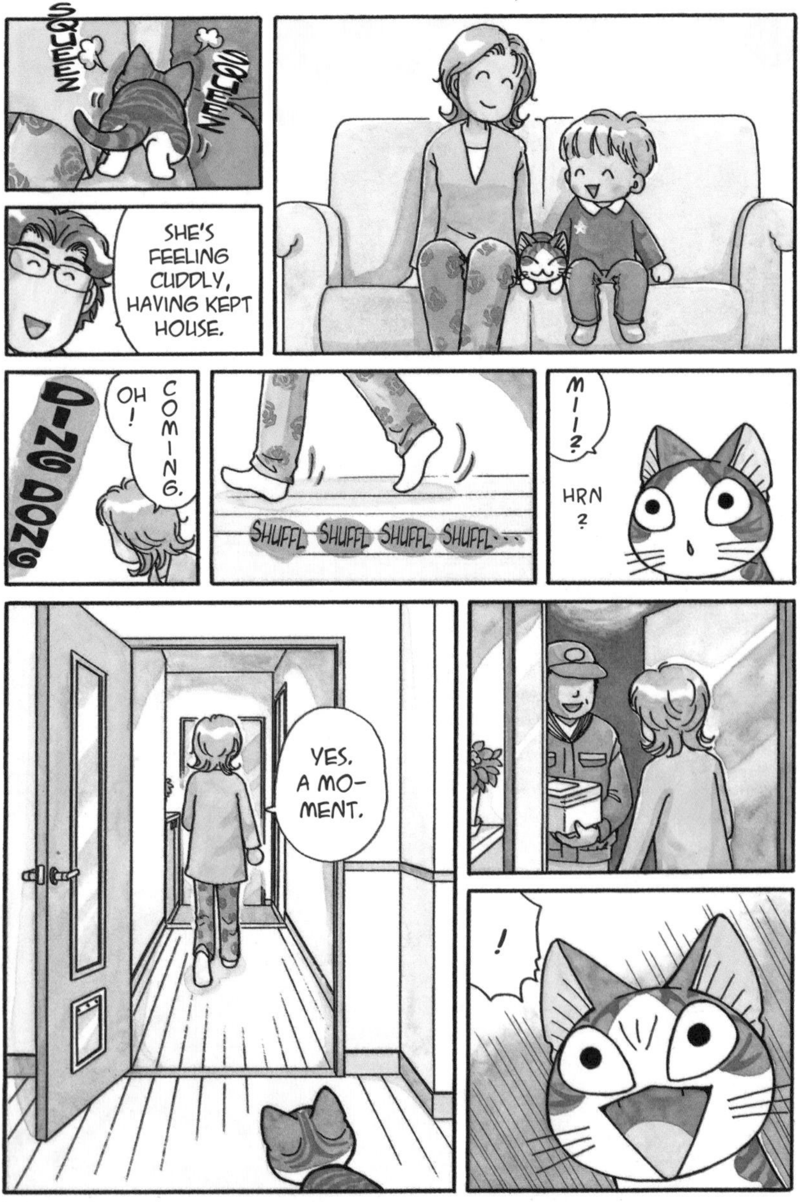
SQUEEN
SQUEEN
SHE'S FEELING CUDDLY, HAVING KEPT HOUSE.
DING DONG
OH!
COMING.
SHUFFL SHUFFL SHUFFL SHUFFL...
MI!?
HRN?
YES. A MO-MENT.
!

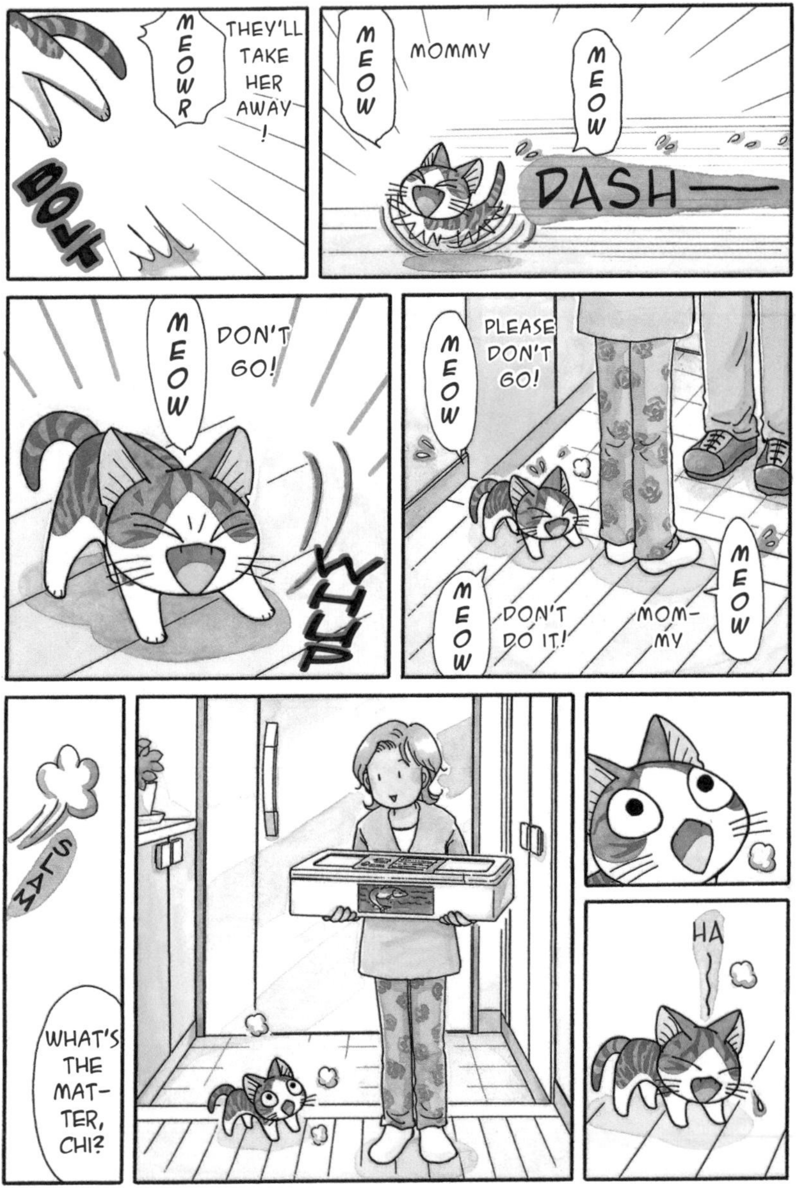
MEOWR
THEY'LL TAKE HER AWAY!
BOLT
MEOW
MOMMY
MEOW
DASH—
MEOW
DON'T GO!
WHUP
MEOW
PLEASE DON'T GO!
MEOW
DON'T DO IT!
MOM-MY
MEOW
SLAM
WHAT'S THE MAT-TER, CHI?
HA

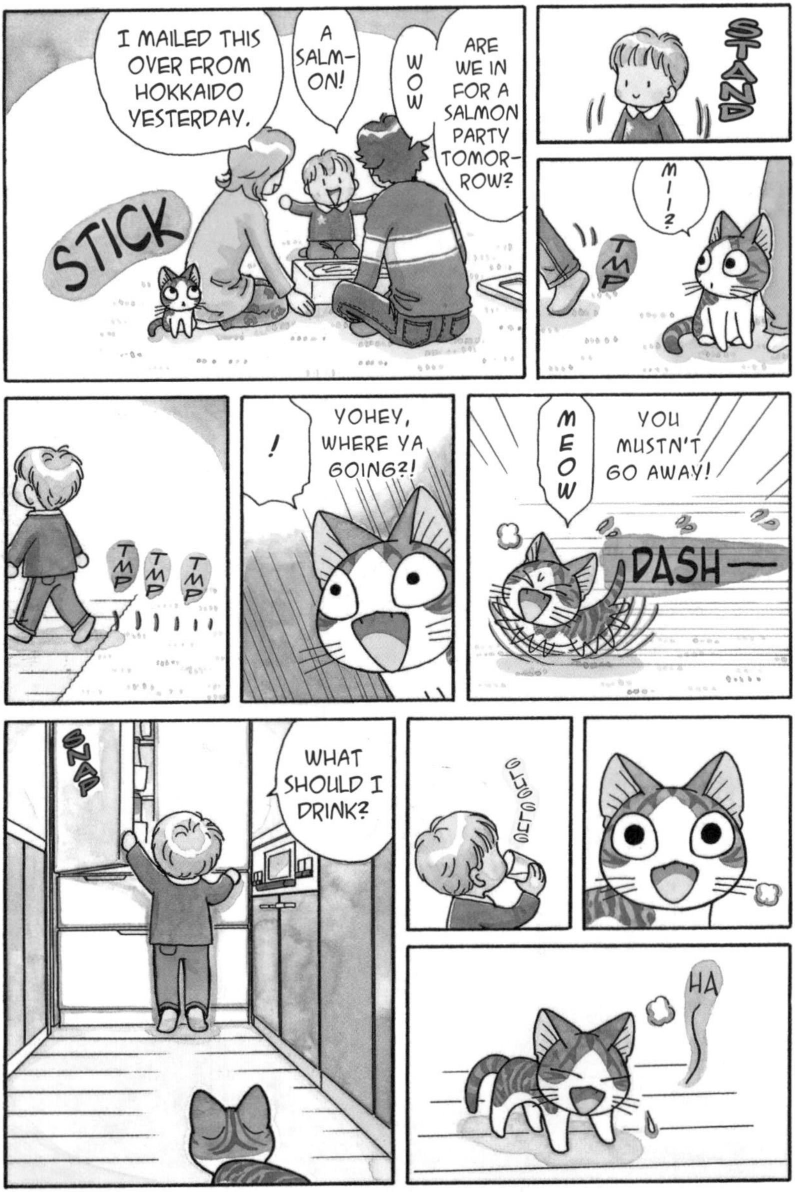
I MAILED THIS OVER FROM HOKKAIDO YESTERDAY.
A SALM-ON!
WOW
ARE WE IN FOR A SALMON PARTY TOMOR-ROW?
STICK
STAND
MII?
TMP
TMP
TMP
TMP
!
YOHEY, WHERE YA GOING?!
MEOW
YOU MUSTN'T GO AWAY!
DASH—
SNAP
WHAT SHOULD I DRINK?
GLUG GLUG
HA

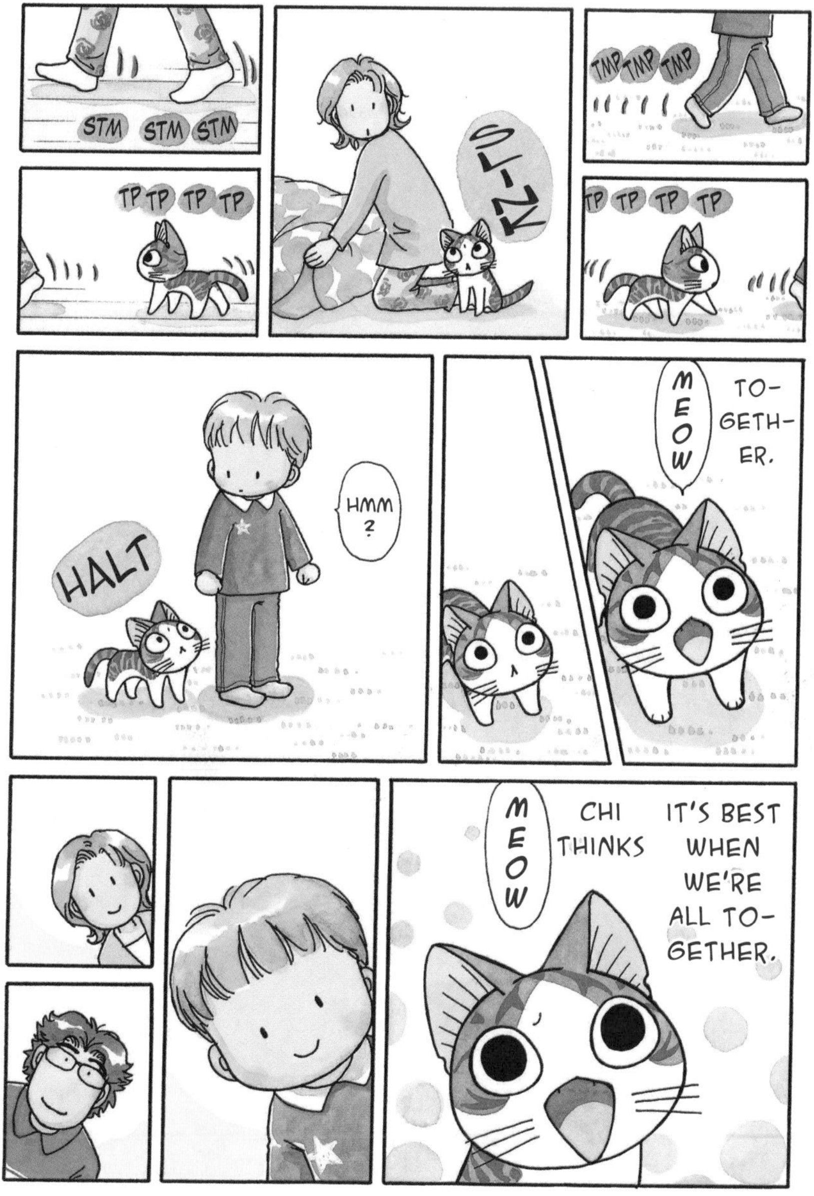
STM STM STM
TP TP TP TP
SLINK
TMP TMP TMP
TP TP TP TP
HALT
HMM?
MEOW
TO-GETH-ER.
MEOW
CHI THINKS IT'S BEST WHEN WE'RE ALL TO-GETHER.

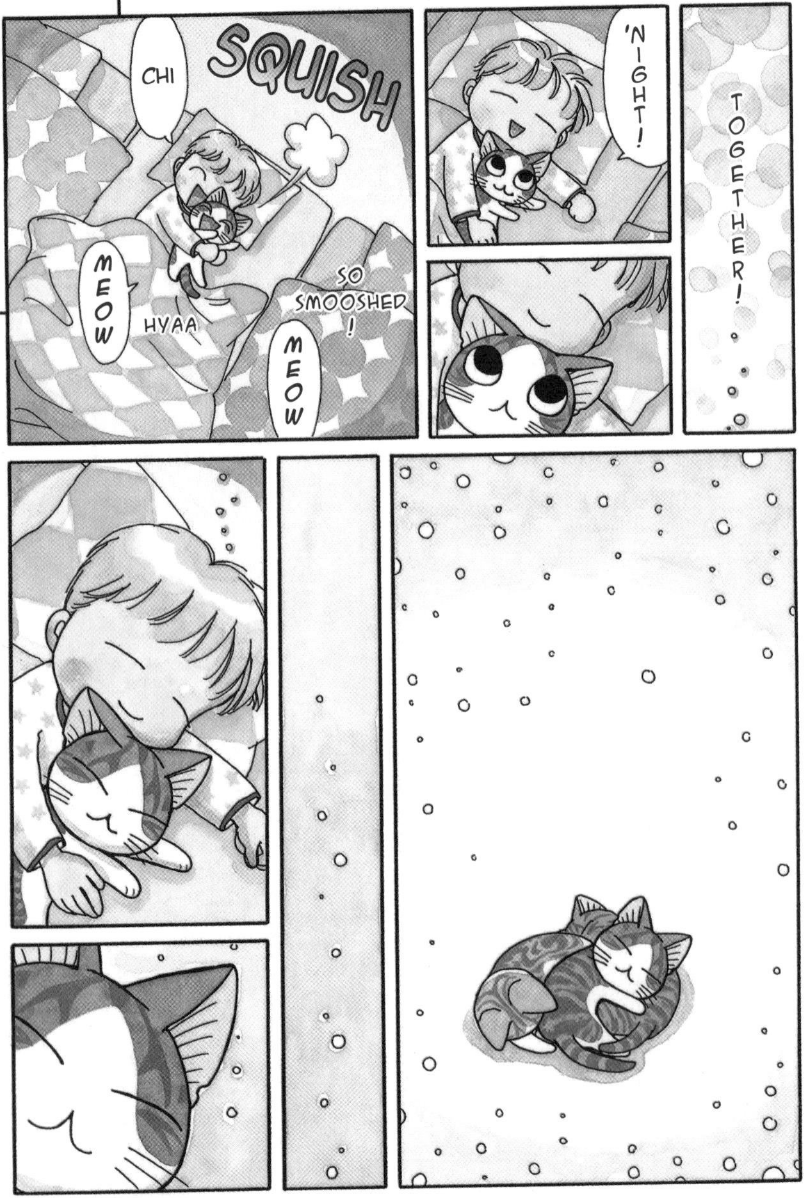
CHI
SQUISH
MEOW
HYAA
SO SMOOSHED!
MEOW
'NIGHT!
TOGETHER!

the end

homemade 192: a cat communes

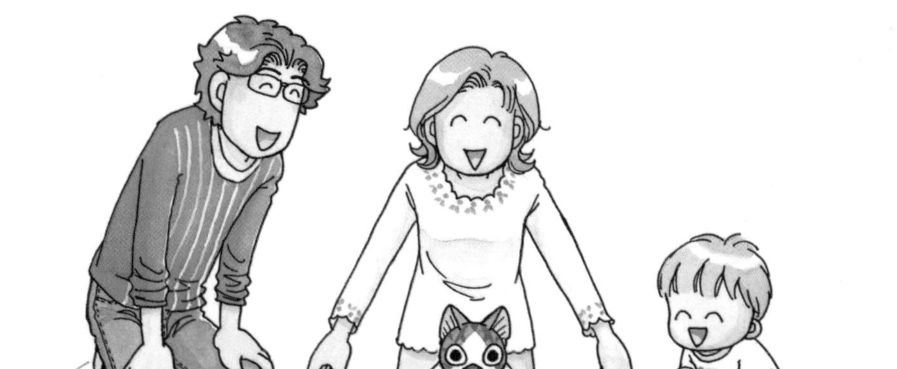

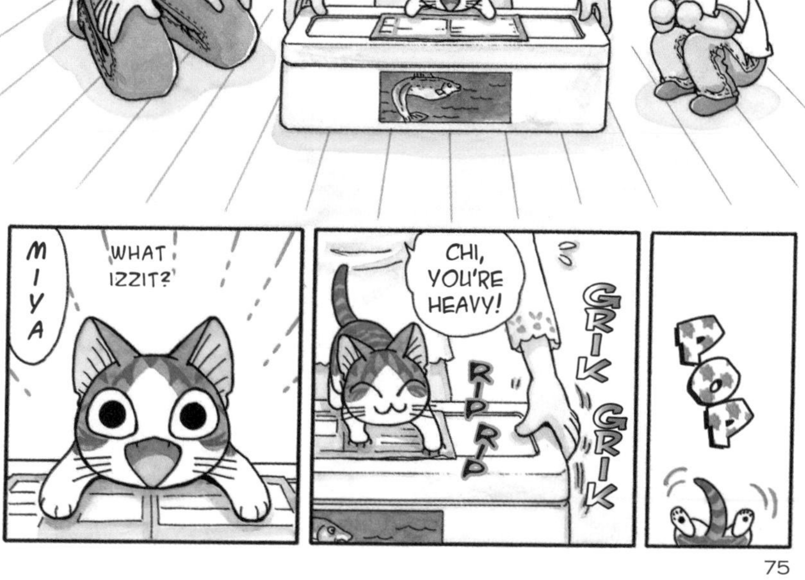
MIYA
WHAT IZZIT?
CHI, YOU'RE HEAVY!
GRIK GRIK GRIK
RIP RIP
POP

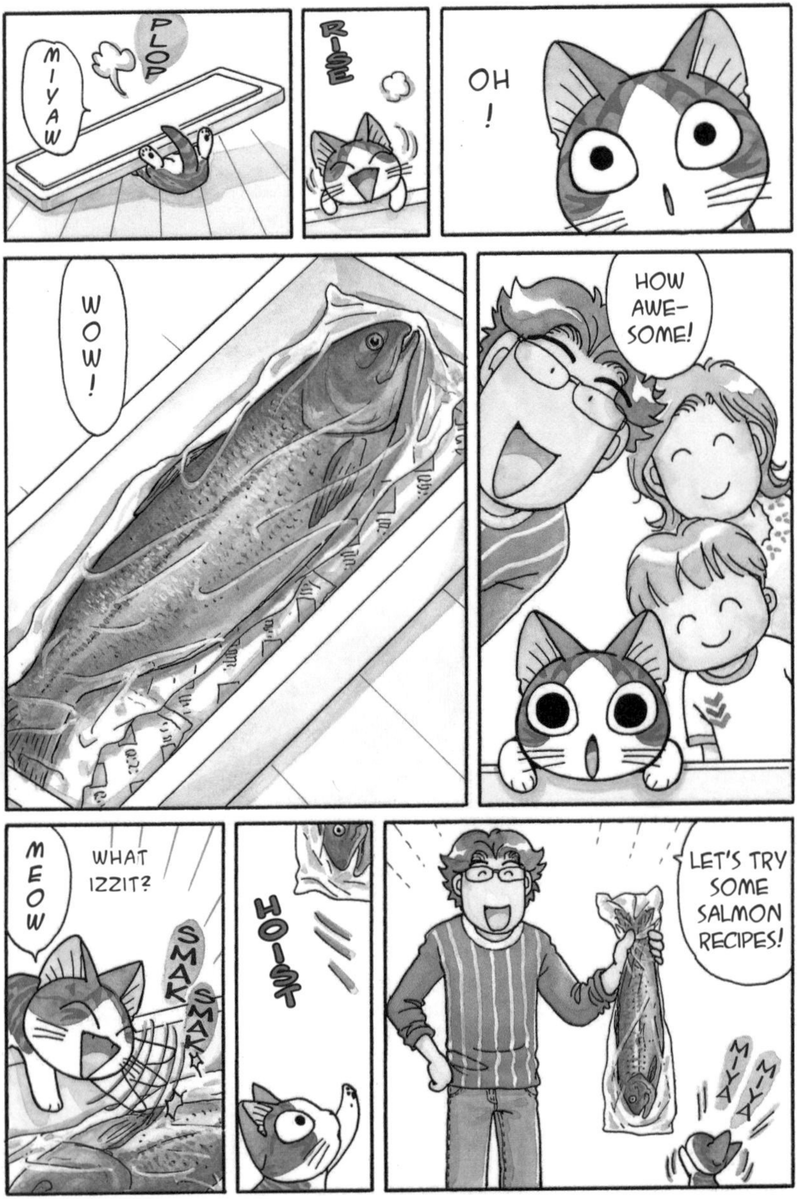
PLOP
MIYAW
RISE
OH!
WOW!
HOW AWESOME!
MEOW
WHAT IZZIT?
SMAK
SMAK
HOIST
LET'S TRY SOME SALMON RECIPES!
MIYA
MIYA

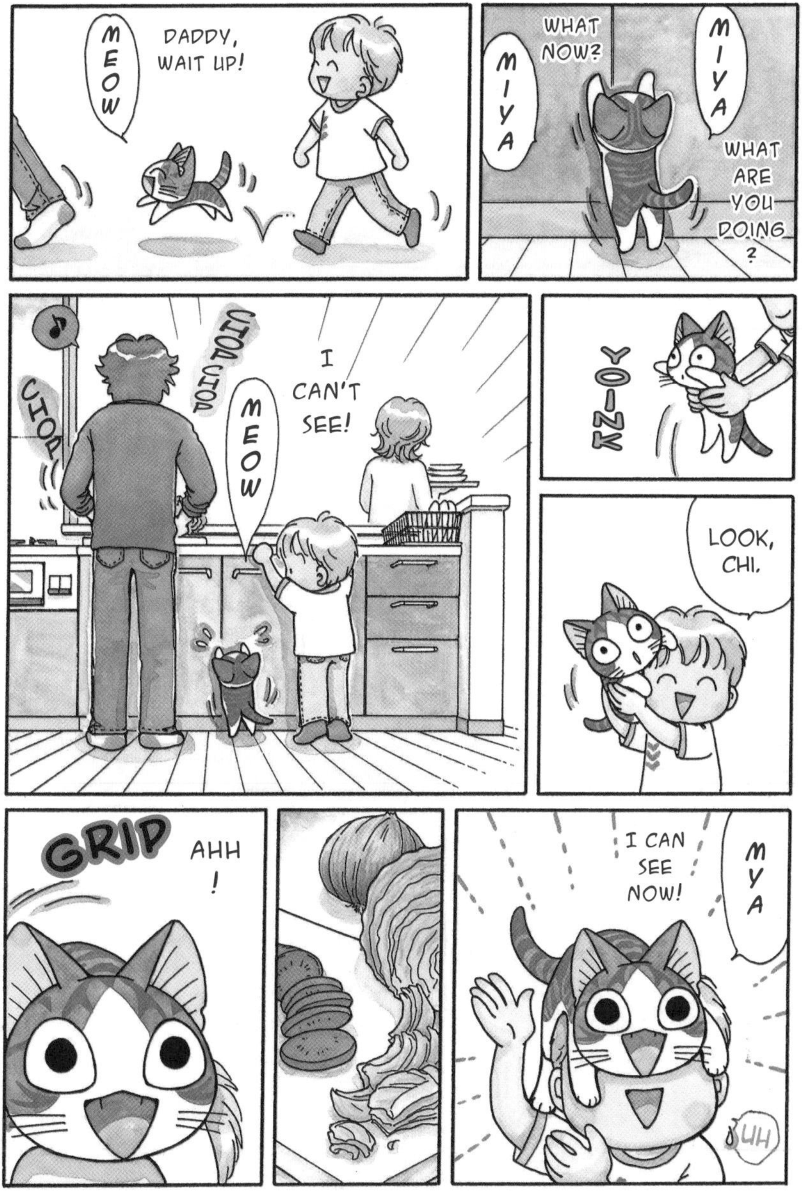
MEOW
DADDY, WAIT UP!
MIYA
WHAT NOW?
MIYA
WHAT ARE YOU DOING?
♪
CHOP
CHOP CHOP
I CAN'T SEE!
MEOW
YOINK
LOOK, CHI.
GRIP
AHH!
I CAN SEE NOW!
MYA
UH

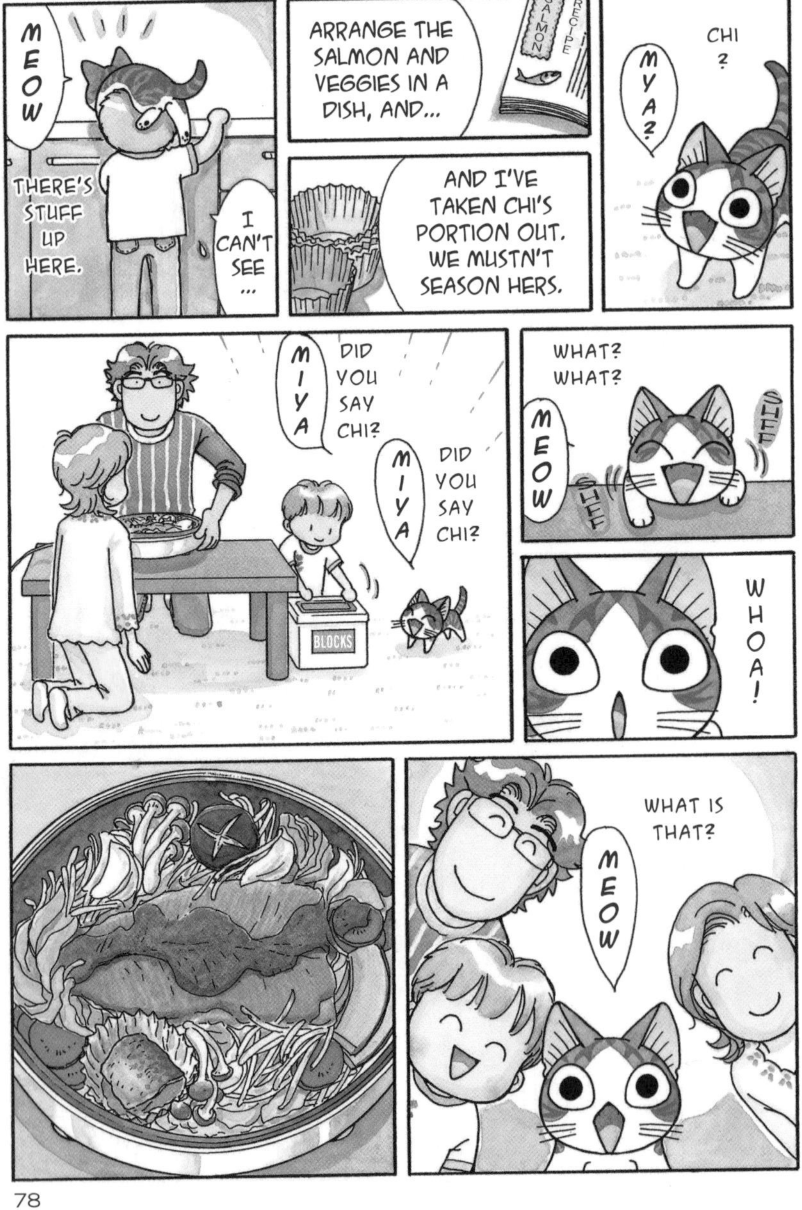
MEOW
THERE'S STUFF UP HERE.
I CAN'T SEE ...
ARRANGE THE SALMON AND VEGGIES IN A DISH, AND...
SALMON
RECIPE
AND I'VE TAKEN CHI'S PORTION OUT. WE MUSTN'T SEASON HERS.
MYA?
CHI?
MIYA
DID YOU SAY CHI?
MIYA
DID YOU SAY CHI?
BLOCKS
WHAT? WHAT?
MEOW
SHFF
SHFF
WHOA!
MEOW
WHAT IS THAT?

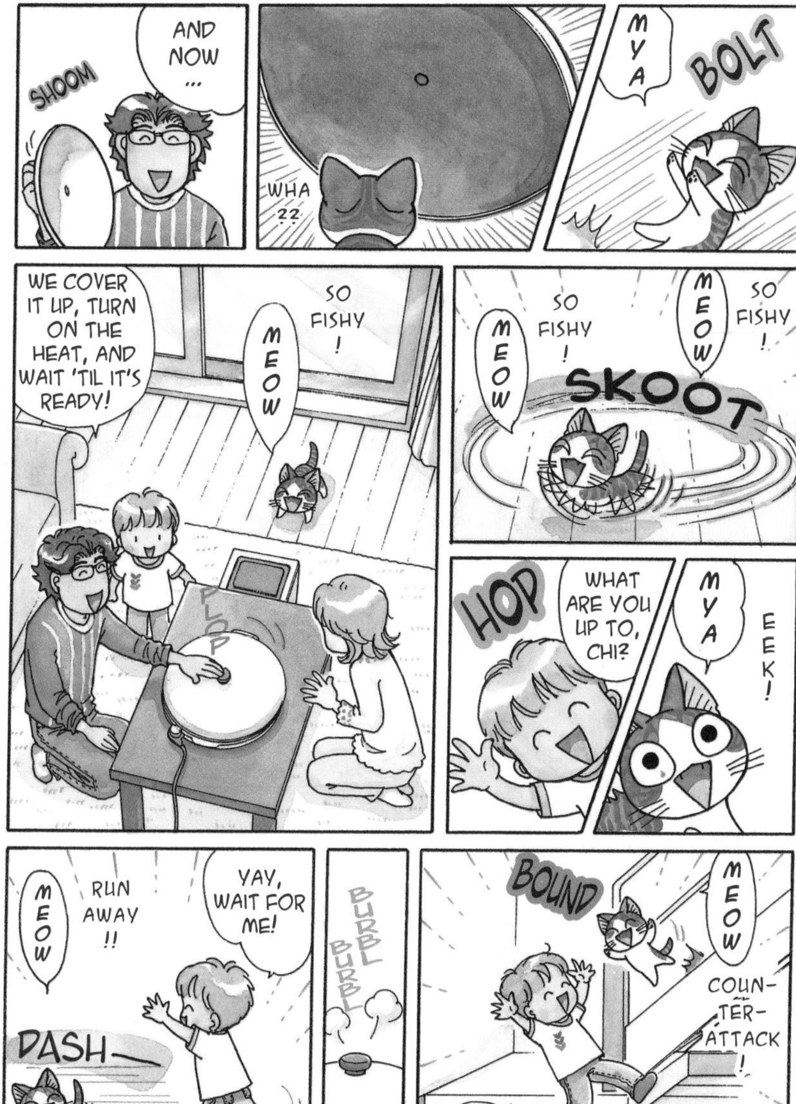

SHOOM
AND NOW ...
WHA ??
MYA
BOLT
WE COVER IT UP, TURN ON THE HEAT, AND WAIT 'TIL IT'S READY!
MEOW
SO FISHY !
PLOP
MEOW
SO FISHY !
MEOW
SO FISHY !
SKOOT
HOP
WHAT ARE YOU UP TO, CHI?
MYA
EEK!
MEOW
RUN AWAY !!
YAY, WAIT FOR ME!
DASH—
BURBL
BURBL
BOUND
MEOW
COUNTER-ATTACK !
WOAH !

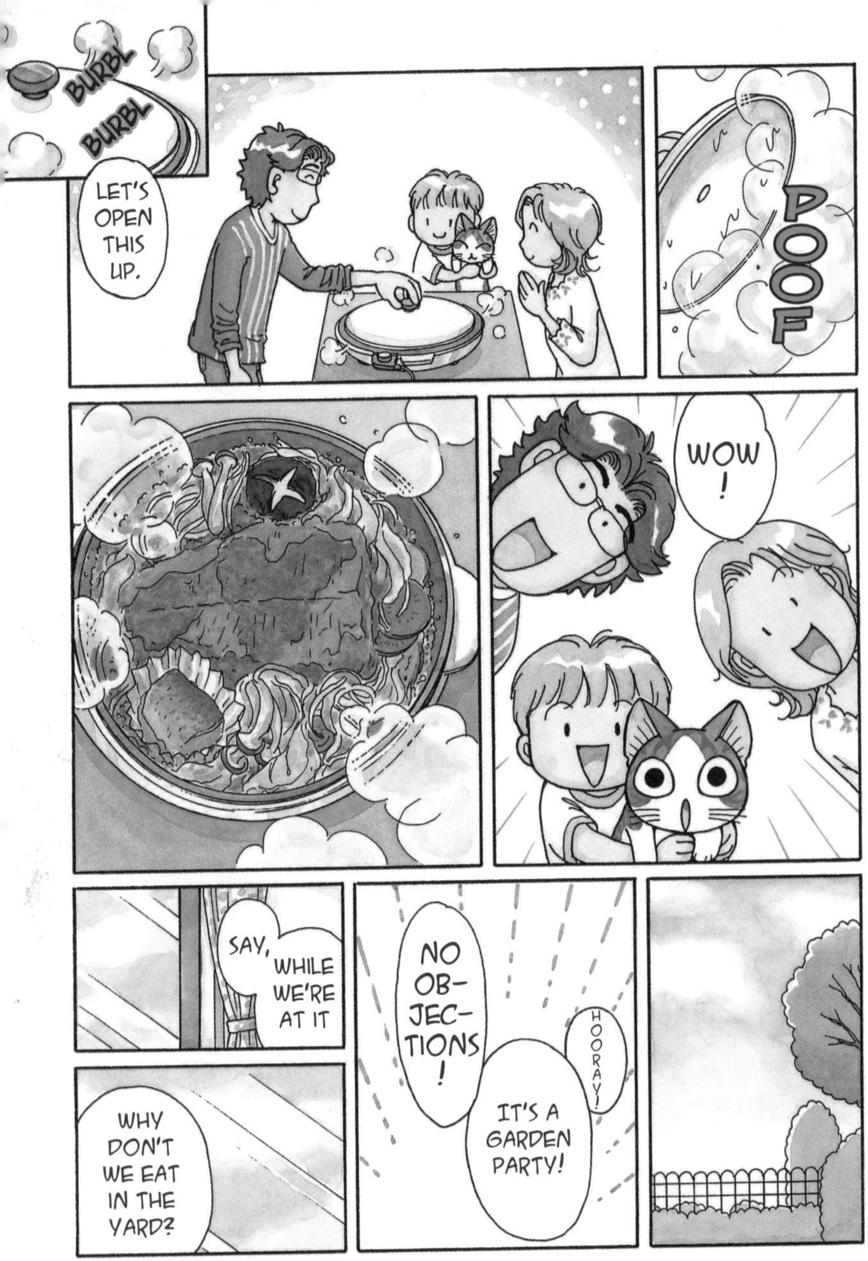
BURBL
BURBL
LET'S OPEN THIS UP.
POOF
WOW!
SAY, WHILE WE'RE AT IT
WHY DON'T WE EAT IN THE YARD?
NO OBJECTIONS!
HOORAY!
IT'S A GARDEN PARTY!

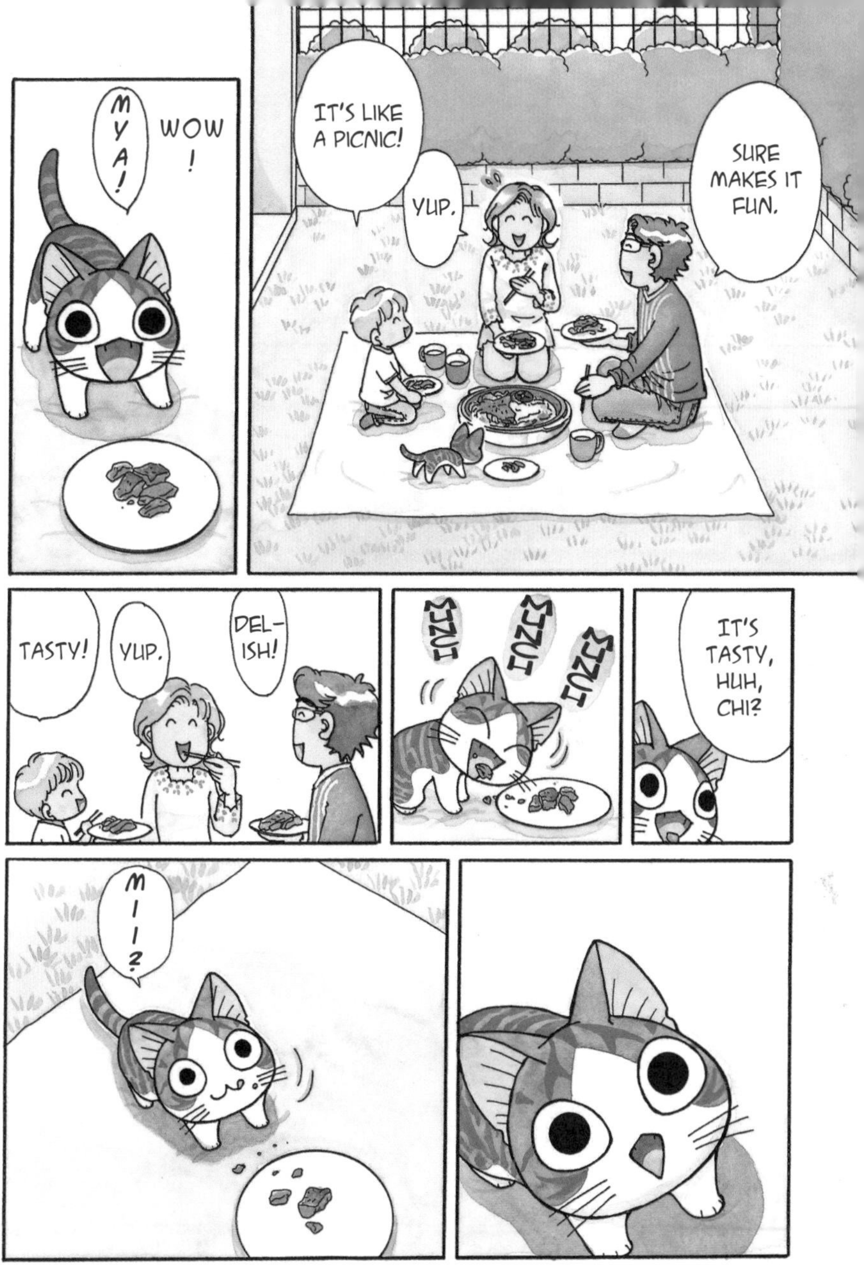
MYA!
WOW!
IT'S LIKE A PICNIC!
YUP.
SURE MAKES IT FUN.
TASTY!
YUP.
DEL-ISH!
MUNCH
MUNCH
MUNCH
IT'S TASTY, HUH, CHI?
MII?

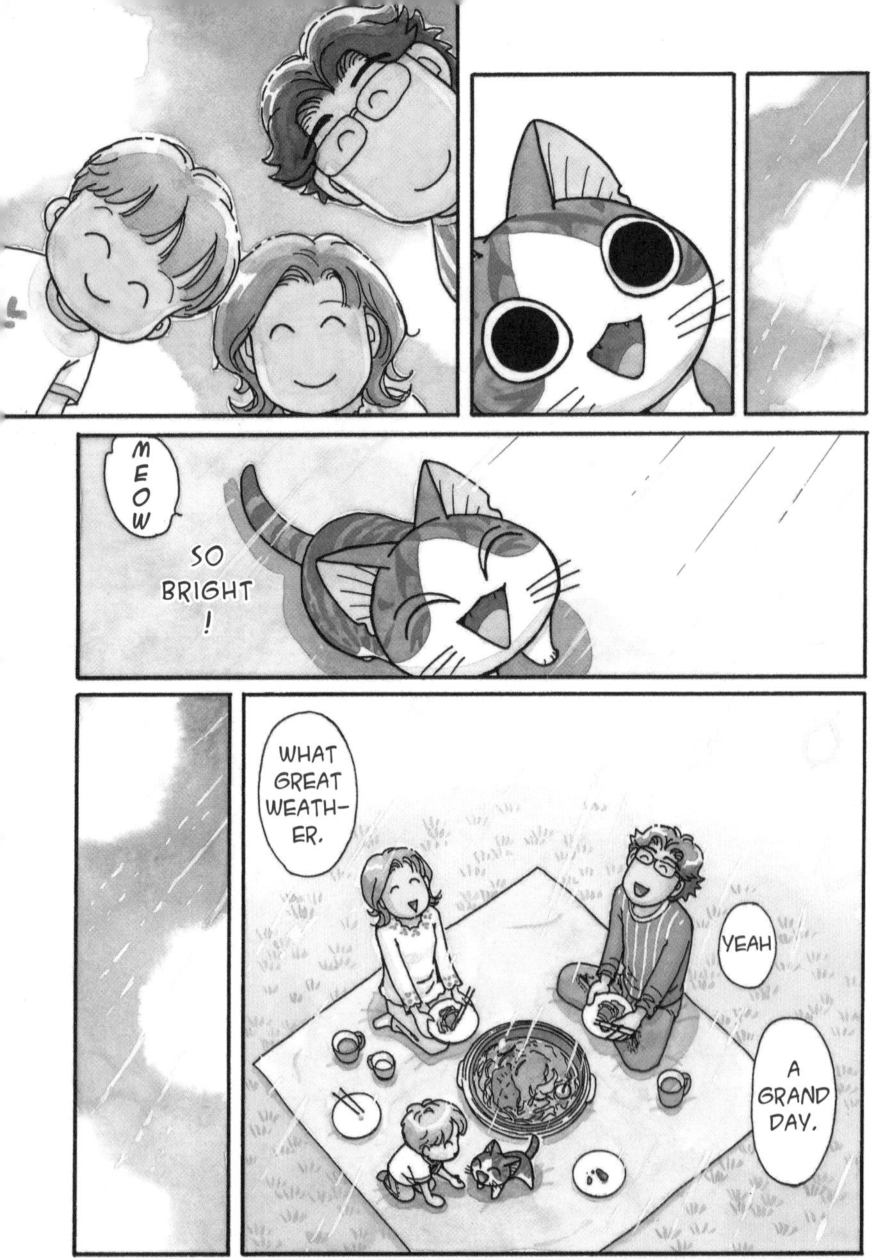
MEOW
SO BRIGHT!
WHAT GREAT WEATH-ER.
YEAH
A GRAND DAY.

the end

homemade 193: a cat is surprised

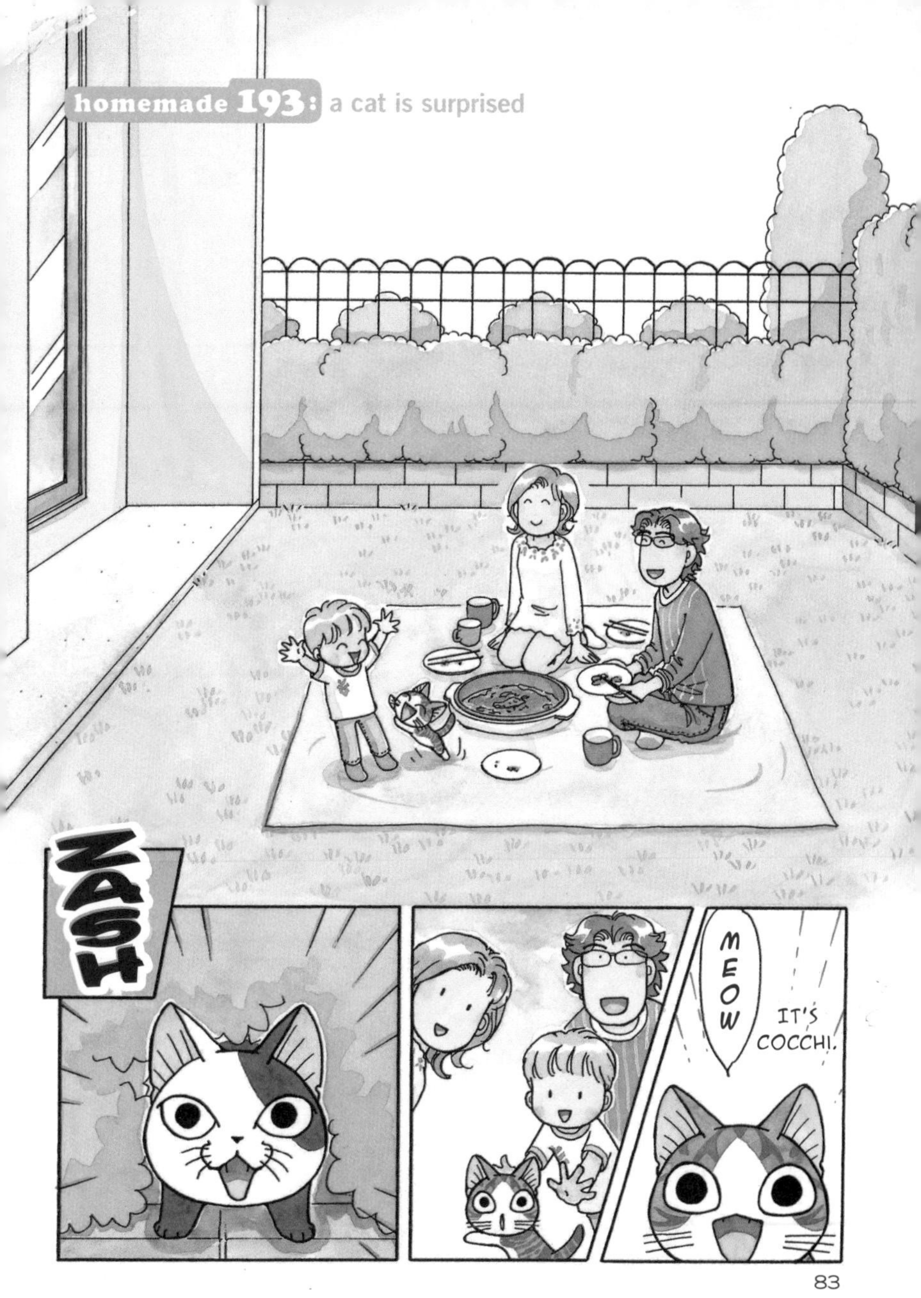
ZASH
MEOW
IT'S COCCHI.

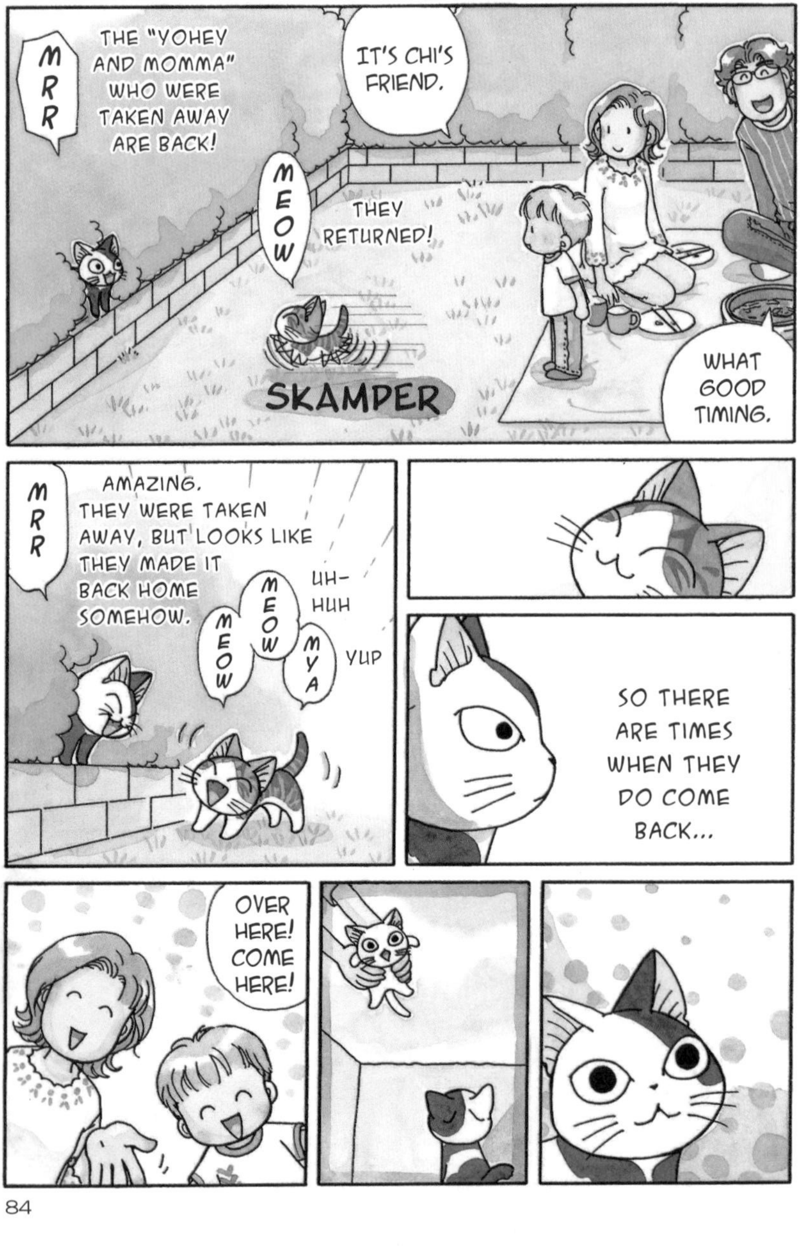
MRR
THE "YOHEY AND MOMMA" WHO WERE TAKEN AWAY ARE BACK!
IT'S CHI'S FRIEND.
MEOW
THEY RETURNED!
SKAMPER
WHAT GOOD TIMING.
MRR
AMAZING. THEY WERE TAKEN AWAY, BUT LOOKS LIKE THEY MADE IT BACK HOME SOMEHOW.
MEOW
MEOW
UH-HUH
MYA
YUP
SO THERE ARE TIMES WHEN THEY DO COME BACK...
OVER HERE! COME HERE!

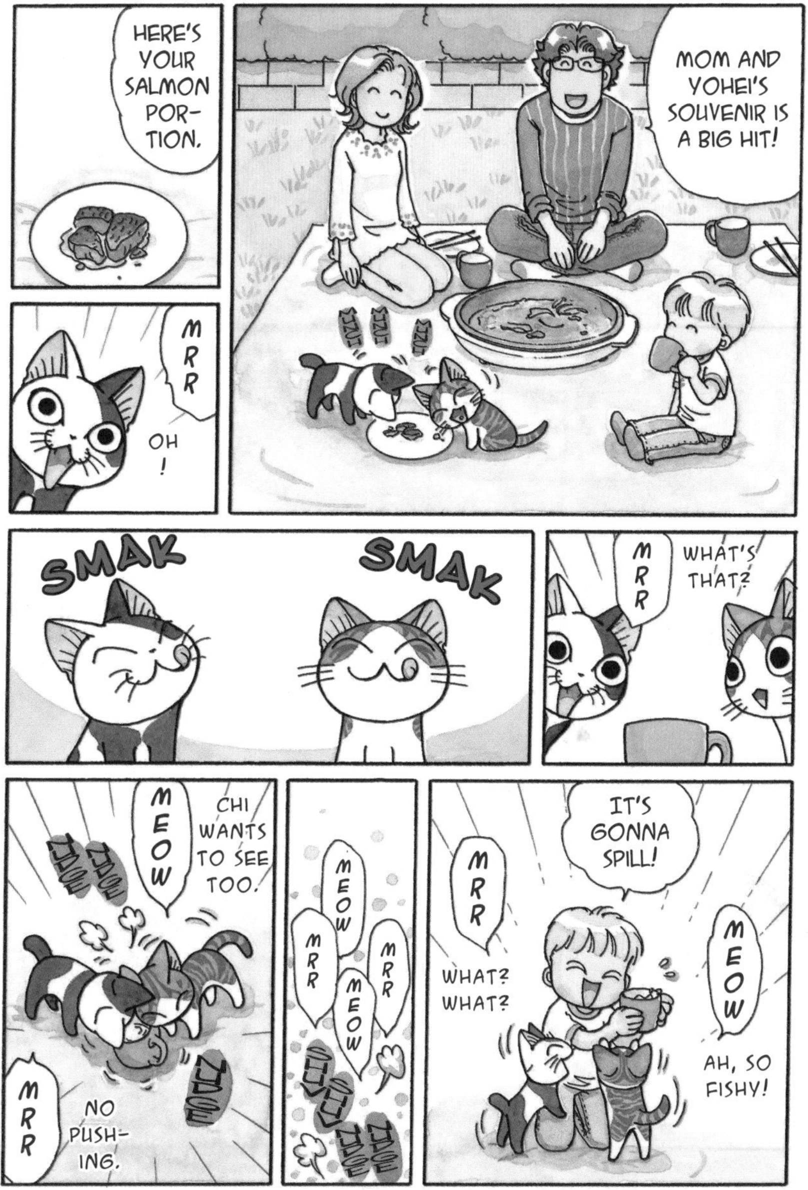
HERE'S YOUR SALMON PORTION.
MRR
OH!
MOM AND YOHEI'S SOUVENIR IS A BIG HIT!
SMAK
SMAK
MRR
WHAT'S THAT?
MEOW
CHI WANTS TO SEE TOO.
MRR
NO PUSHING.
MEOW
MRR
MRR
MEOW
MRR
IT'S GONNA SPILL!
WHAT? WHAT?
MEOW
AH, SO FISHY!

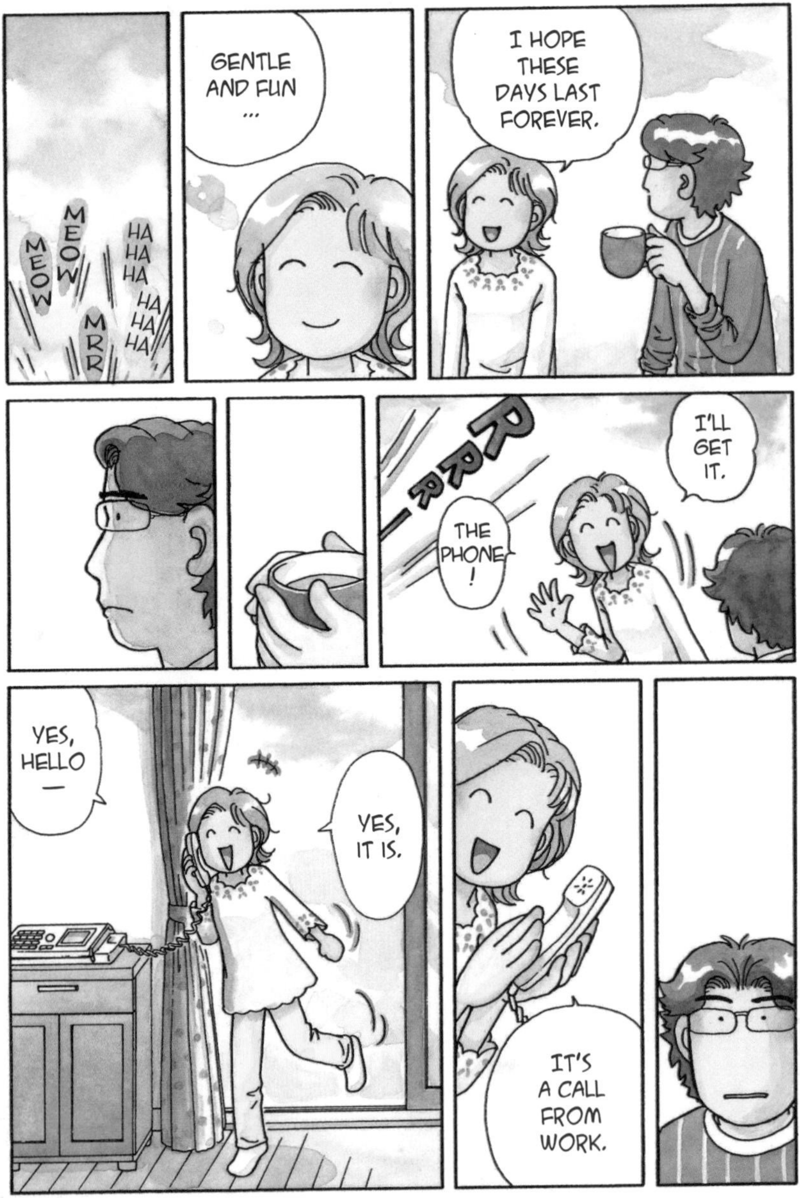

MEOW
MEOW
HA HA HA HA HA HA
MRR
GENTLE AND FUN ...
I HOPE THESE DAYS LAST FOREVER.
RRRR—
THE PHONE!
I'LL GET IT.
YES, HELLO —
YES, IT IS.
IT'S A CALL FROM WORK.

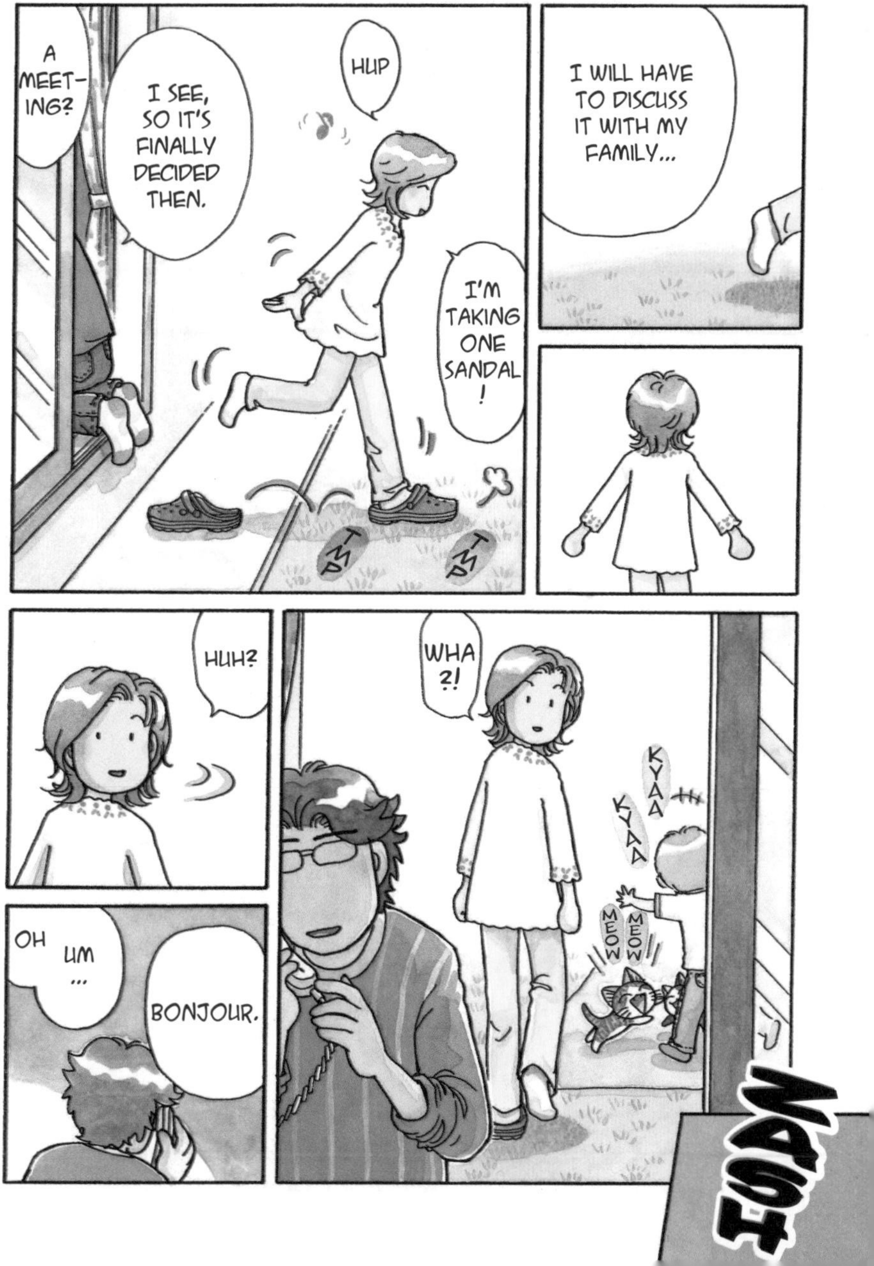
A MEETING?
I SEE, SO IT'S FINALLY DECIDED THEN.
HUP
I'M TAKING ONE SANDAL!
TMP
TMP
I WILL HAVE TO DISCUSS IT WITH MY FAMILY...
HUH?
OH UM ...
BONJOUR.
WHA?!
KYAA
KYAA
MEOW
MEOW
WASH

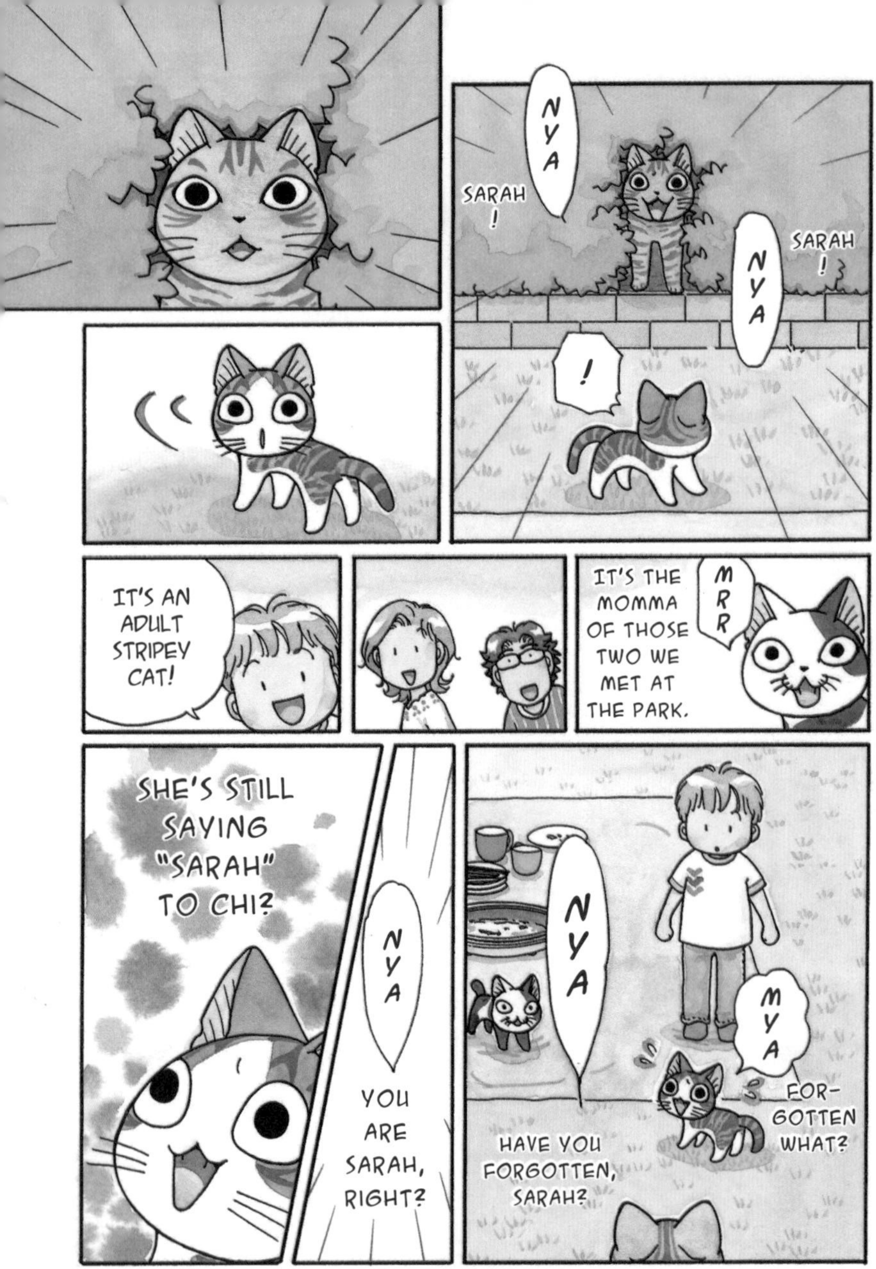
NYA
SARAH!
NYA
SARAH!
!
IT'S AN ADULT STRIPEY CAT!
IT'S THE MOMMA OF THOSE TWO WE MET AT THE PARK.
MRR
SHE'S STILL SAYING "SARAH" TO CHI?
NYA
YOU ARE SARAH, RIGHT?
NYA
HAVE YOU FORGOTTEN, SARAH?
MYA
FOR-GOTTEN WHAT?

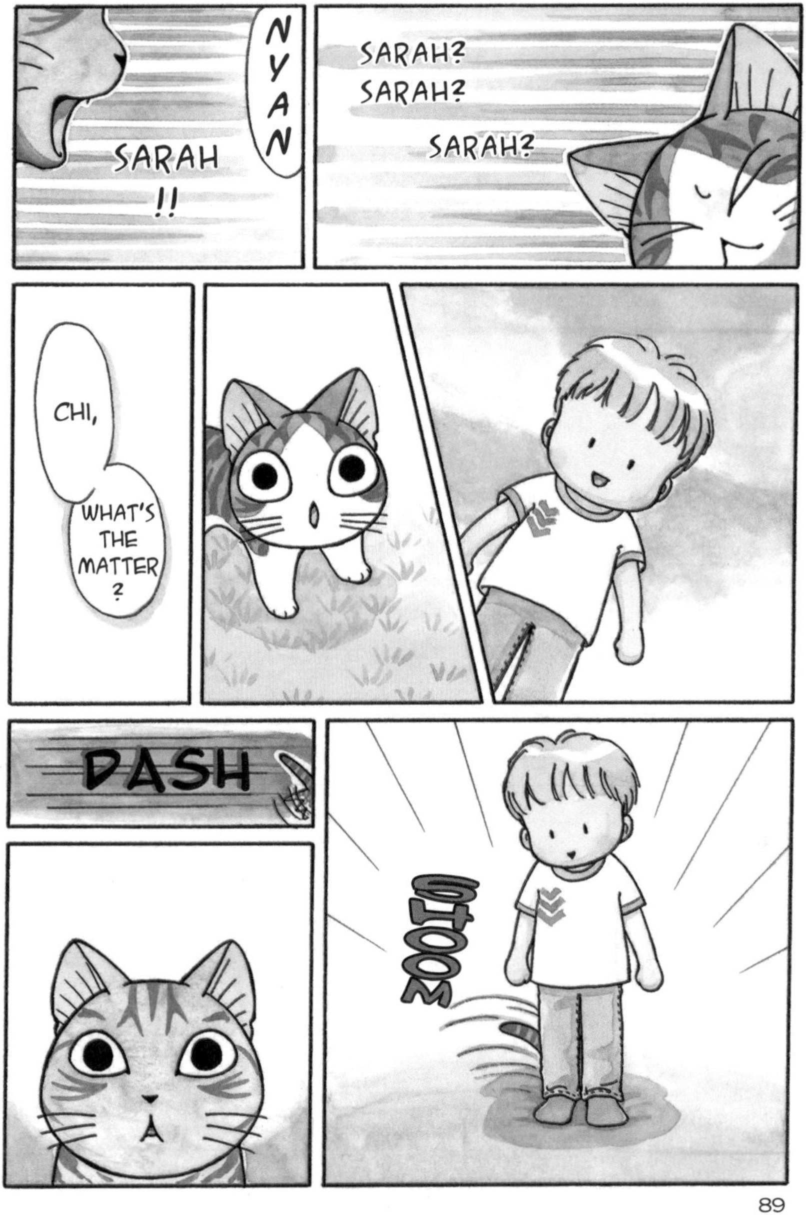
SARAH
!!
NYAN
SARAH?
SARAH?
SARAH?
CHI,
WHAT'S THE MATTER?
DASH
WHOOSH

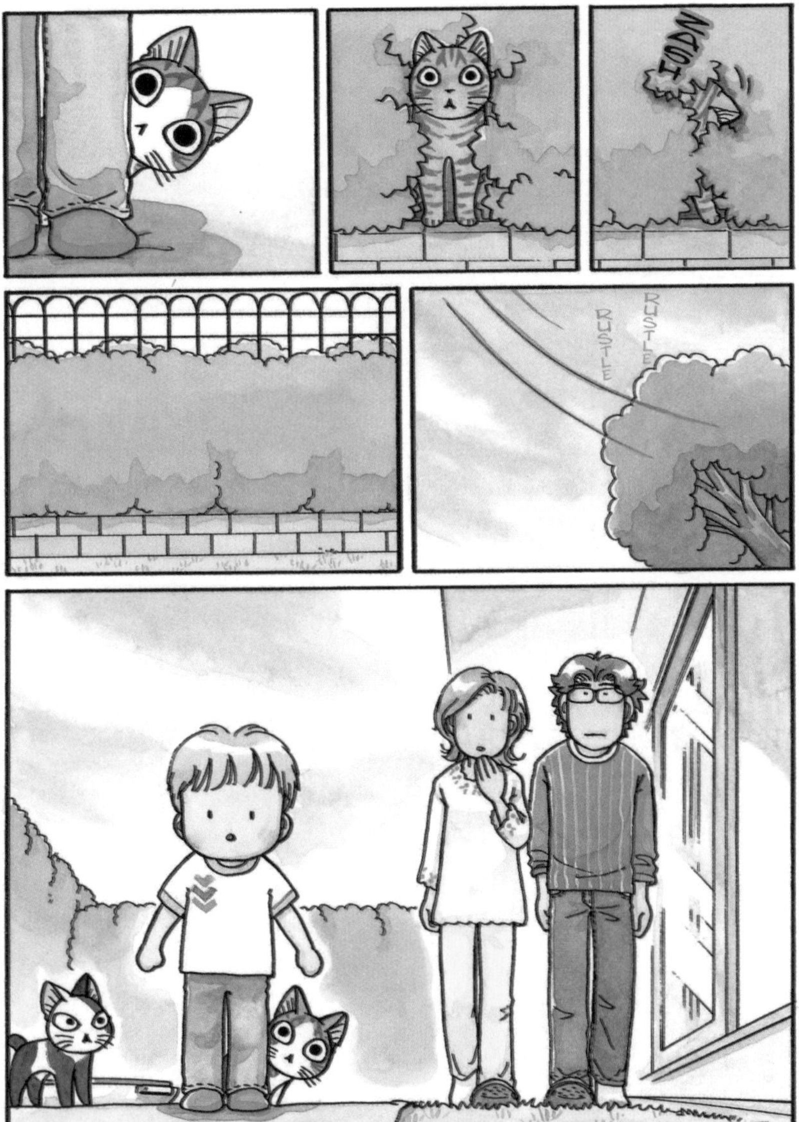
RUSTLE
RUSTLE

the end

homemade 194: a cat is compelled

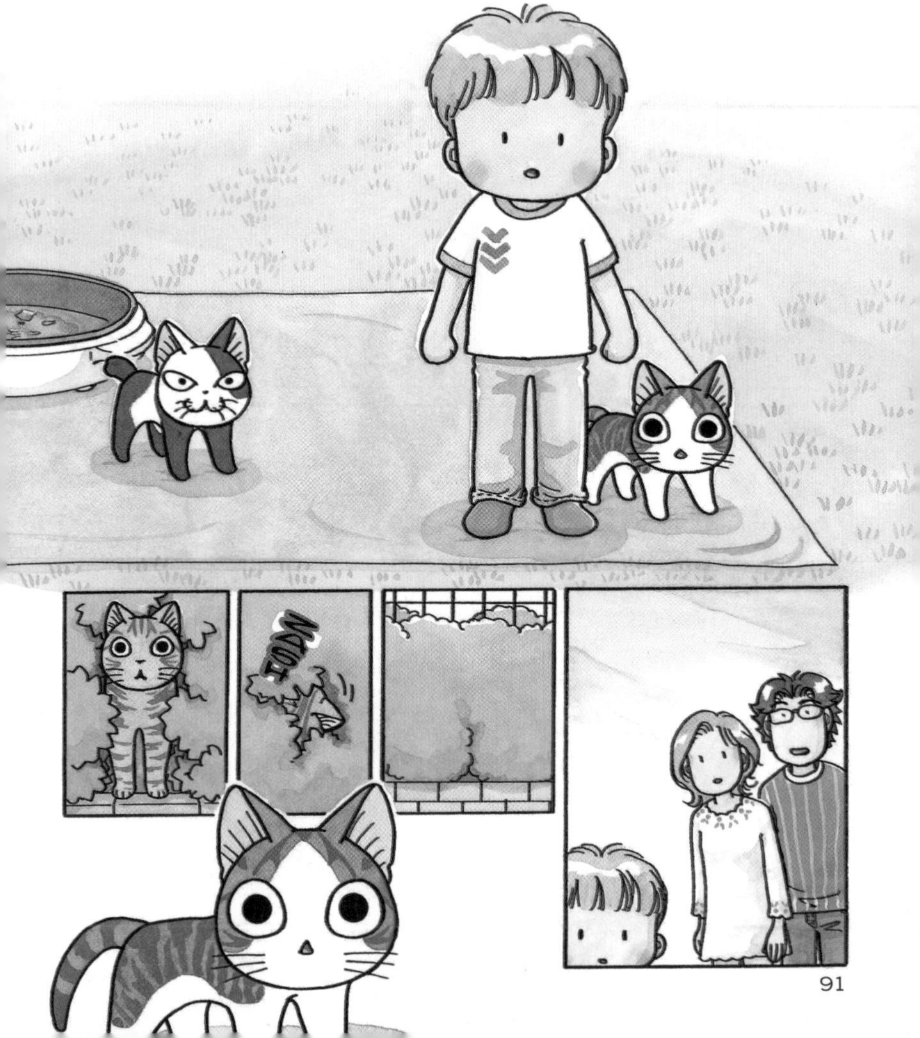

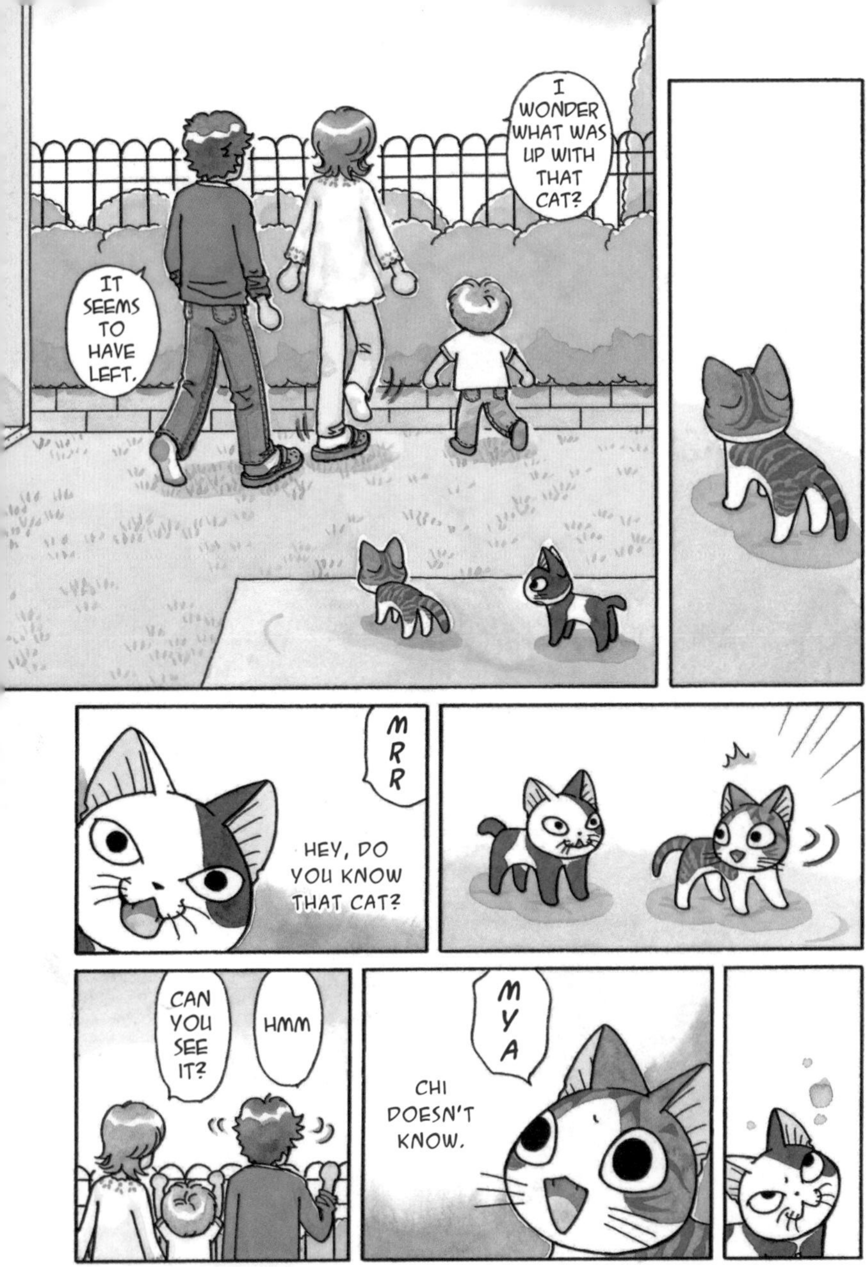
I WONDER WHAT WAS UP WITH THAT CAT?
IT SEEMS TO HAVE LEFT.
MRR
HEY, DO YOU KNOW THAT CAT?
CAN YOU SEE IT?
HMM
MYA
CHI DOESN'T KNOW.

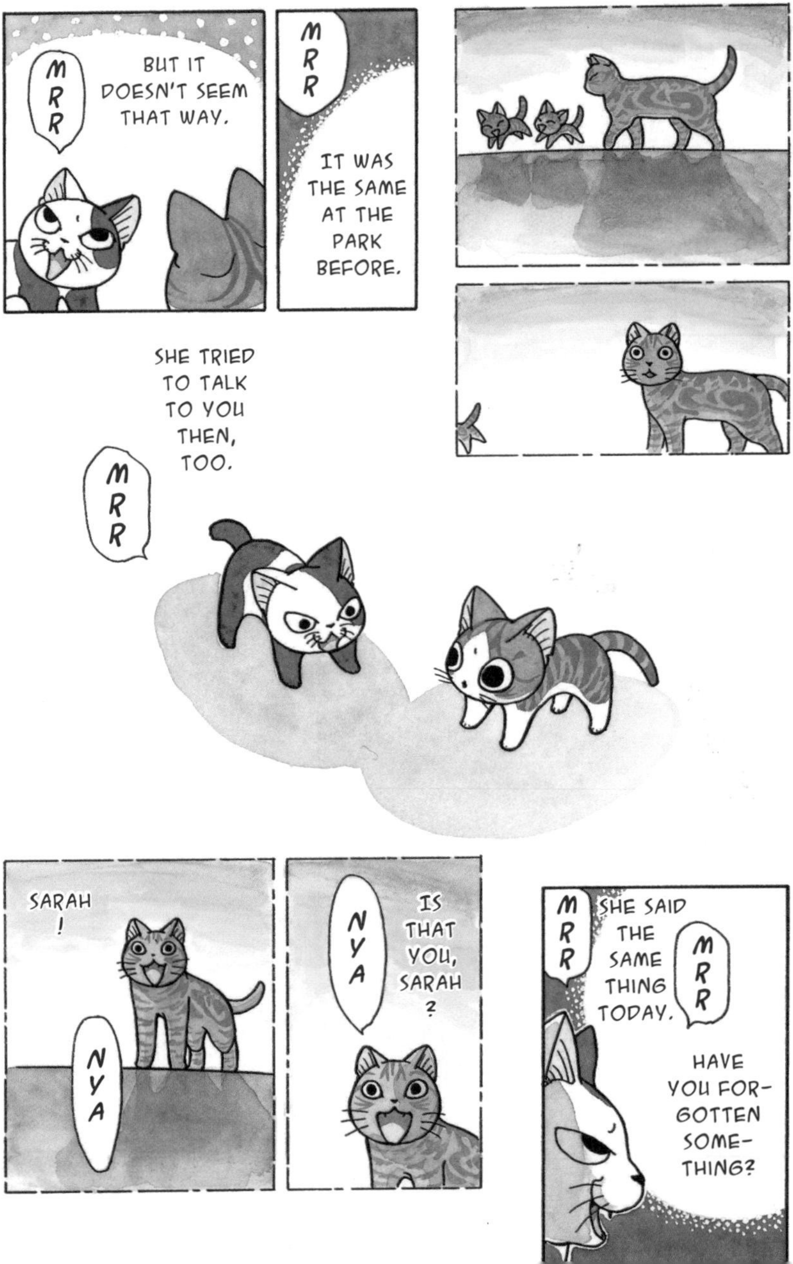
MRR
BUT IT DOESN'T SEEM THAT WAY.
MRR
IT WAS THE SAME AT THE PARK BEFORE.
SHE TRIED TO TALK TO YOU THEN, TOO.
MRR
SARAH!
NYA
NYA
IS THAT YOU, SARAH?
MRR
SHE SAID THE SAME THING TODAY.
MRR
HAVE YOU FORGOTTEN SOMETHING?

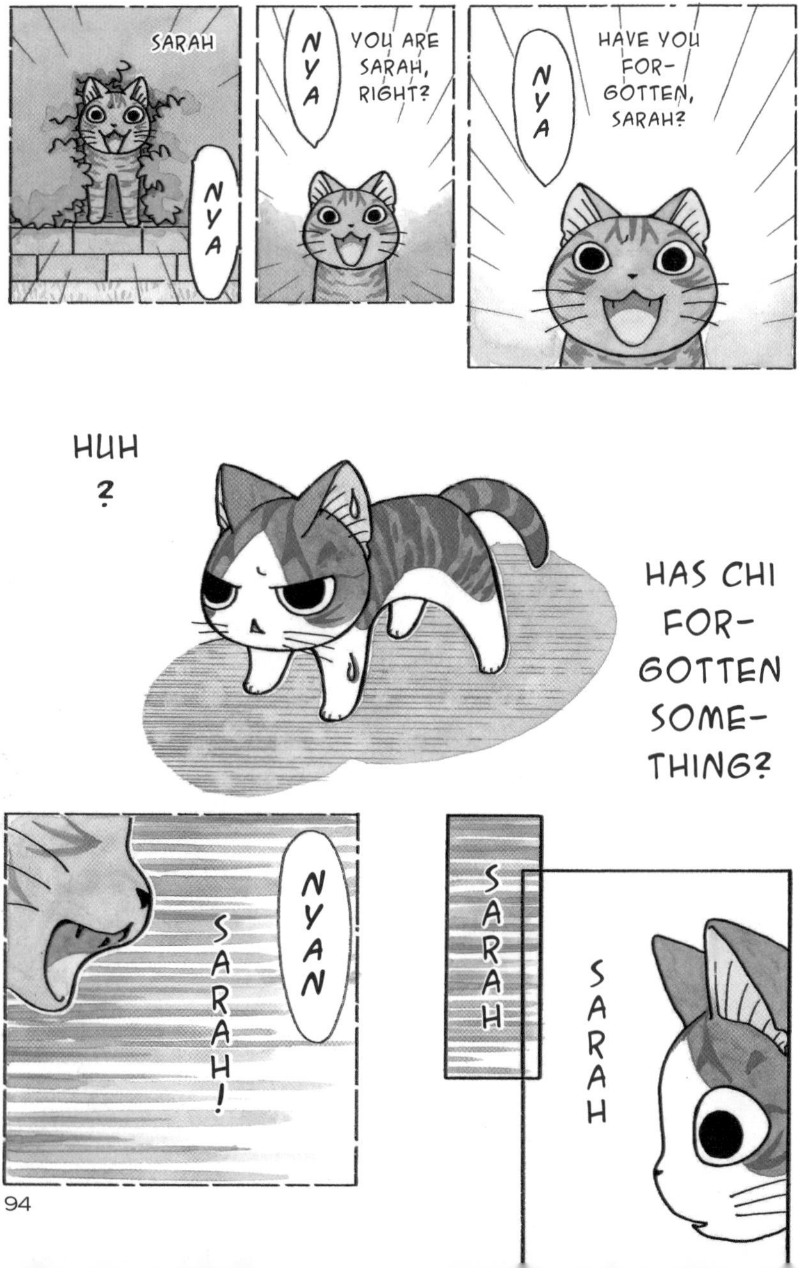
SARAH
NYA
NYA
YOU ARE SARAH, RIGHT?
NYA
HAVE YOU FOR-GOTTEN, SARAH?
HUH ?
HAS CHI FOR-GOTTEN SOME-THING?
NYAN
SARAH!
SARAH
SARAH

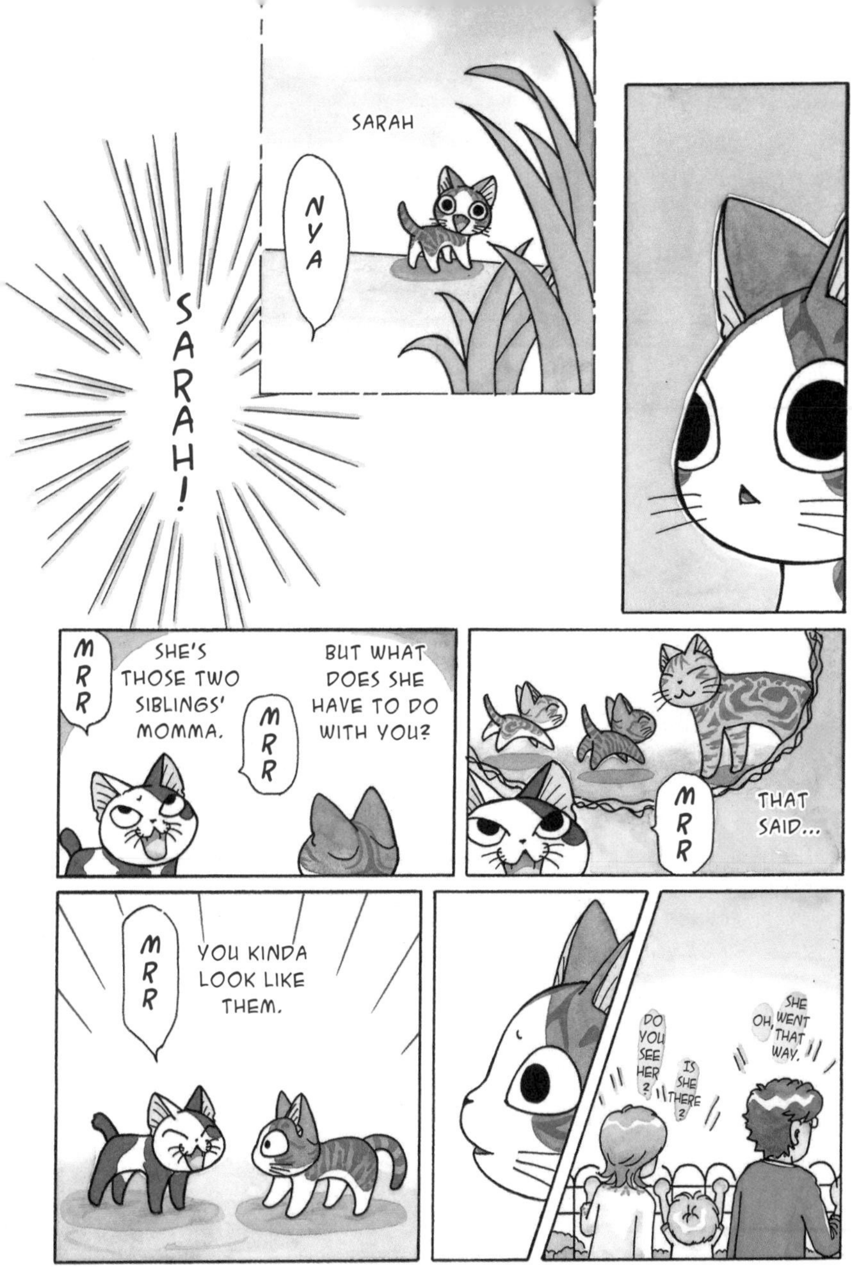
SARAH!
SARAH
NYA
MRR
SHE'S THOSE TWO SIBLINGS' MOMMA.
MRR
BUT WHAT DOES SHE HAVE TO DO WITH YOU?
MRR
THAT SAID...
MRR
YOU KINDA LOOK LIKE THEM.
DO YOU SEE HER?
IS SHE THERE?
OH, SHE WENT THAT WAY.

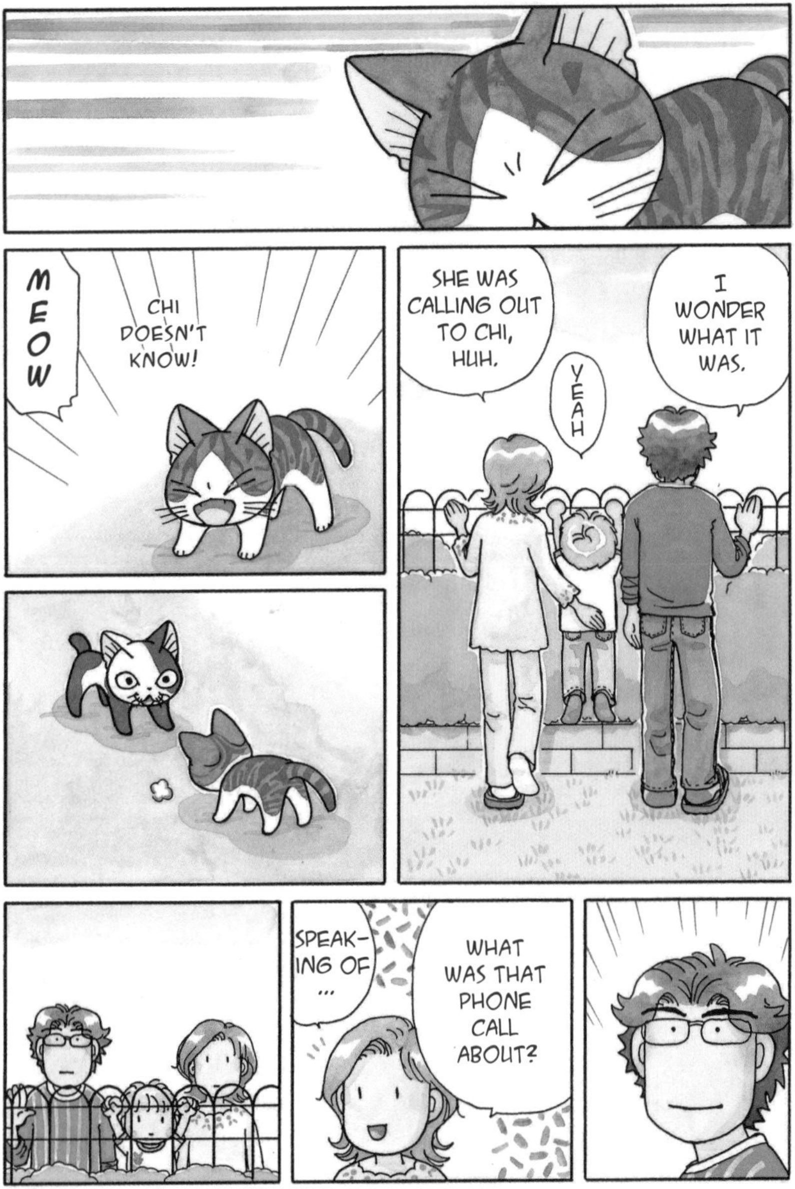
MEOW
CHI DOESN'T KNOW!
SHE WAS CALLING OUT TO CHI, HUH.
YEAH
I WONDER WHAT IT WAS.
SPEAK-ING OF ...
WHAT WAS THAT PHONE CALL ABOUT?

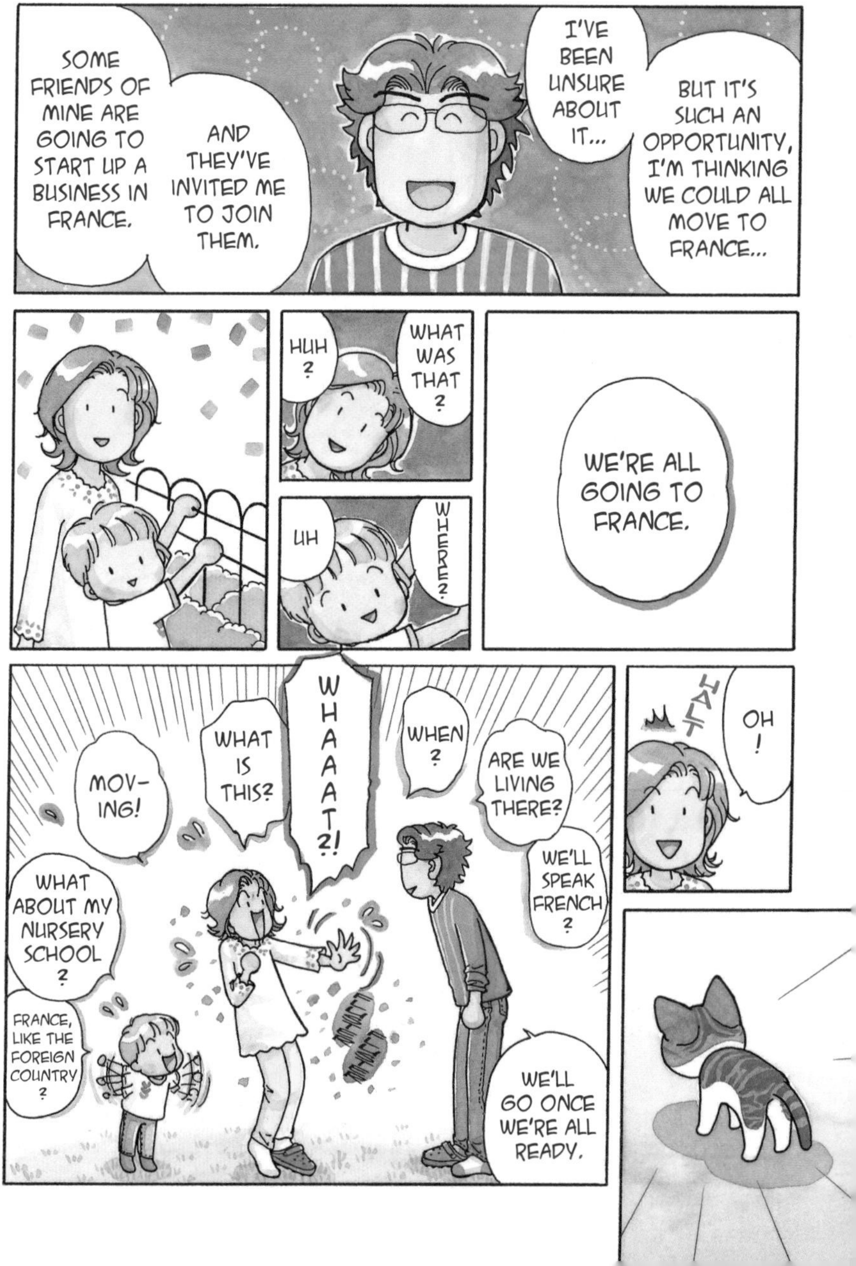
SOME FRIENDS OF MINE ARE GOING TO START UP A BUSINESS IN FRANCE.
AND THEY'VE INVITED ME TO JOIN THEM.
I'VE BEEN UNSURE ABOUT IT...
BUT IT'S SUCH AN OPPORTUNITY, I'M THINKING WE COULD ALL MOVE TO FRANCE...
HUH?
WHAT WAS THAT?
UH
WHERE?
WE'RE ALL GOING TO FRANCE.
MOV-ING!
WHAT IS THIS?
WHAAAAT?!
WHEN?
ARE WE LIVING THERE?
WE'LL SPEAK FRENCH?
WHAT ABOUT MY NURSERY SCHOOL?
FRANCE, LIKE THE FOREIGN COUNTRY?
WE'LL GO ONCE WE'RE ALL READY.
HALT
OH!

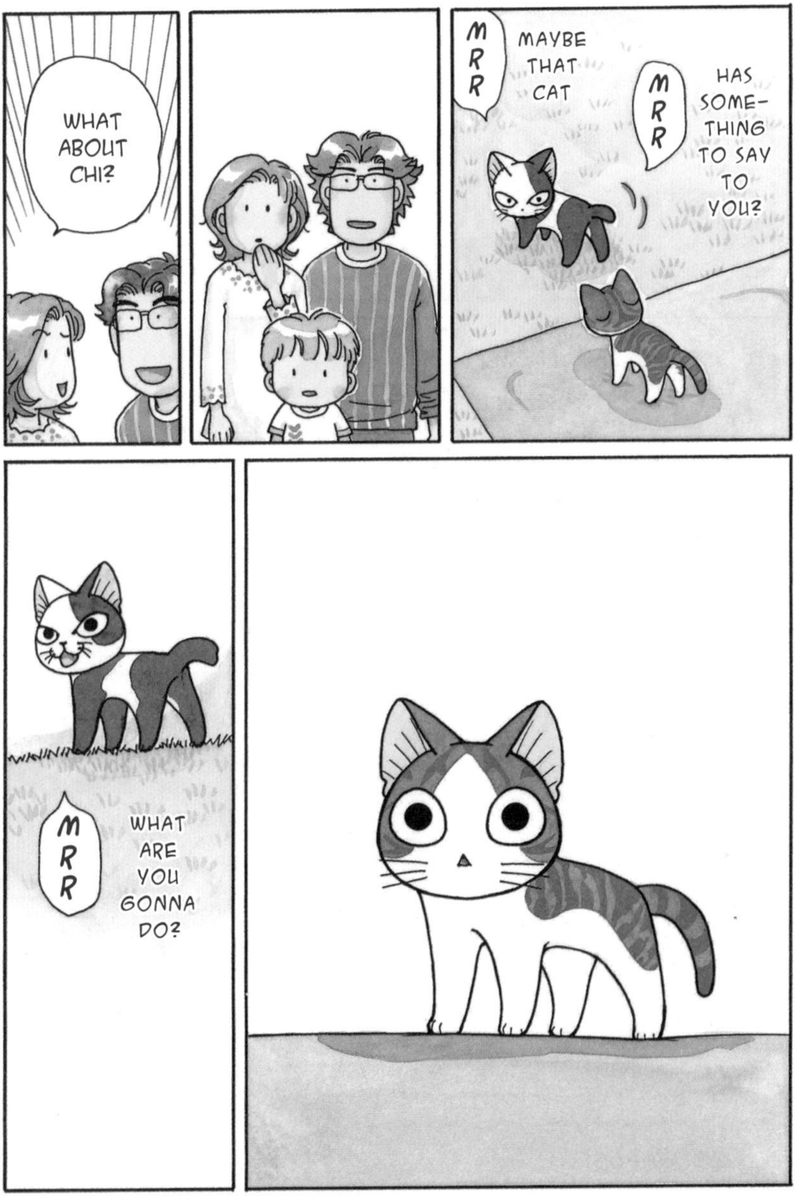
WHAT ABOUT CHI?
MRR
MAYBE THAT CAT
MRR
HAS SOME-THING TO SAY TO YOU?
MRR
WHAT ARE YOU GONNA DO?

the end

homemade 195: a cat recalls

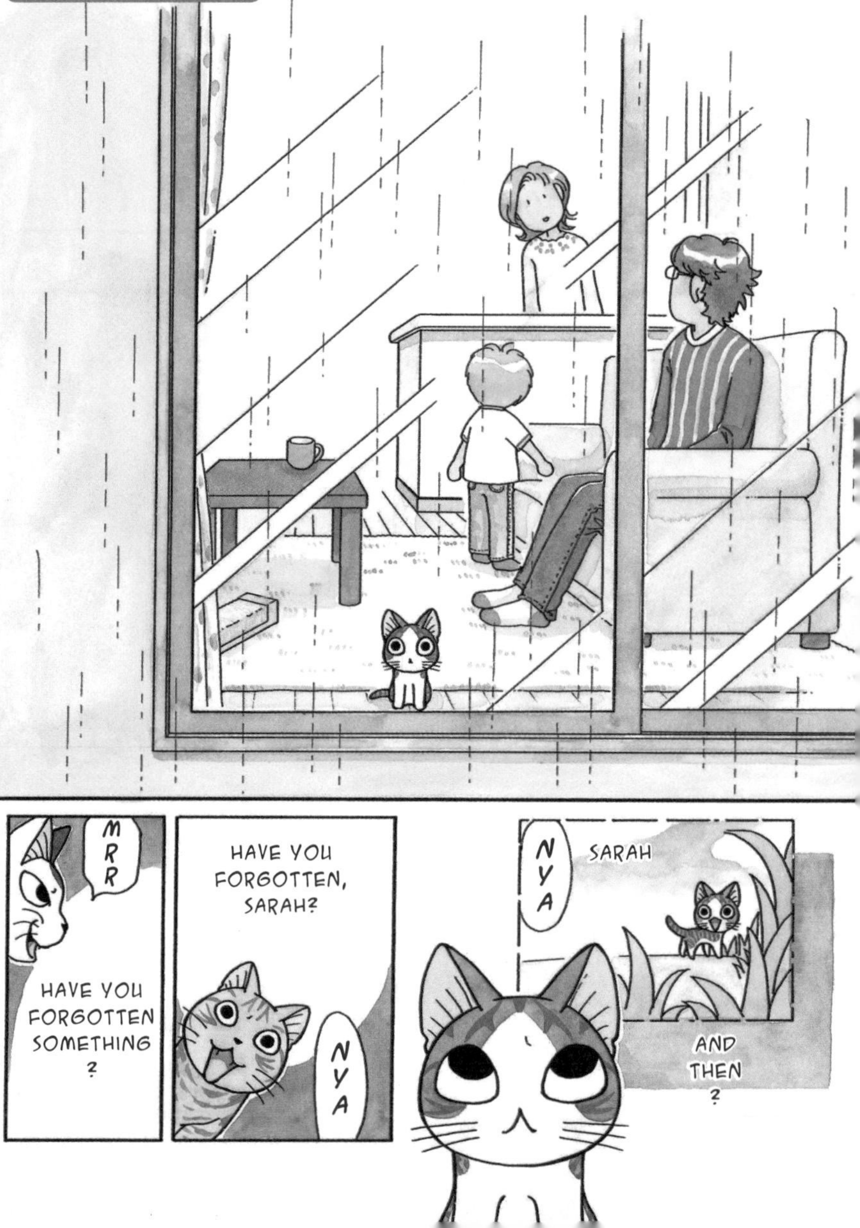
MRR
HAVE YOU FORGOTTEN SOMETHING?
HAVE YOU FORGOTTEN, SARAH?
NYA
NYA
SARAH
AND THEN?

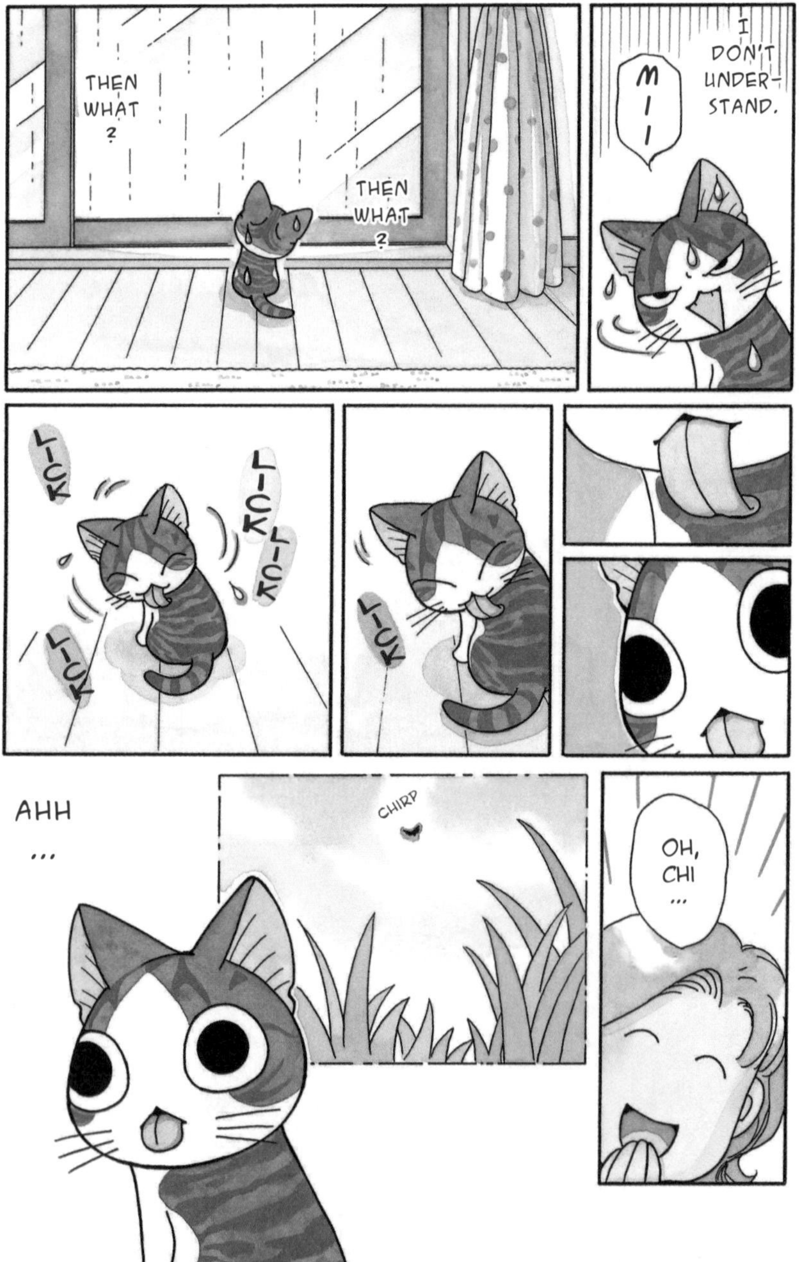
THEN WHAT ?
THEN WHAT ?
MII
I DON'T UNDER-STAND.
LICK
LICK LICK
LICK
LICK
AHH ...
CHIRP
OH, CHI ...

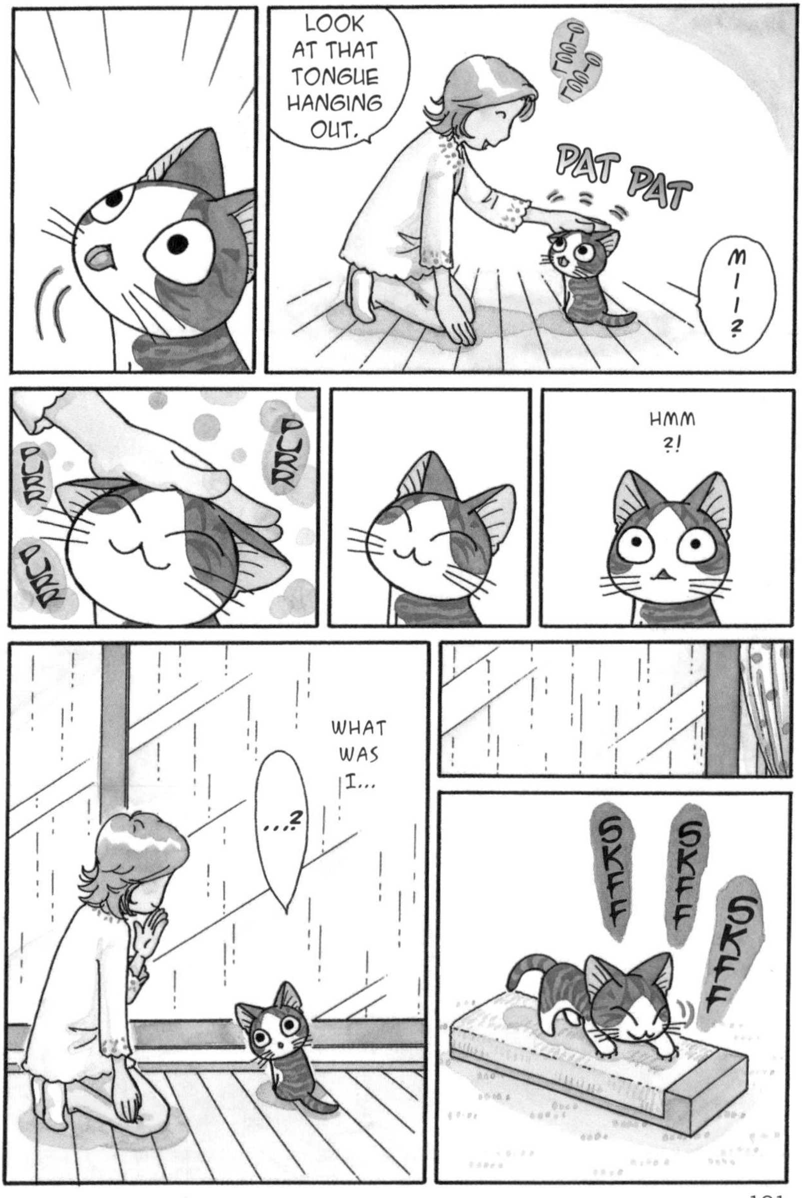
LOOK AT THAT TONGUE HANGING OUT.
GIGGLE GIGGLE
PAT PAT
MII?
PURR
PURR
PURR
HMM ?!
WHAT WAS I...
...?
SKFF
SKFF
SKFF

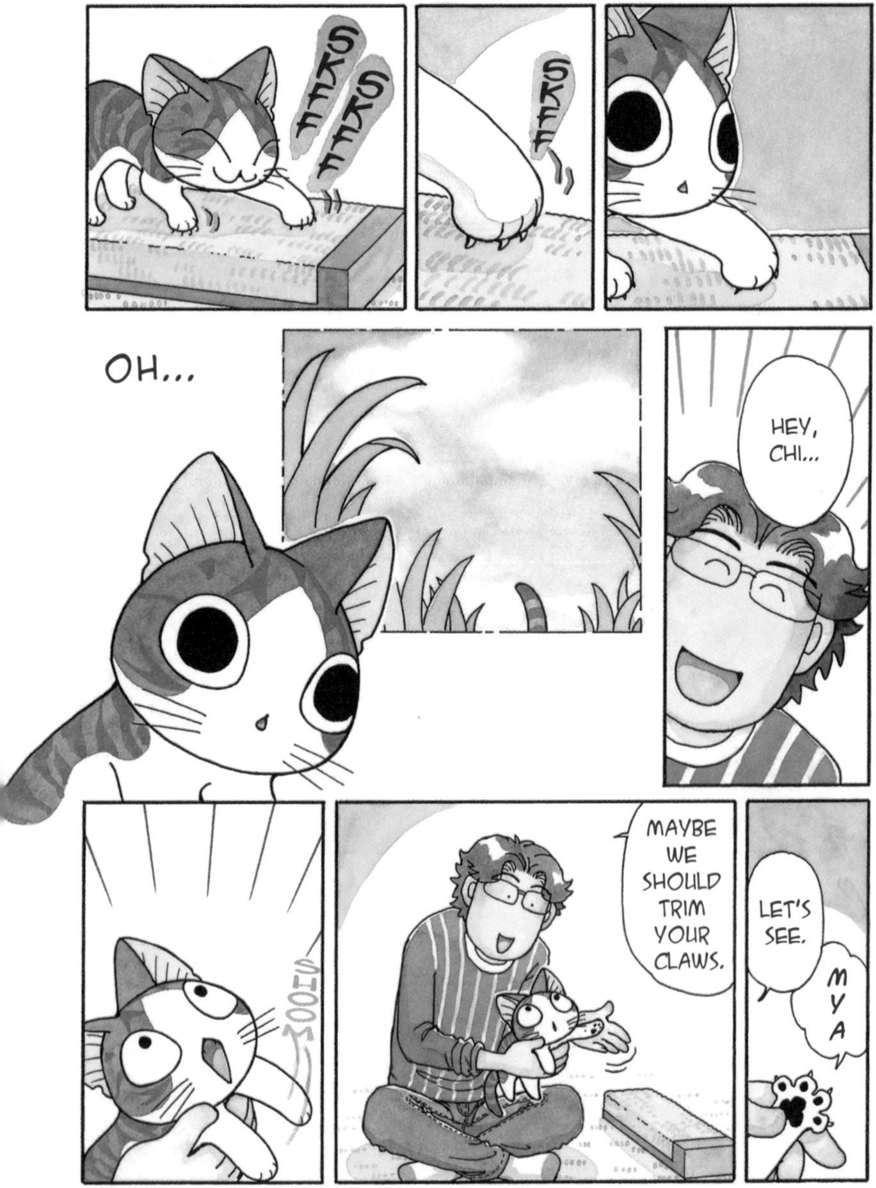
SKFF
SKFF
SKFF
OH...
HEY, CHI...
SHOOM
MAYBE WE SHOULD TRIM YOUR CLAWS.
LET'S SEE.
MYA

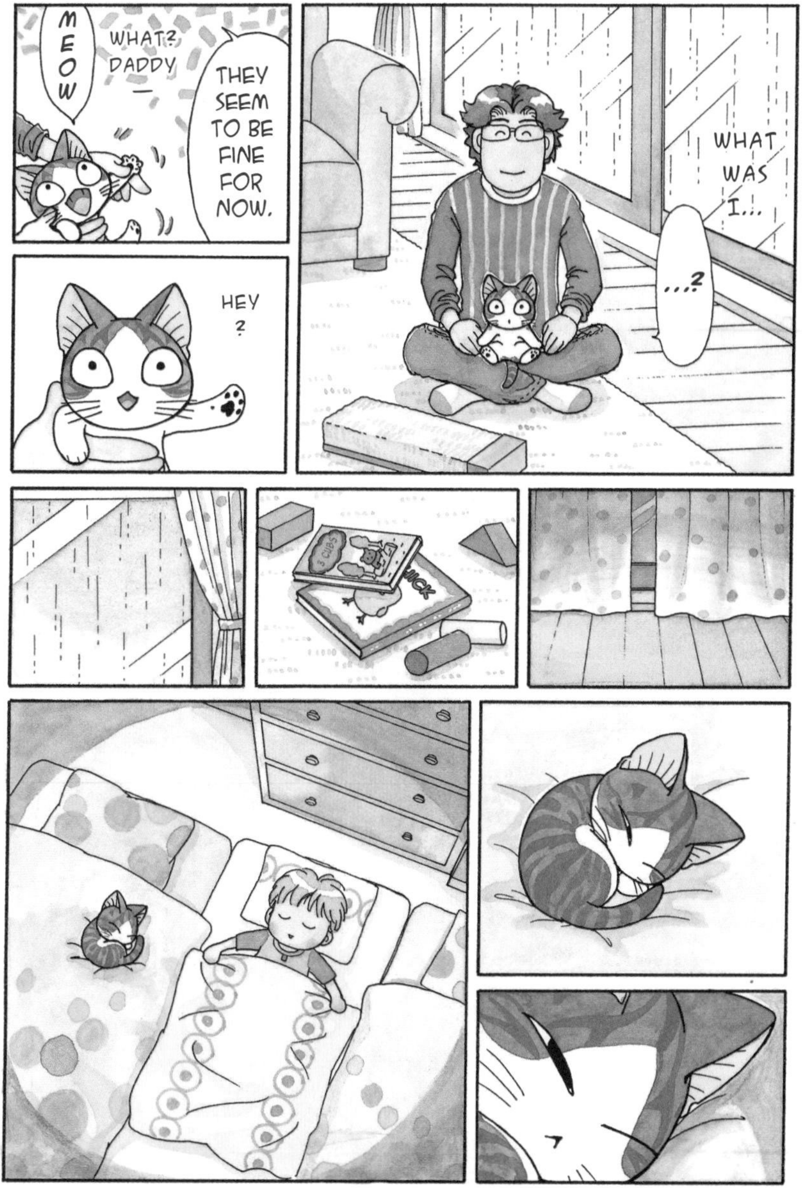
MEOW
WHAT? DADDY —
THEY SEEM TO BE FINE FOR NOW.
HEY?
WHAT WAS I...
...?
3 CUBS

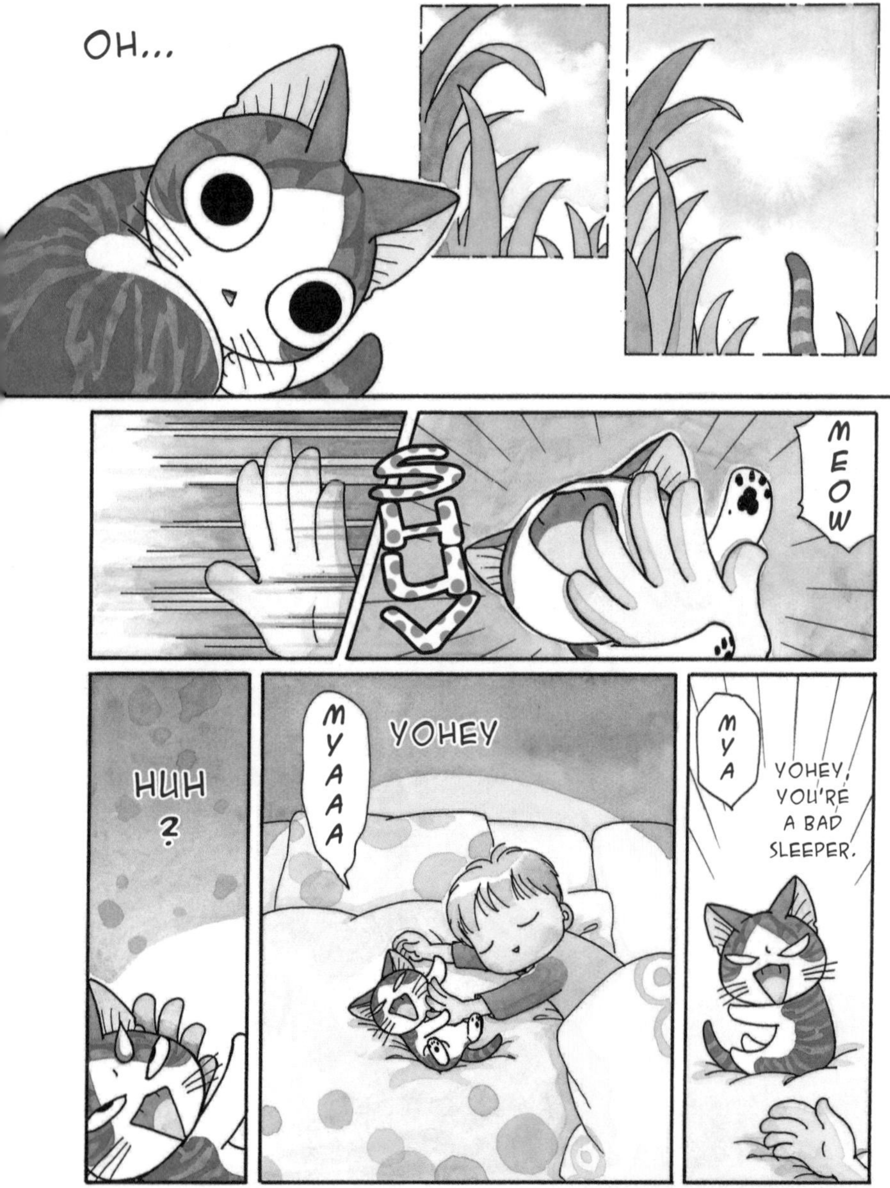
OH...
MEOW
SHU
HUH ?
MYAAAA
YOHEY
MYA
YOHEY, YOU'RE A BAD SLEEPER.

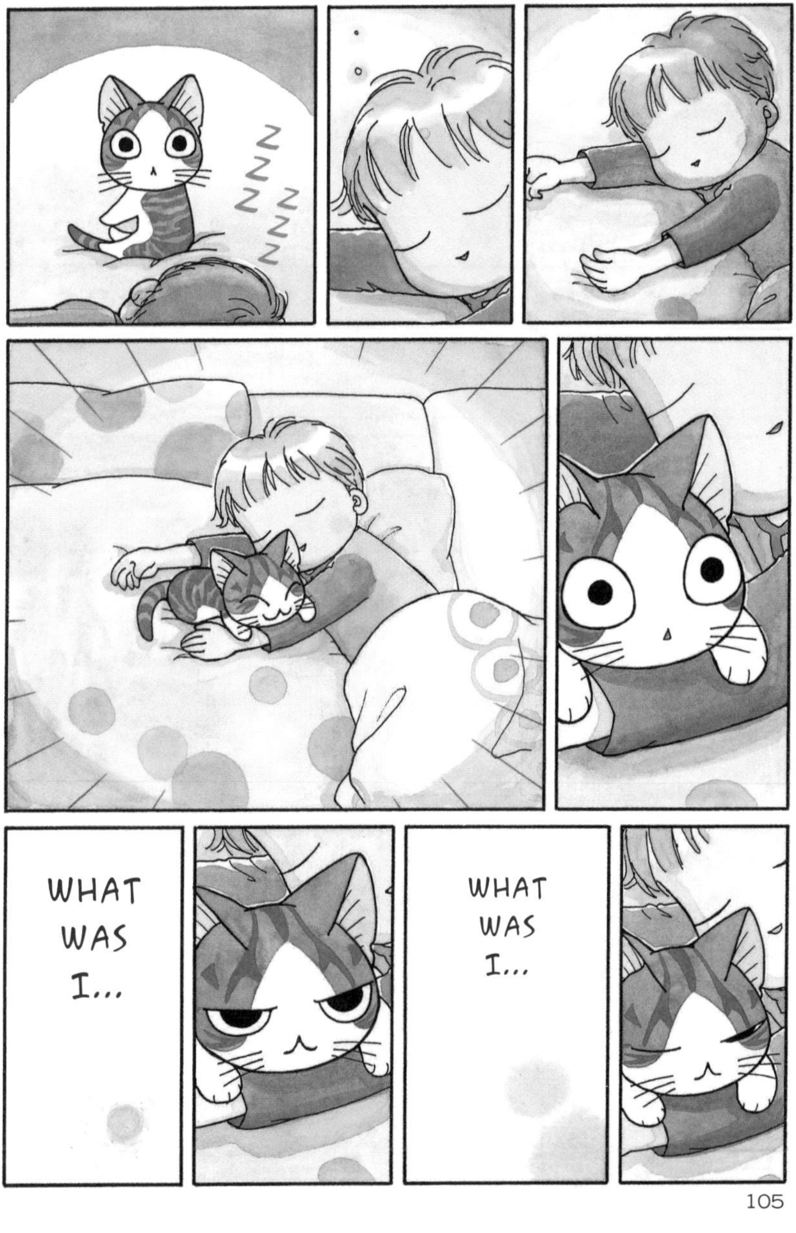
Z Z Z
Z Z Z
WHAT WAS I...
WHAT WAS I...

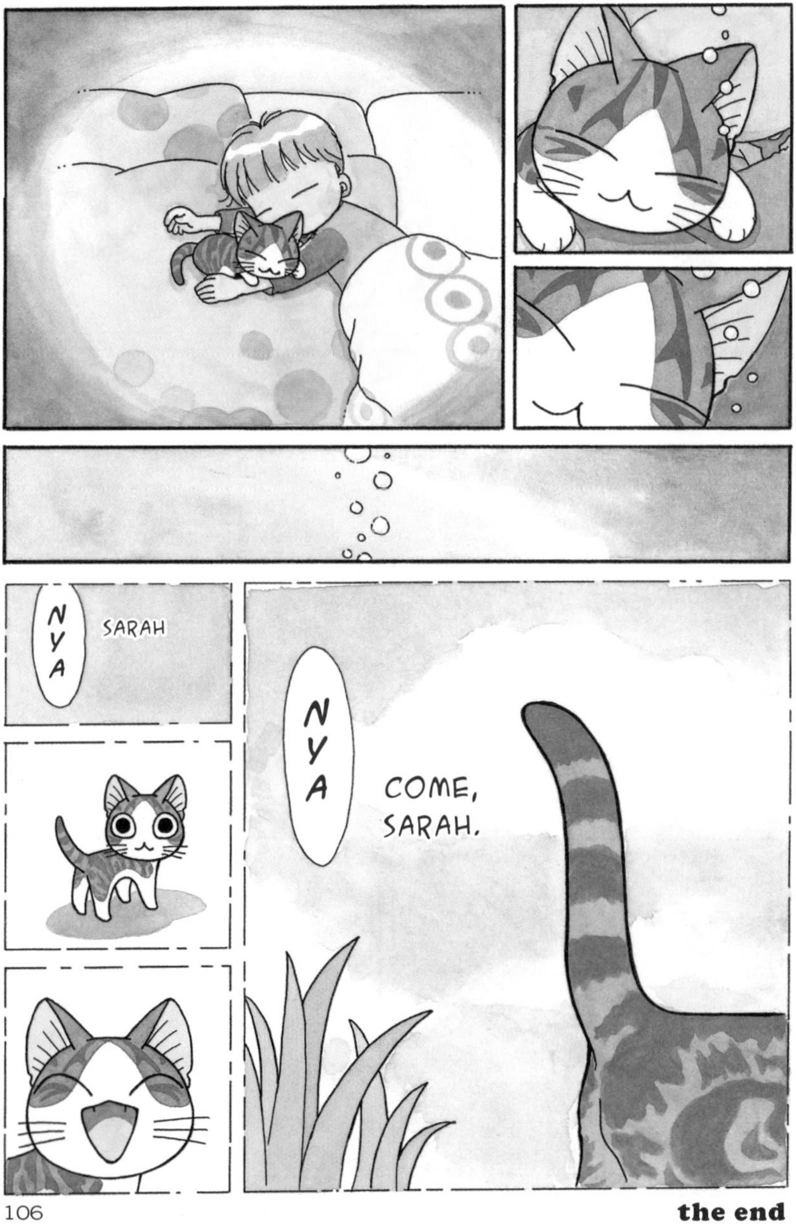
NYA
SARAH
NYA
COME, SARAH.

the end

homemade 196: a cat is lost in thought

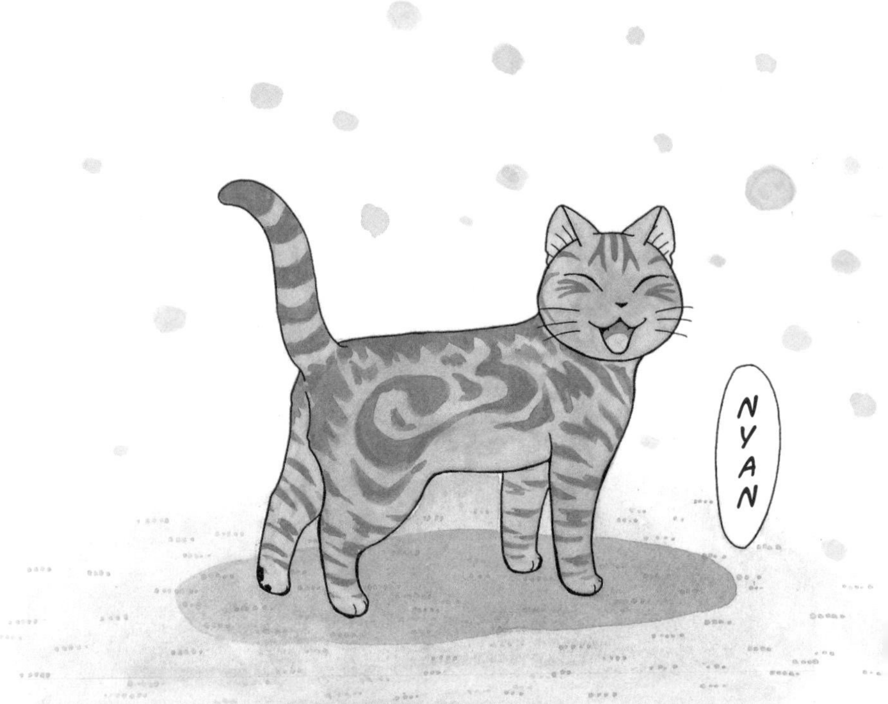
NYAN

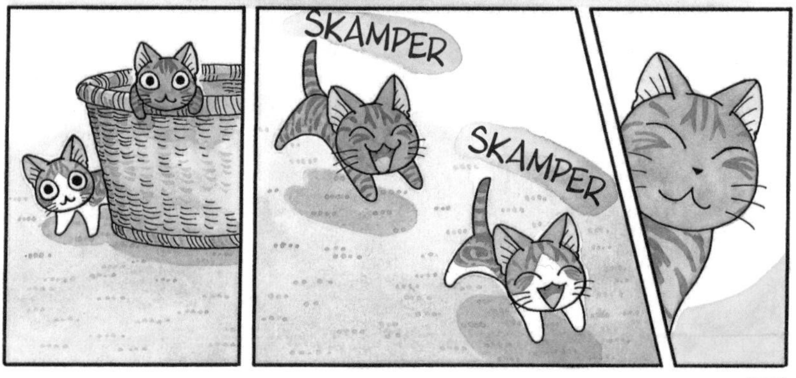
SKAMPER
SKAMPER

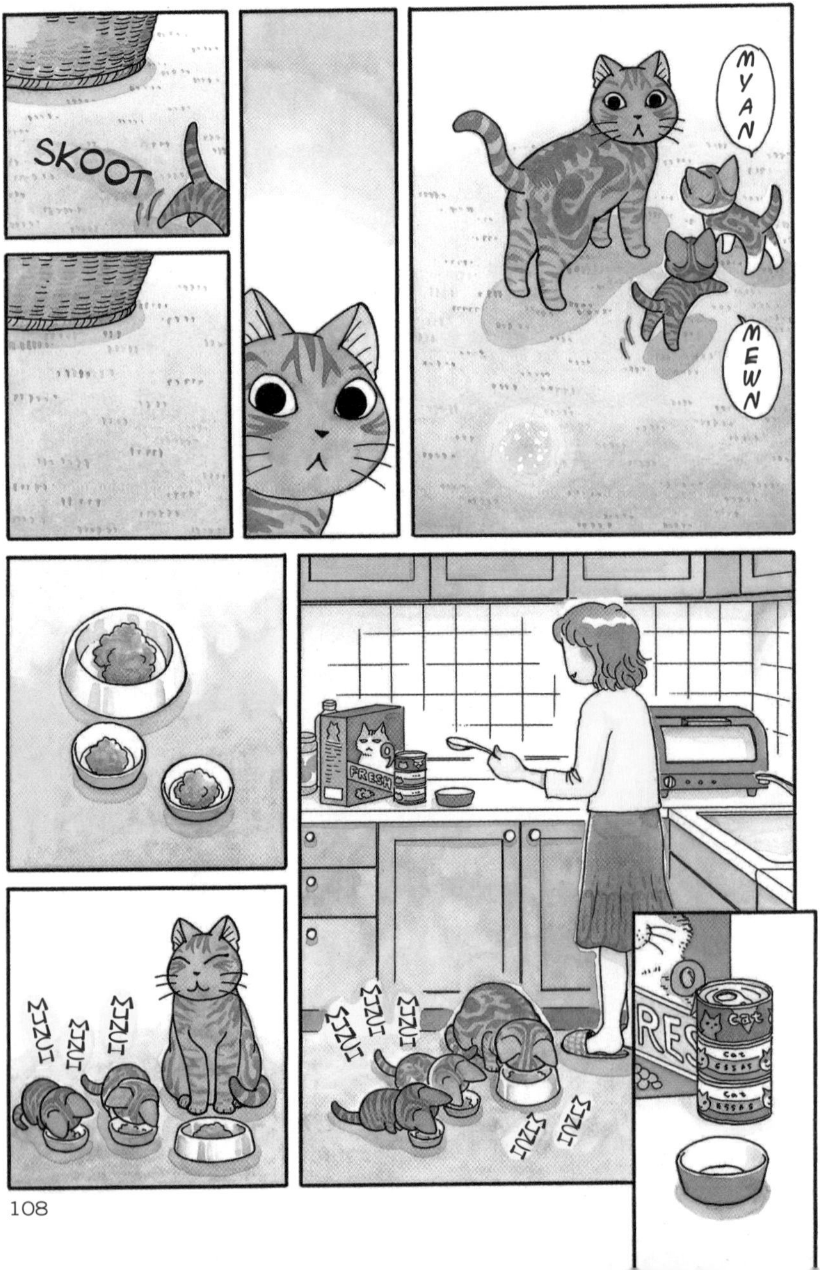
SKOOT
MYAN
MEWN
MUNCH
MUNCH
MUNCH
FRESH
MUNCH
MUNCH
MUNCH
MUNCH
MUNCH
Cat
Cat
Cat

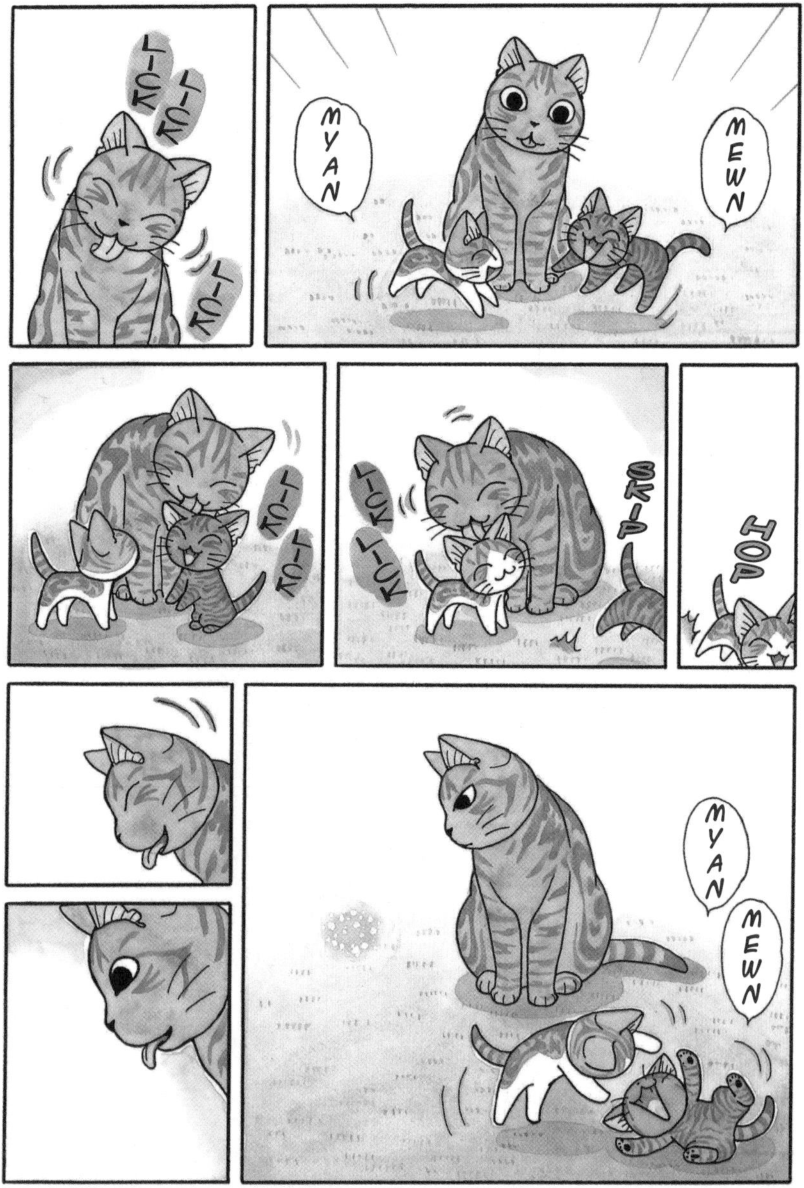
LICK
LICK
LICK
MYAN
MEWN
LICK
LICK
LICK
LICK
SKIP
HOP
MYAN
MEWN

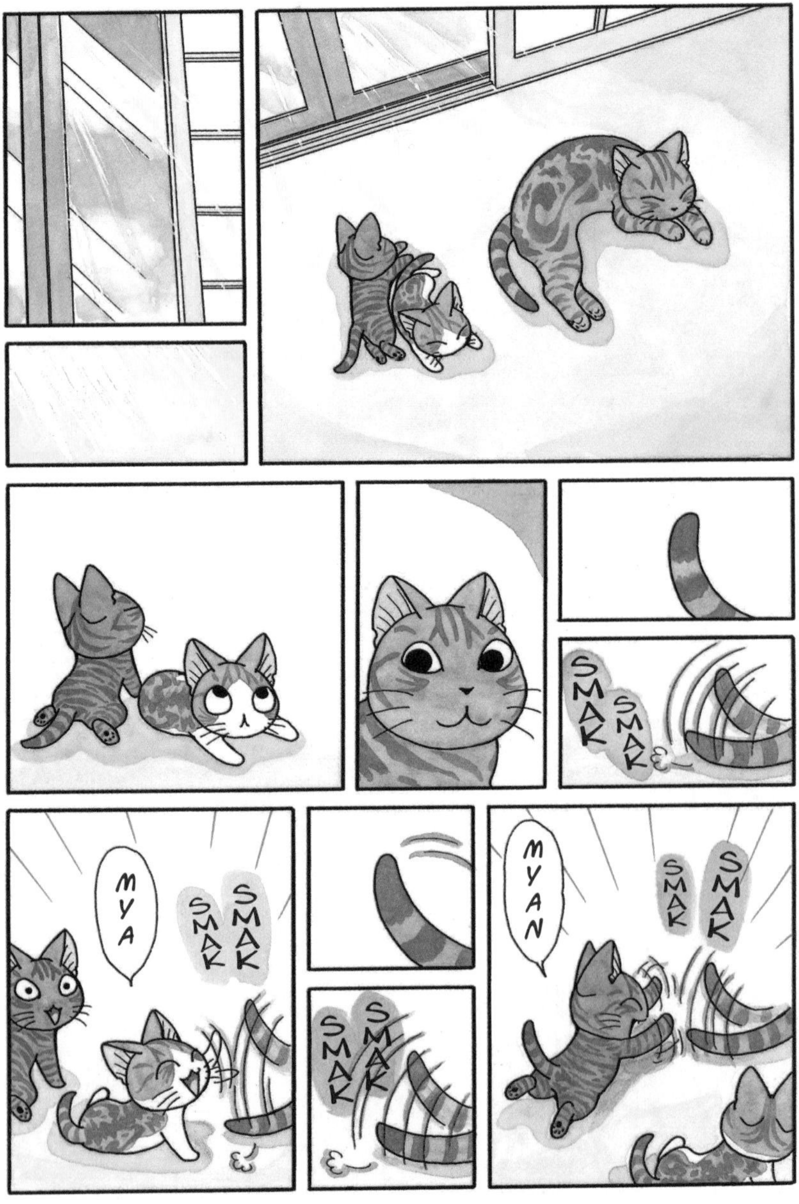
SMAK
SMAK
MYA
SMAK
SMAK
SMAK
SMAK
MYAN
SMAK
SMAK

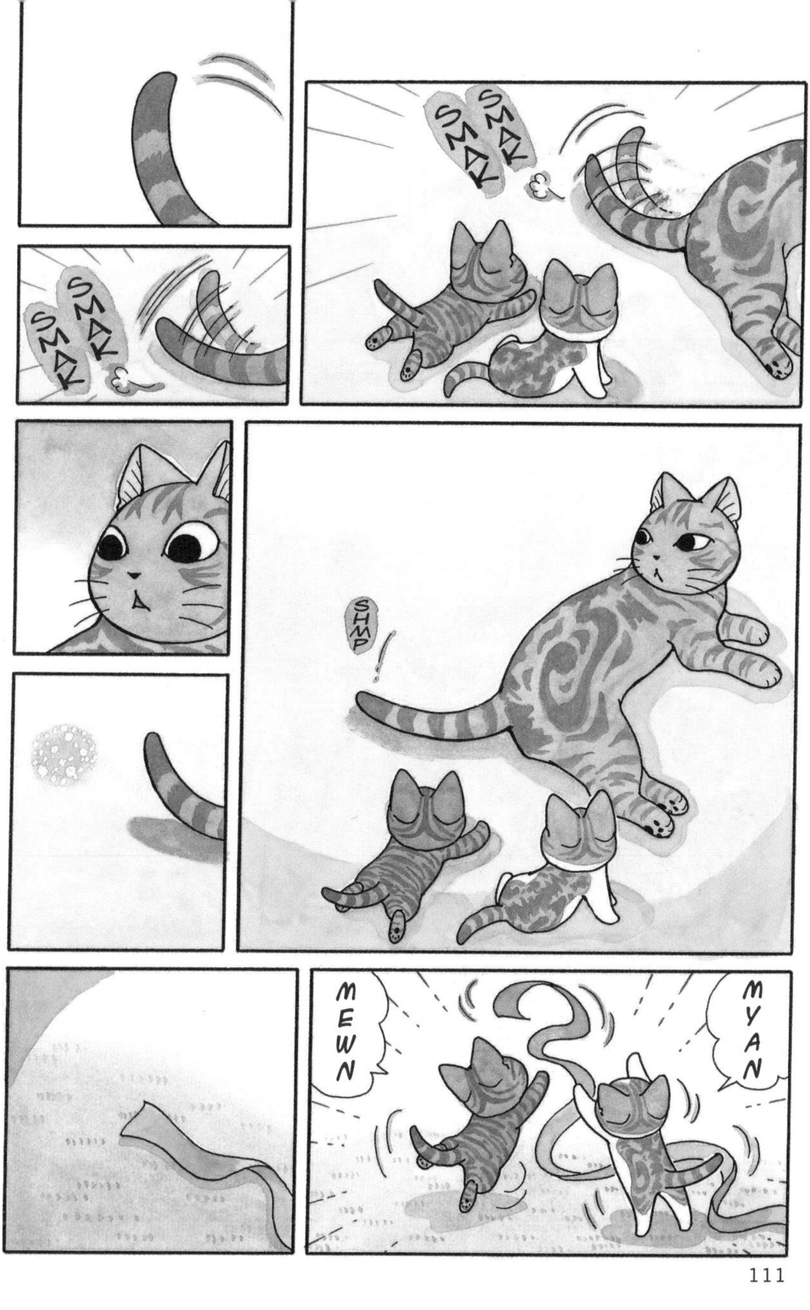
SMAK
SMAK
SMAK
SMAK
SHMP
MEWN
MYAN

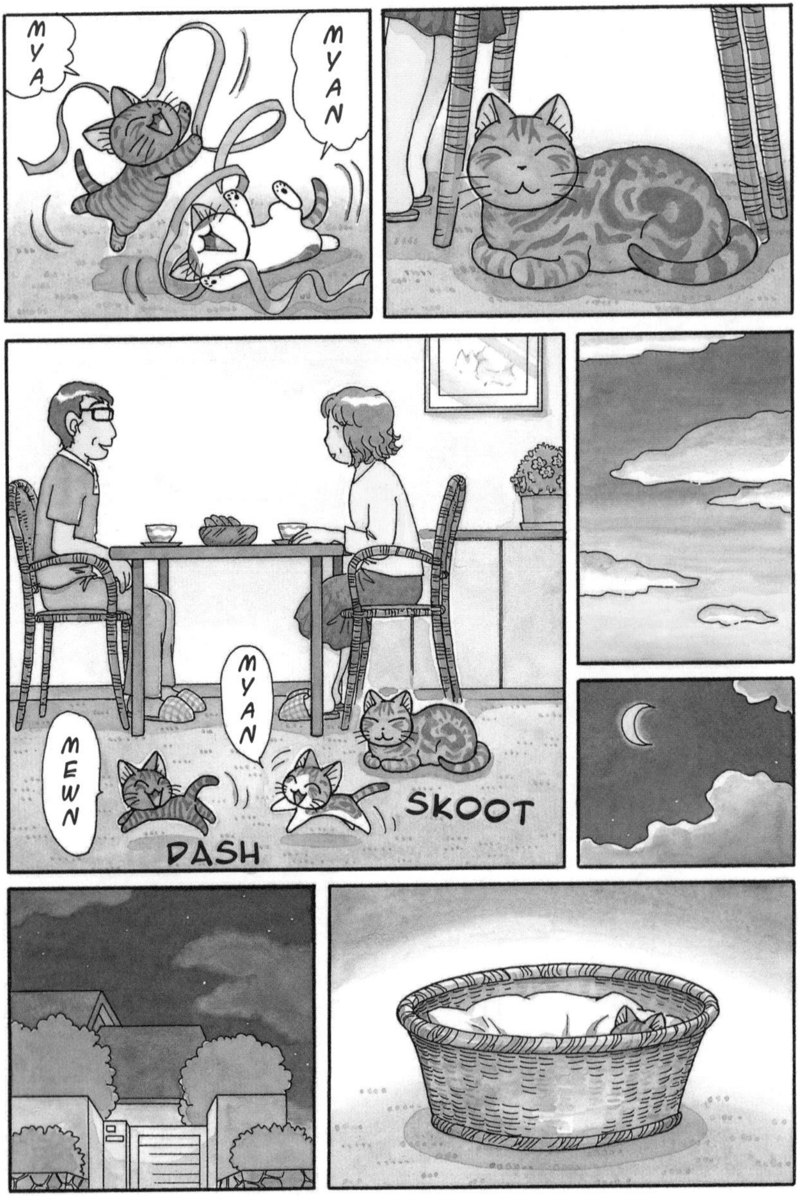
MYA
MYAN
MYAN
MEWN
SKOOT
DASH

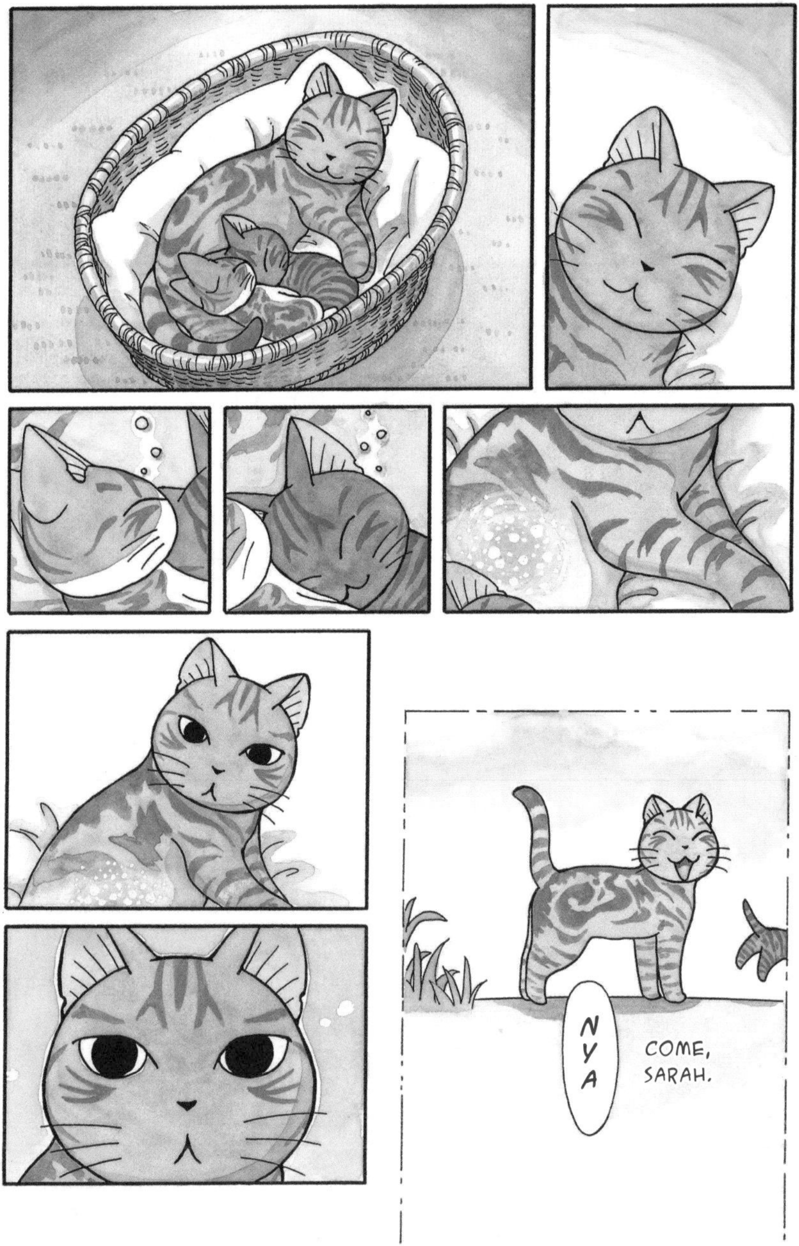
NYA
COME, SARAH.

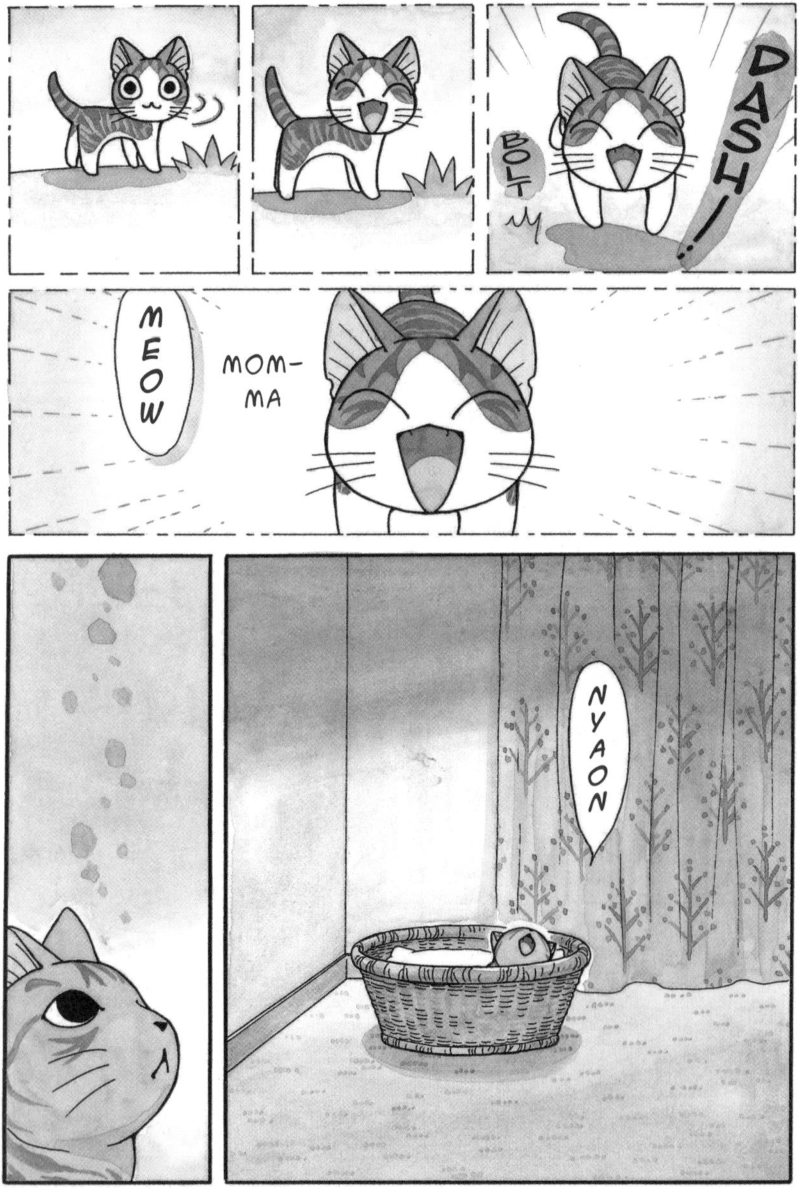
BOLT
DASH!!
MEOW
MOM-
MA
NYAON

the end

homemade 197: a cat is looked for

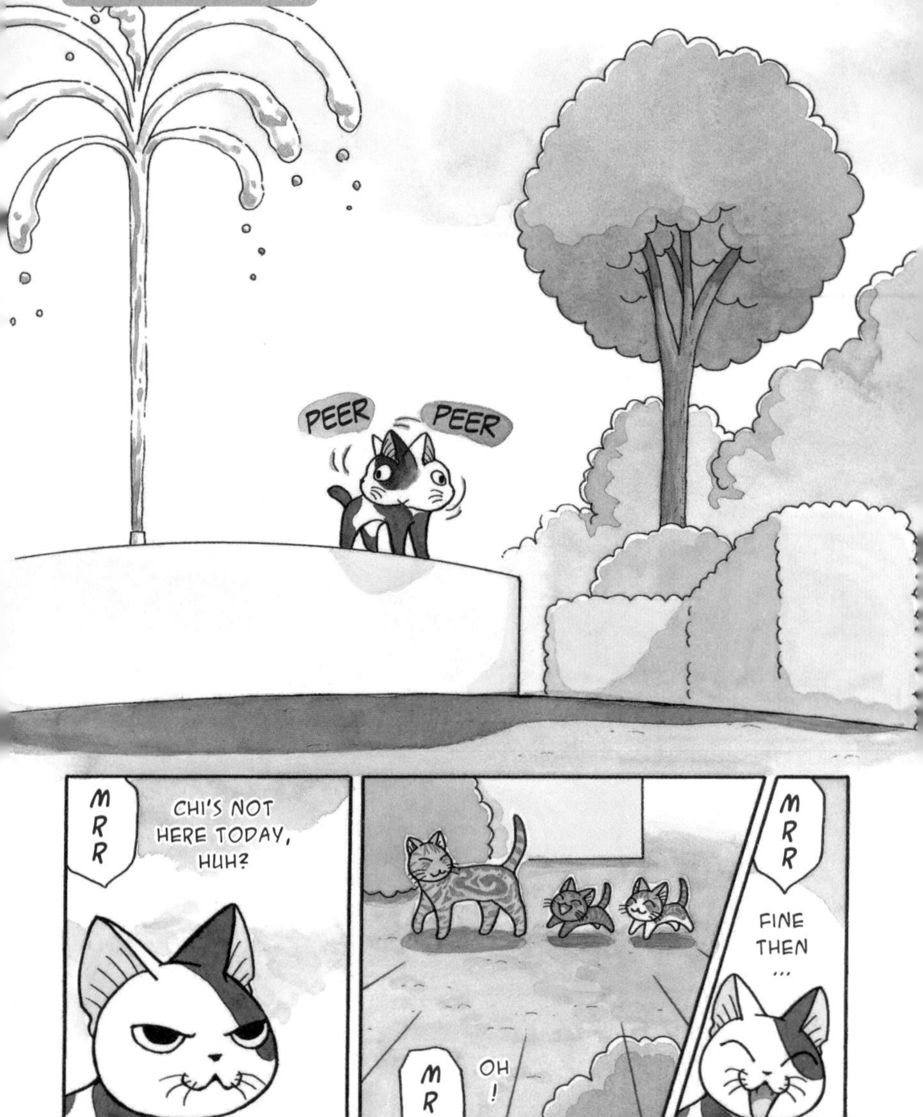
PEER
PEER
MRR
CHI'S NOT HERE TODAY, HUH?
MRR
OH!
MRR
FINE THEN ...

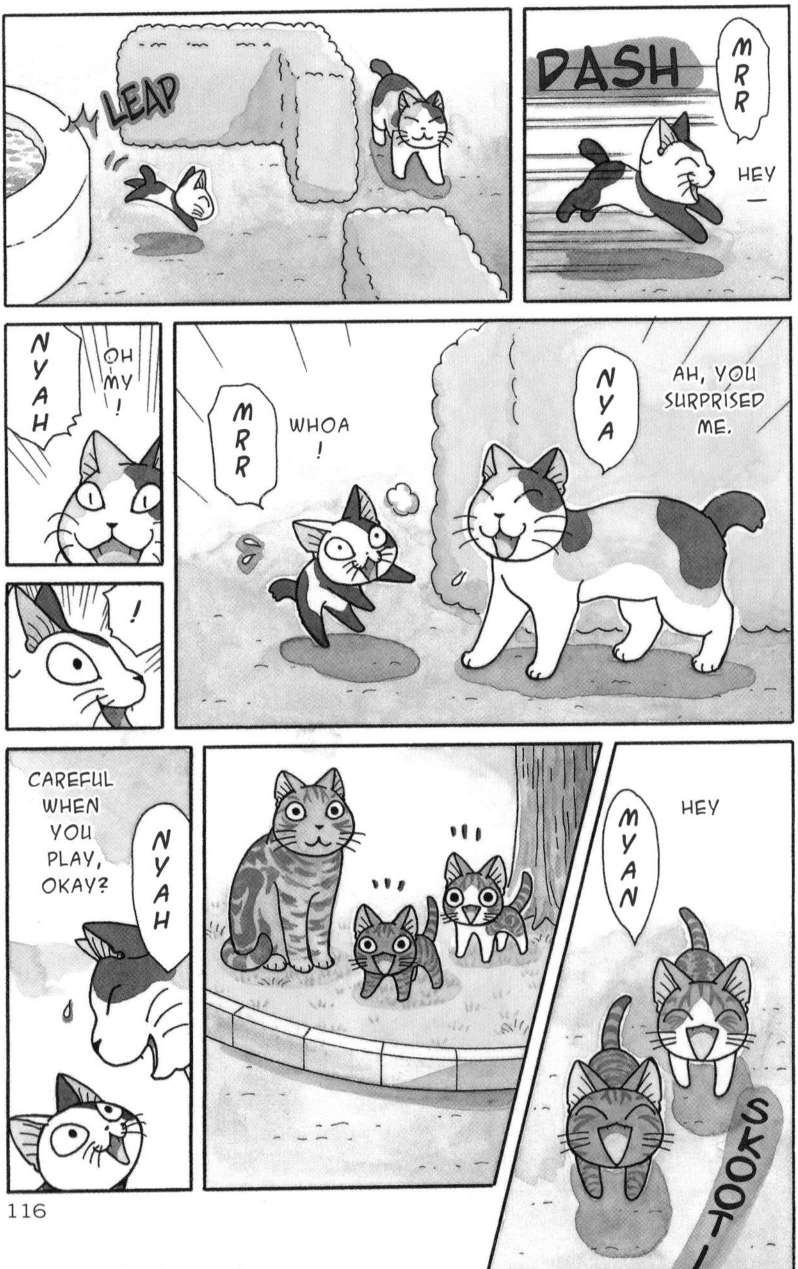
LEAP
DASH
MRR
HEY—
NYAH
OH MY!
!
MRR
WHOA!
NYA
AH, YOU SURPRISED ME.
CAREFUL WHEN YOU PLAY, OKAY?
NYAH
MYAN
HEY
SKOOT

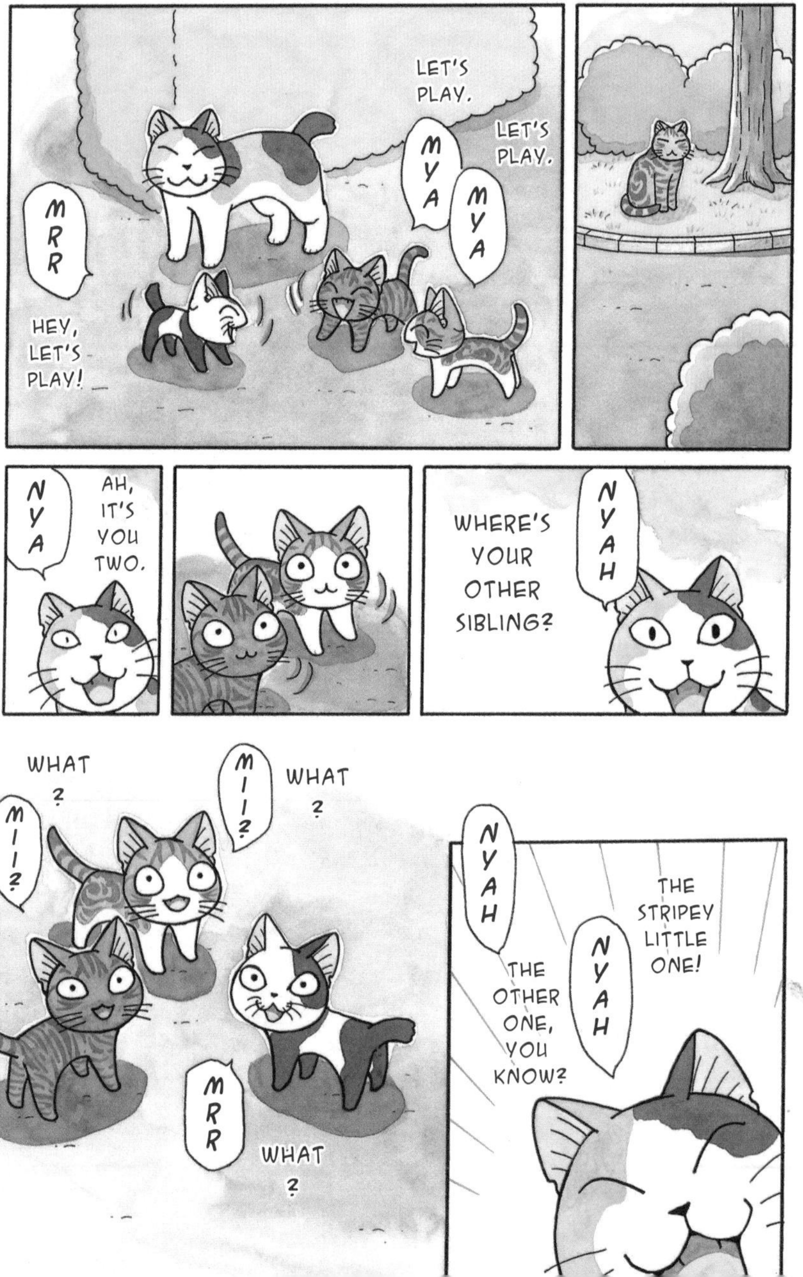
LET'S PLAY.
LET'S PLAY.
MYA
MYA
MRR
HEY, LET'S PLAY!
NYA
AH, IT'S YOU TWO.
WHERE'S YOUR OTHER SIBLING?
NYAH
WHAT?
MII?
MII?
WHAT?
MRR
WHAT?
NYAH
THE STRIPEY LITTLE ONE!
NYAH
THE OTHER ONE, YOU KNOW?

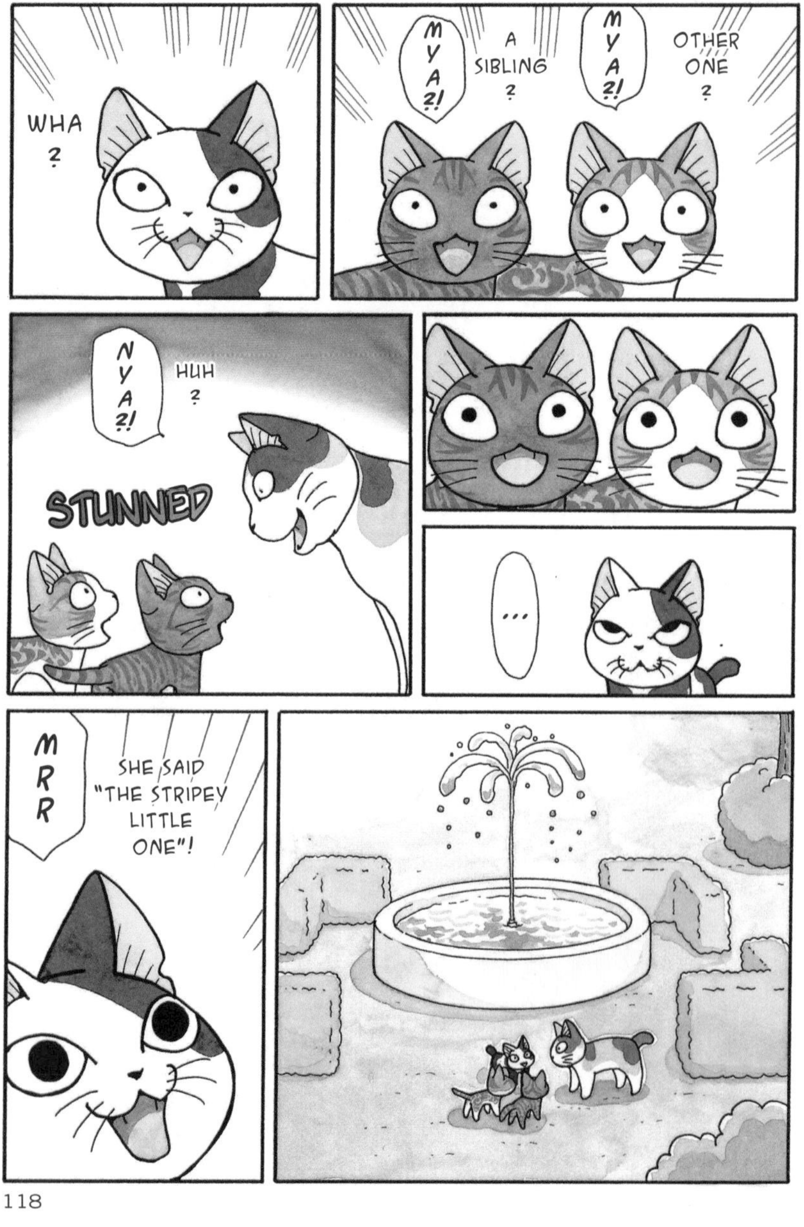
WHA?
MYA?!
A SIBLING?
MYA?!
OTHER ONE?
NYA?!
HUH?
STUNNED
...
MRR
SHE SAID "THE STRIPEY LITTLE ONE"!

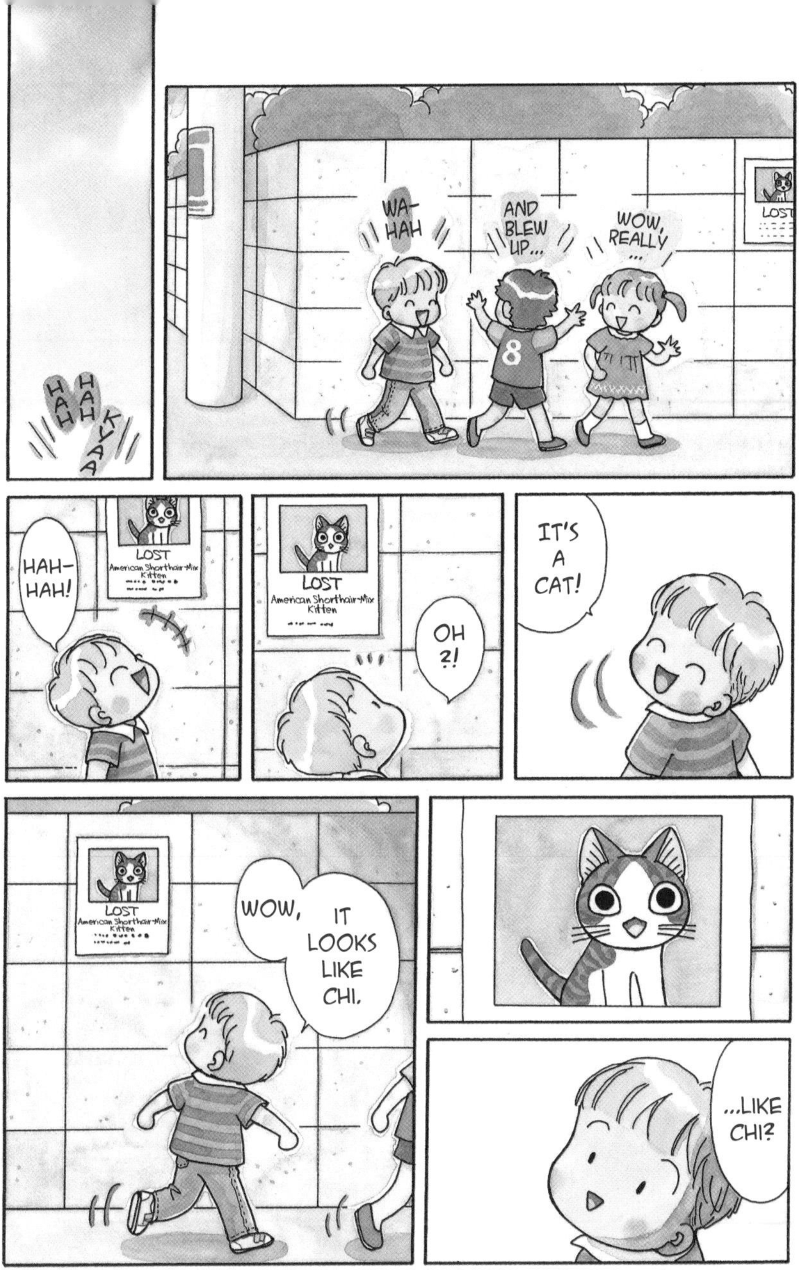
HAH HAH KYAA
WA-HAH
AND BLEW UP...
WOW, REALLY...
LOST
HAH-HAH!
LOST American Shorthair-Mix Kitten
LOST American Shorthair-Mix Kitten
OH ?!
IT'S A CAT!
LOST American Shorthair-Mix Kitten
WOW, IT LOOKS LIKE CHI.
...LIKE CHI?

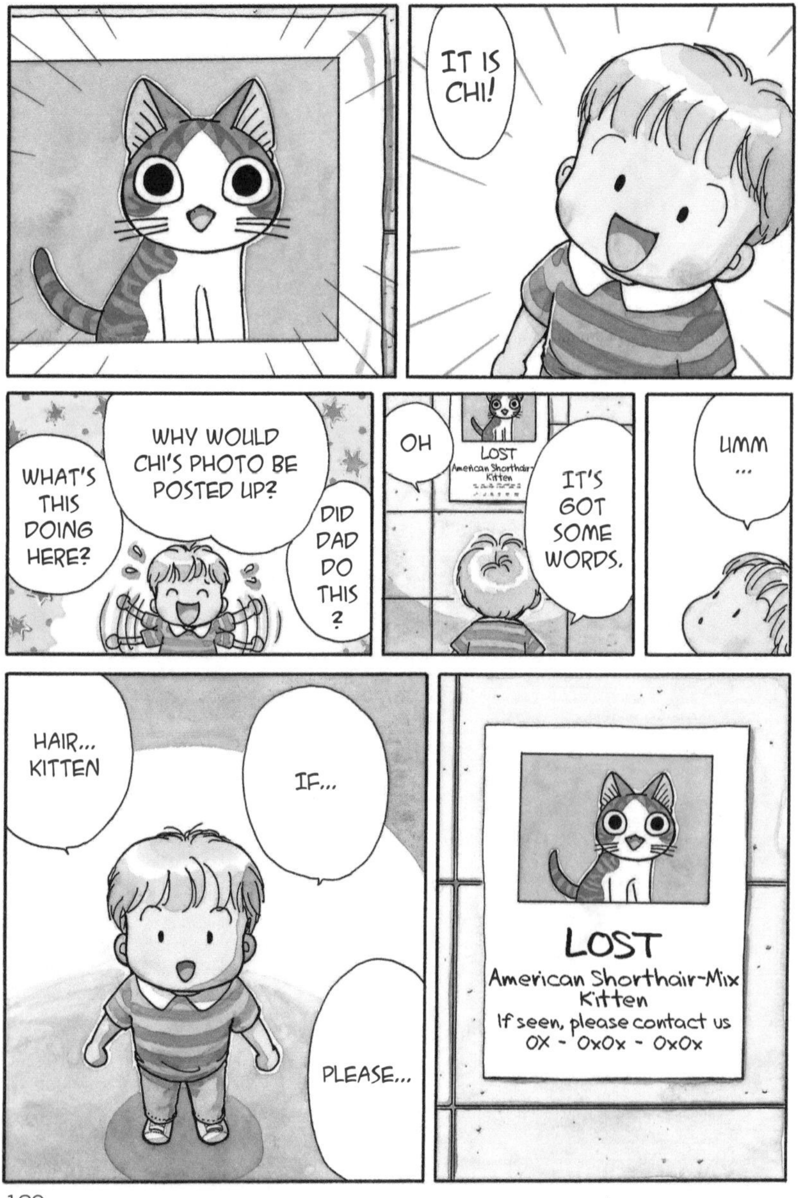
IT IS CHI!
WHAT'S THIS DOING HERE?
WHY WOULD CHI'S PHOTO BE POSTED UP?
DID DAD DO THIS?
OH
LOST
American Shorthair Kitten
IT'S GOT SOME WORDS.
UMM ...
HAIR... KITTEN
IF...
PLEASE...
LOST
American Shorthair-Mix Kitten
If seen, please contact us
OX - OxOx - OxOx

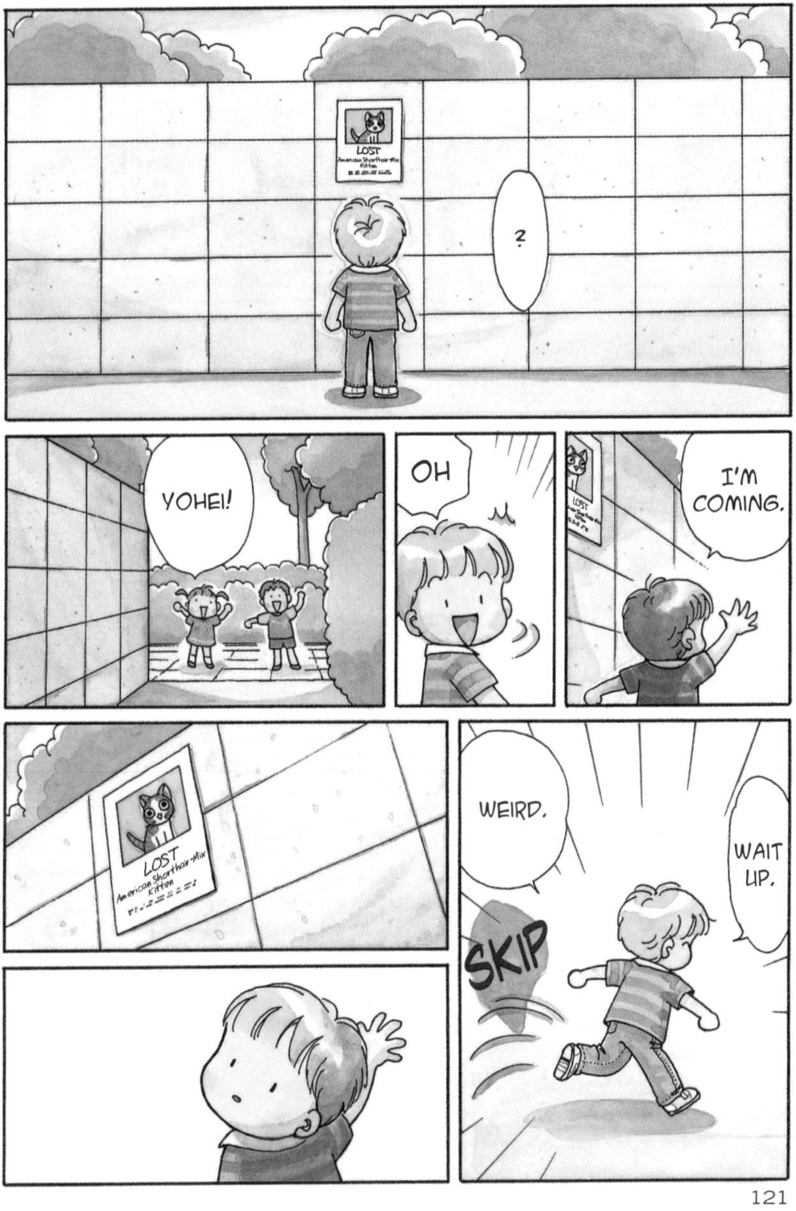
?
YOHEI!
OH
I'M COMING.
LOST
American Shorthair-Mix Kitten
WEIRD.
WAIT UP.
SKIP

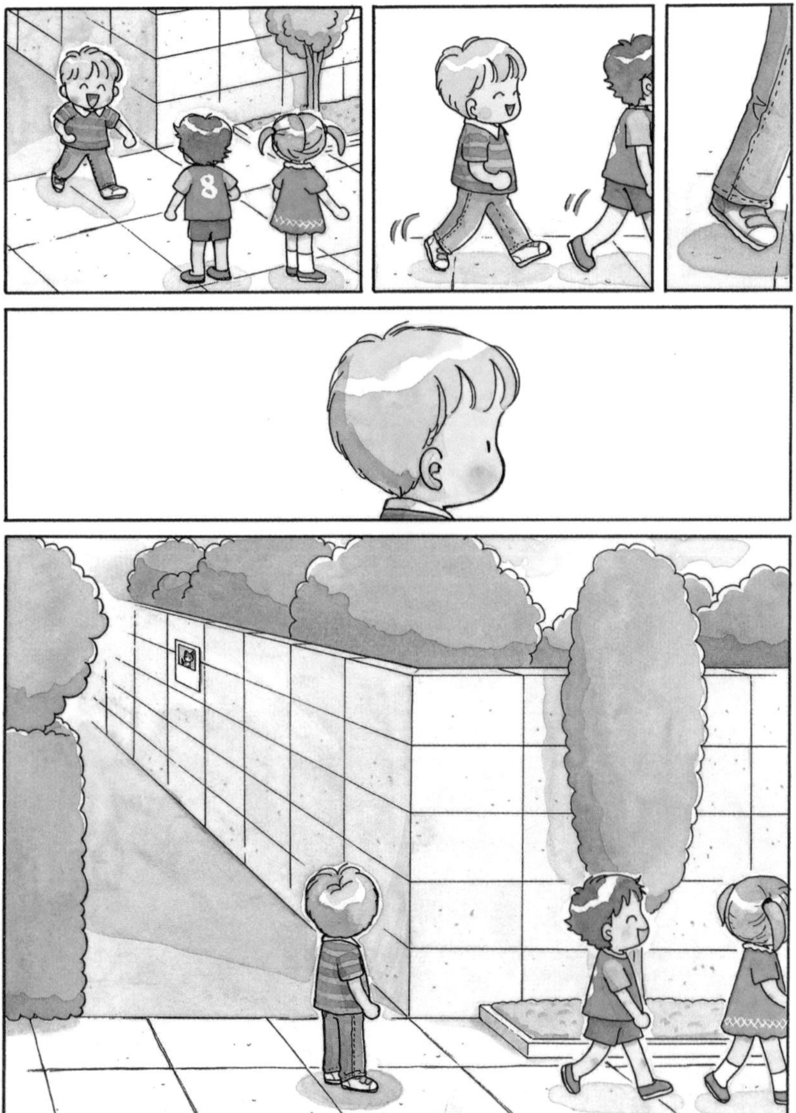
8

the end

homemade 198: a cat is rejected

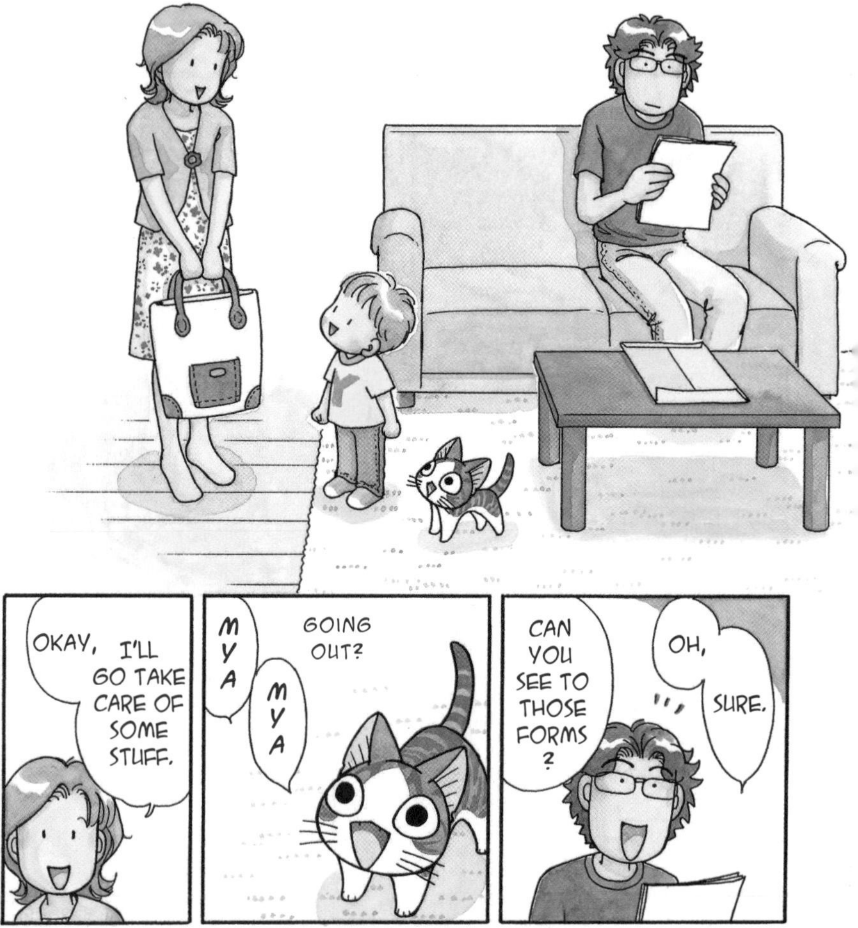
OKAY, I'LL GO TAKE CARE OF SOME STUFF.
MYA
GOING OUT?
MYA
CAN YOU SEE TO THOSE FORMS?
OH,
SURE.

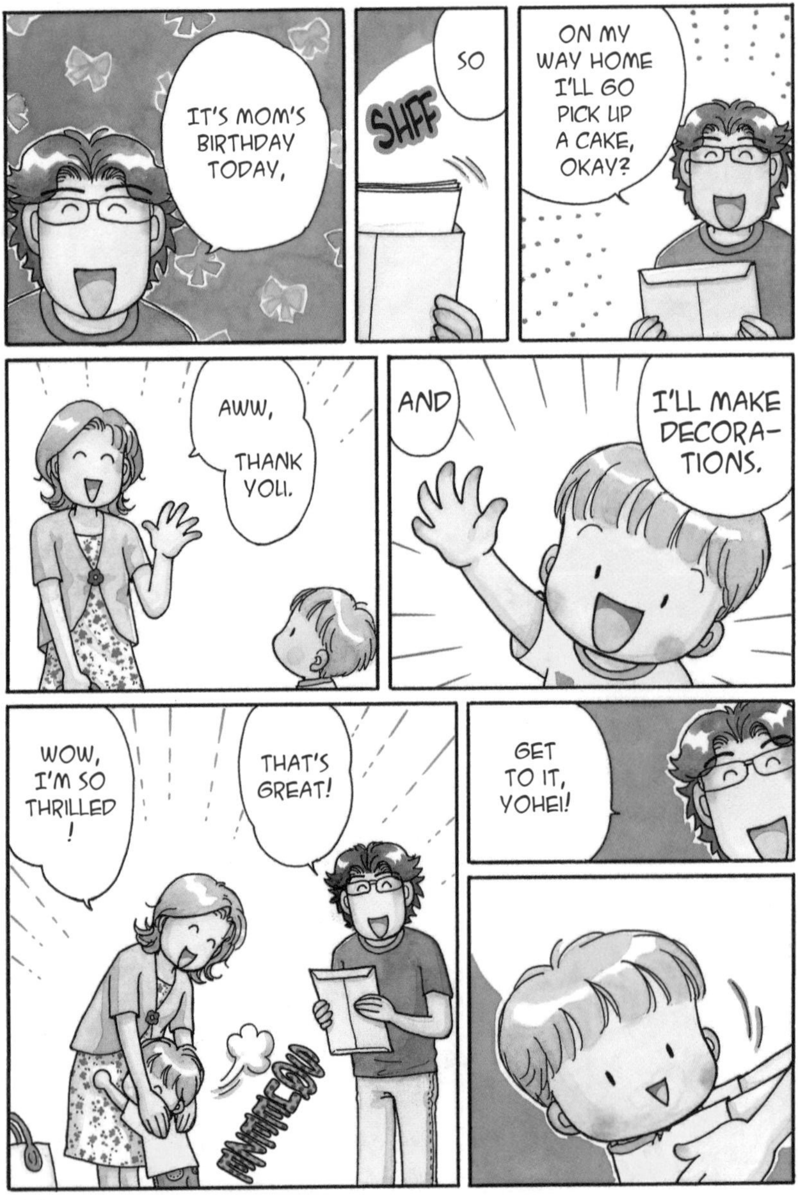
IT'S MOM'S BIRTHDAY TODAY,
SO
SHFF
ON MY WAY HOME I'LL GO PICK UP A CAKE, OKAY?
AWW,
THANK YOU.
AND
I'LL MAKE DECORA-TIONS.
WOW, I'M SO THRILLED!
THAT'S GREAT!
GET TO IT, YOHEI!

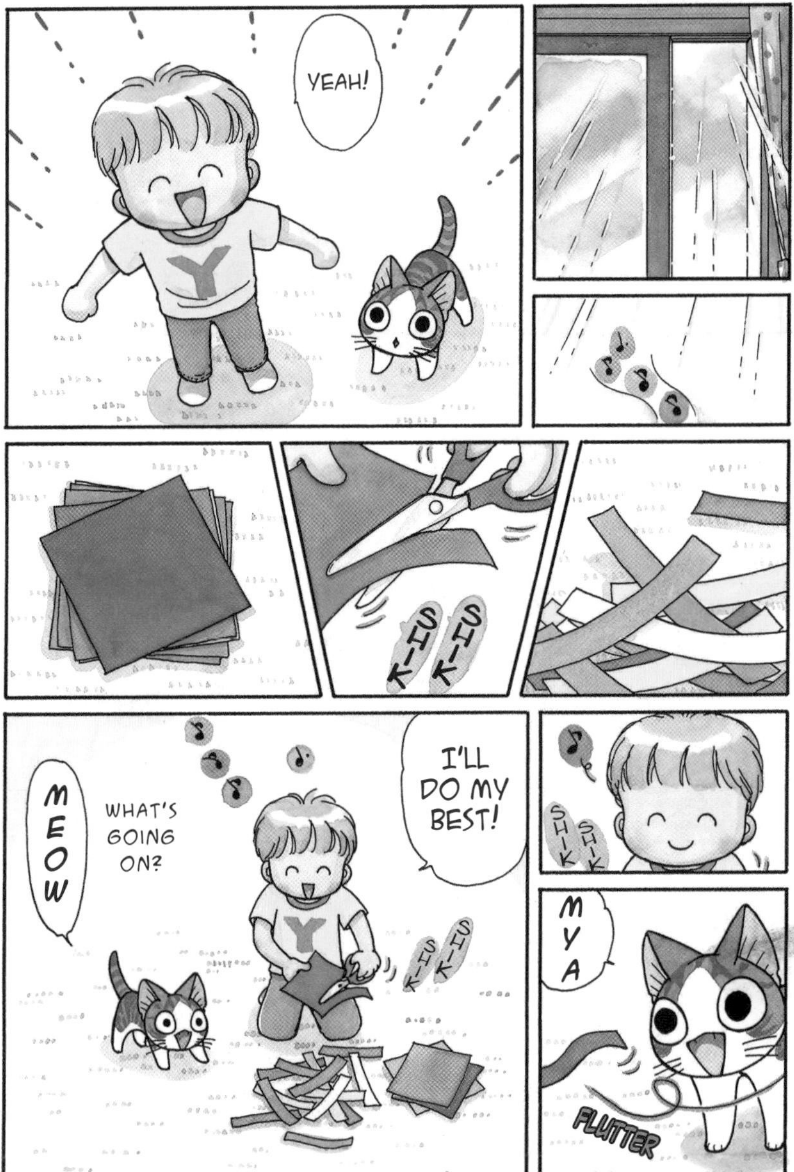
YEAH!
SHIK SHIK
MEOW
WHAT'S GOING ON?
I'LL DO MY BEST!
SHIK SHIK
SHIK SHIK
MYA
FLUTTER

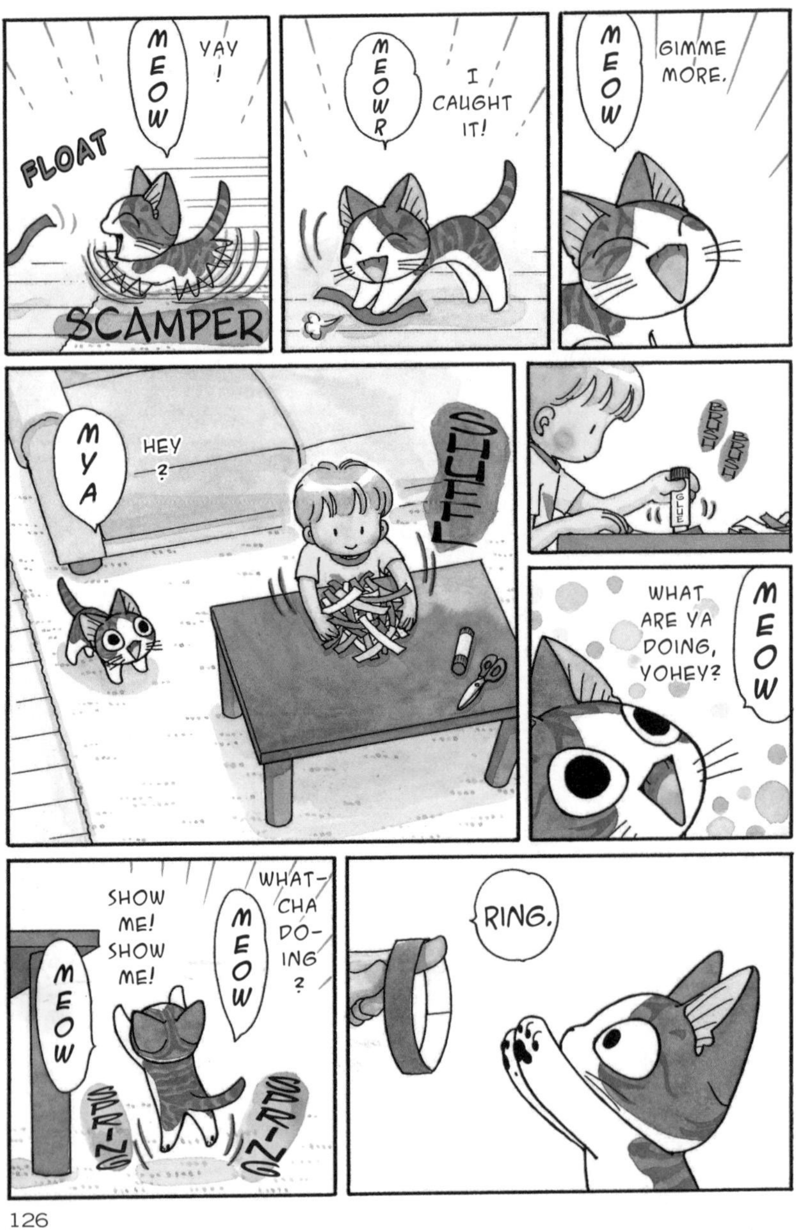
MEOW
YAY!
FLOAT
SCAMPER
MEOWR
I CAUGHT IT!
MEOW
GIMME MORE.
MYA
HEY?
SHUFFL
BRUSH
BRUSH
GLUE
WHAT ARE YA DOING, YOHEY?
MEOW
SHOW ME! SHOW ME!
MEOW
WHAT-CHA DO-ING?
MEOW
SPRING
SPRING
RING.

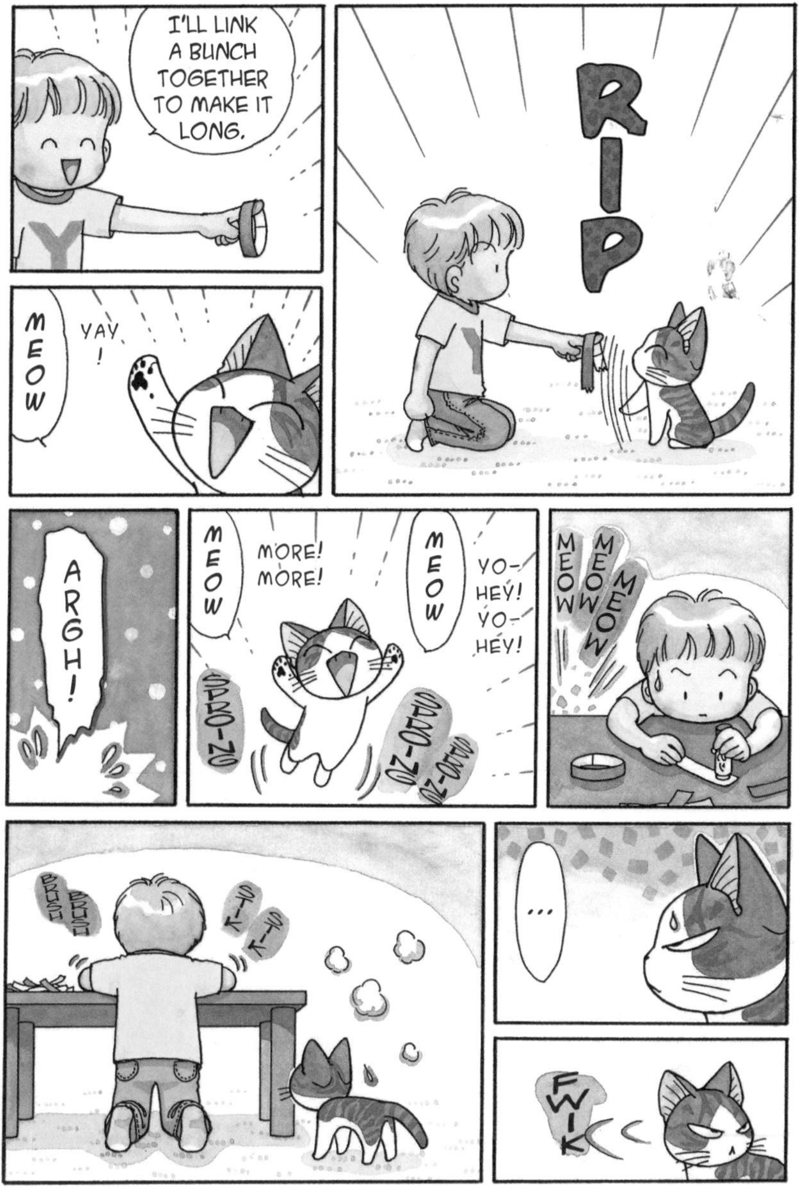
I'LL LINK A BUNCH TOGETHER TO MAKE IT LONG.
MEOW
YAY!
RIP
ARGH!
MEOW
MORE! MORE!
MEOW
YO-HEY! YO-HEY!
SPROING
SPRO-ING
SPRO-ING
MEOW
MEOW
MEOW
BRUSH
BRUSH
STIK
STIK
...
FWIK

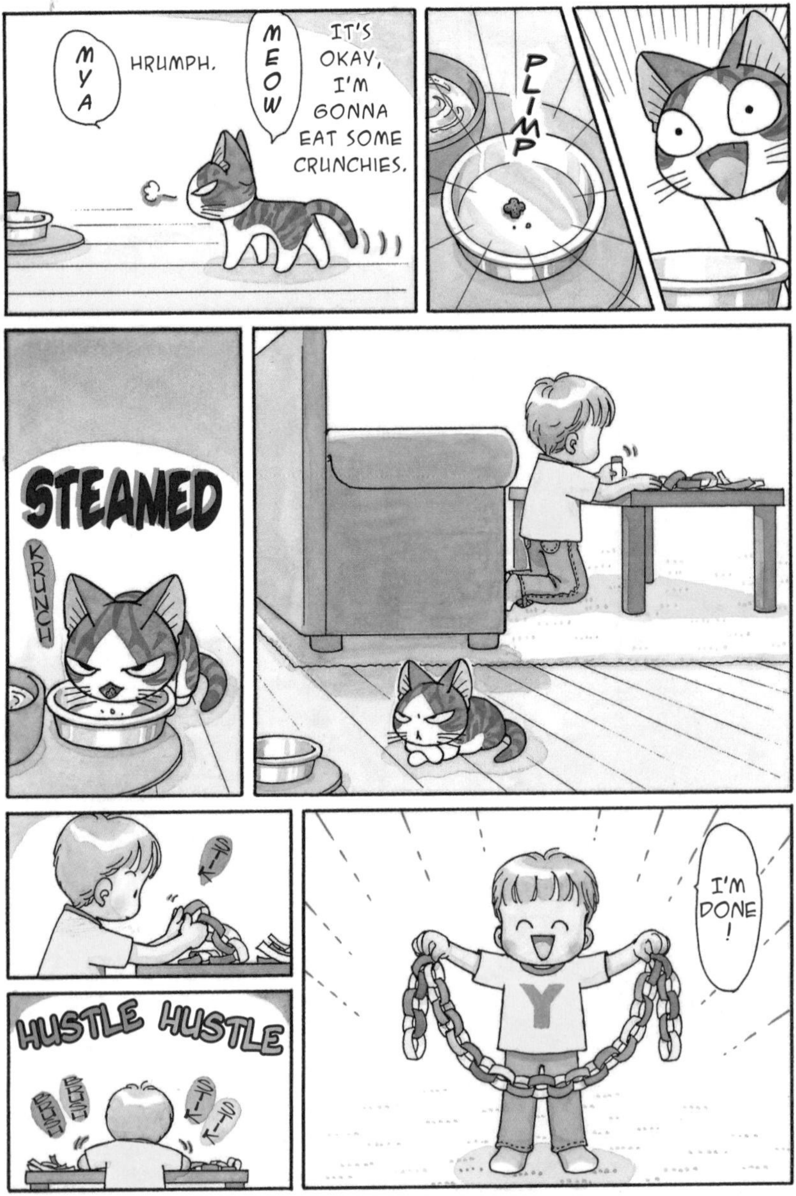
MYA
HRUMPH.
MEOW
IT'S OKAY, I'M GONNA EAT SOME CRUNCHIES.
PLIMP
STEAMED
KRUNCH
STI-K
HUSTLE HUSTLE
BRUSH
BRUSH
STI-K
STI-K
I'M DONE!

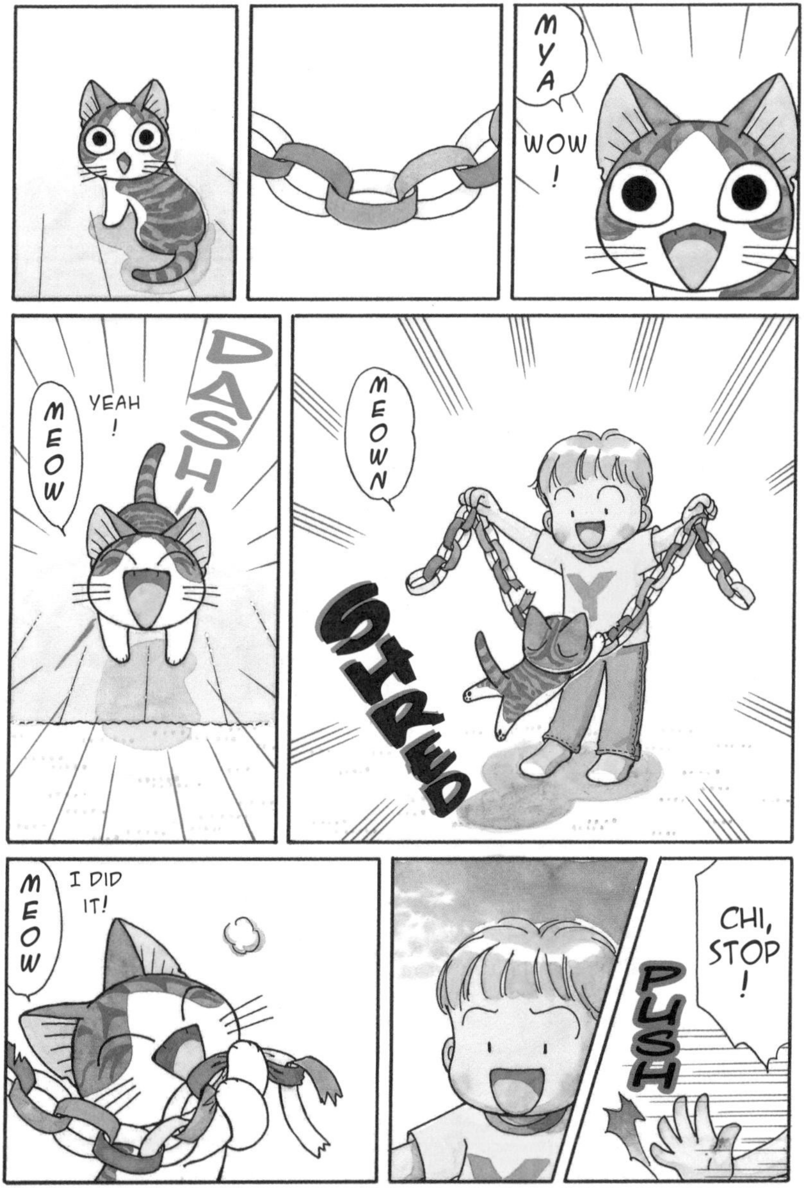
MYA
WOW!
MEOW
YEAH!
DASH
MEOWN
SHRED
MEOW
I DID IT!
PUSH
CHI, STOP!

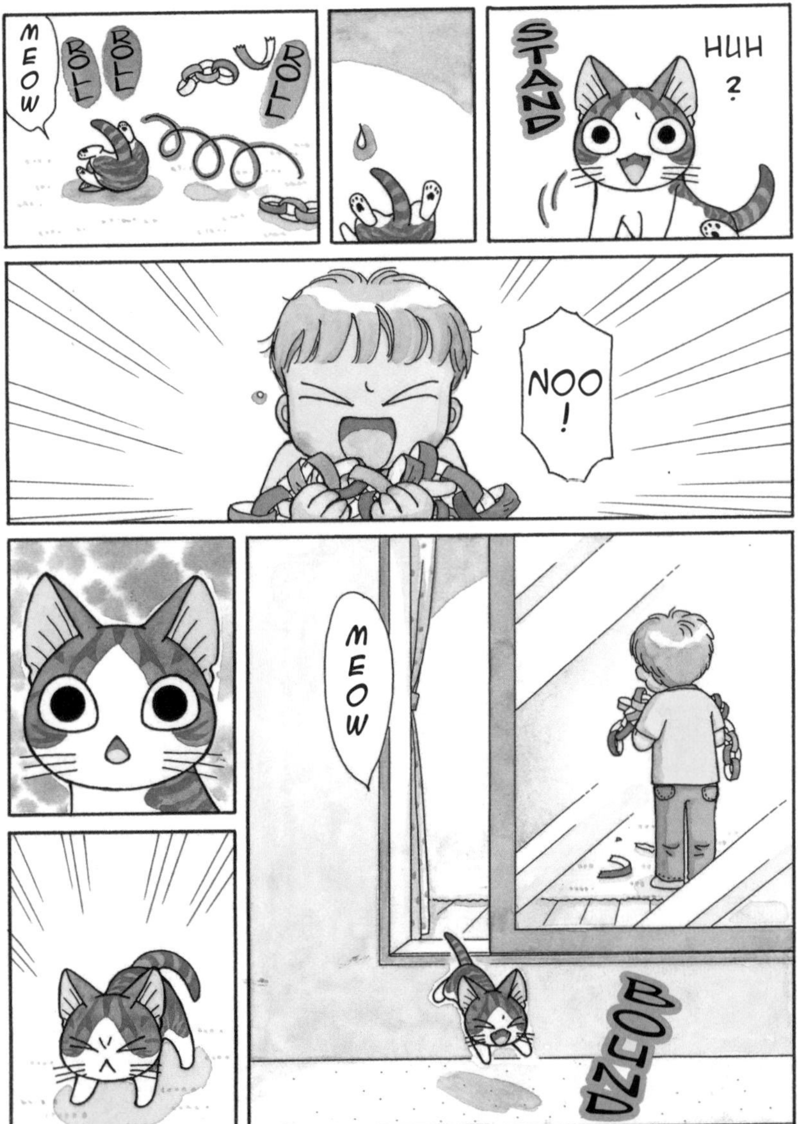
MEOW
ROLL
ROLL
ROLL
STAND
HUH?
NOO!
MEOW
BOUND

the end

homemade 199: a cat is irritable

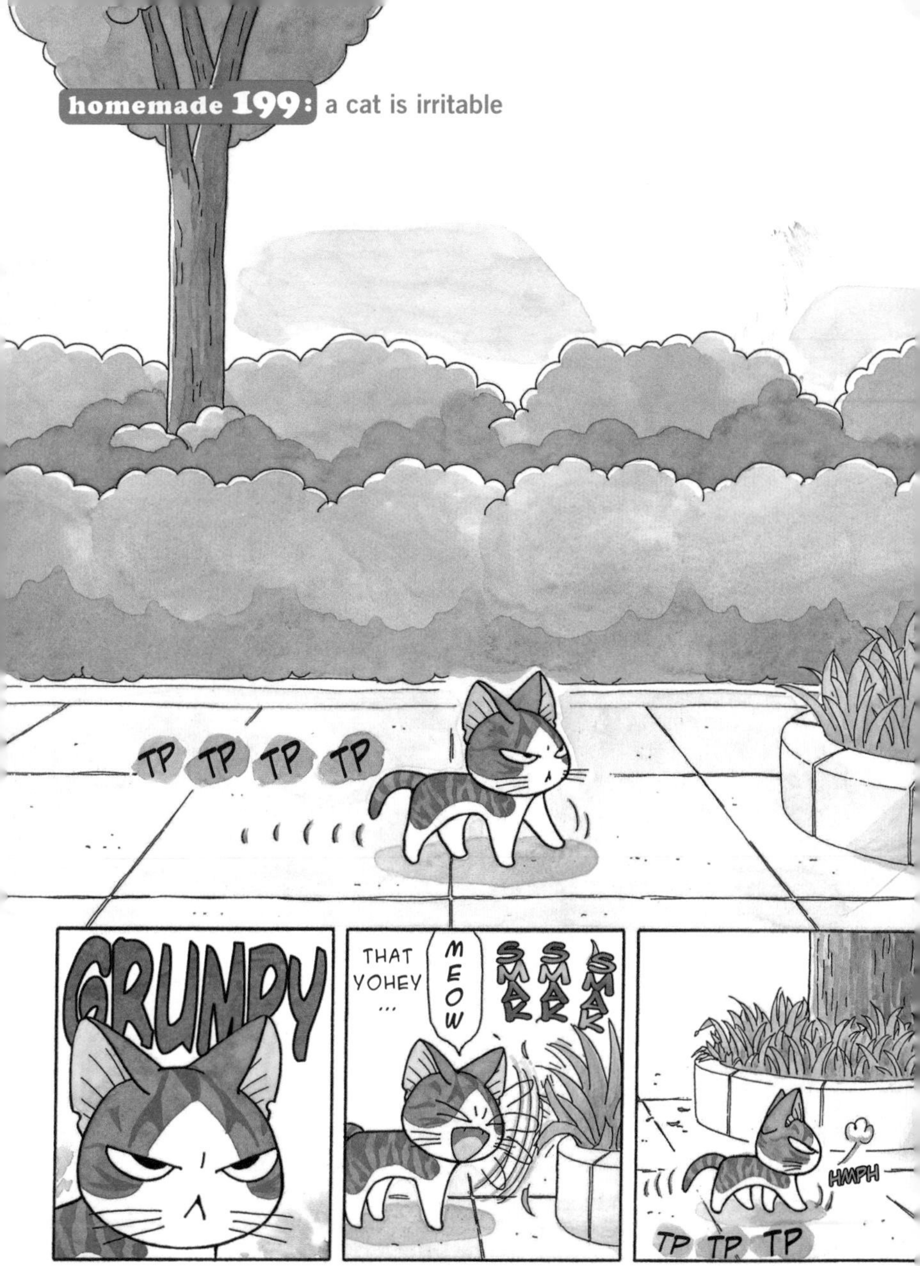
TP TP TP TP
GRUMPY
THAT YOHEY ...
MEOW
SMAK SMAK SMAK
HMPH
TP TP TP

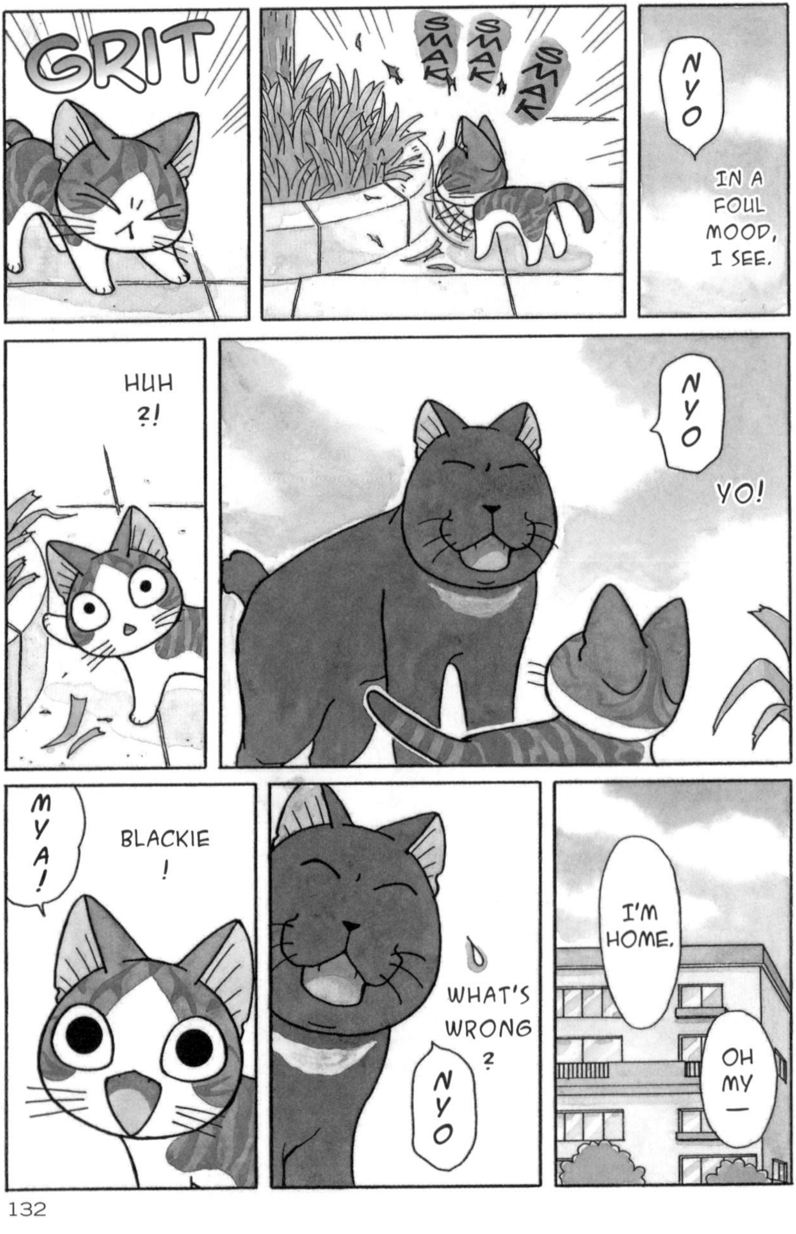
GRIT
SMAK SMAK SMAK
NYO
IN A FOUL MOOD, I SEE.
HUH ?!
NYO
YO!
MYA!
BLACKIE !
NYO
WHAT'S WRONG ?
I'M HOME.
OH MY —

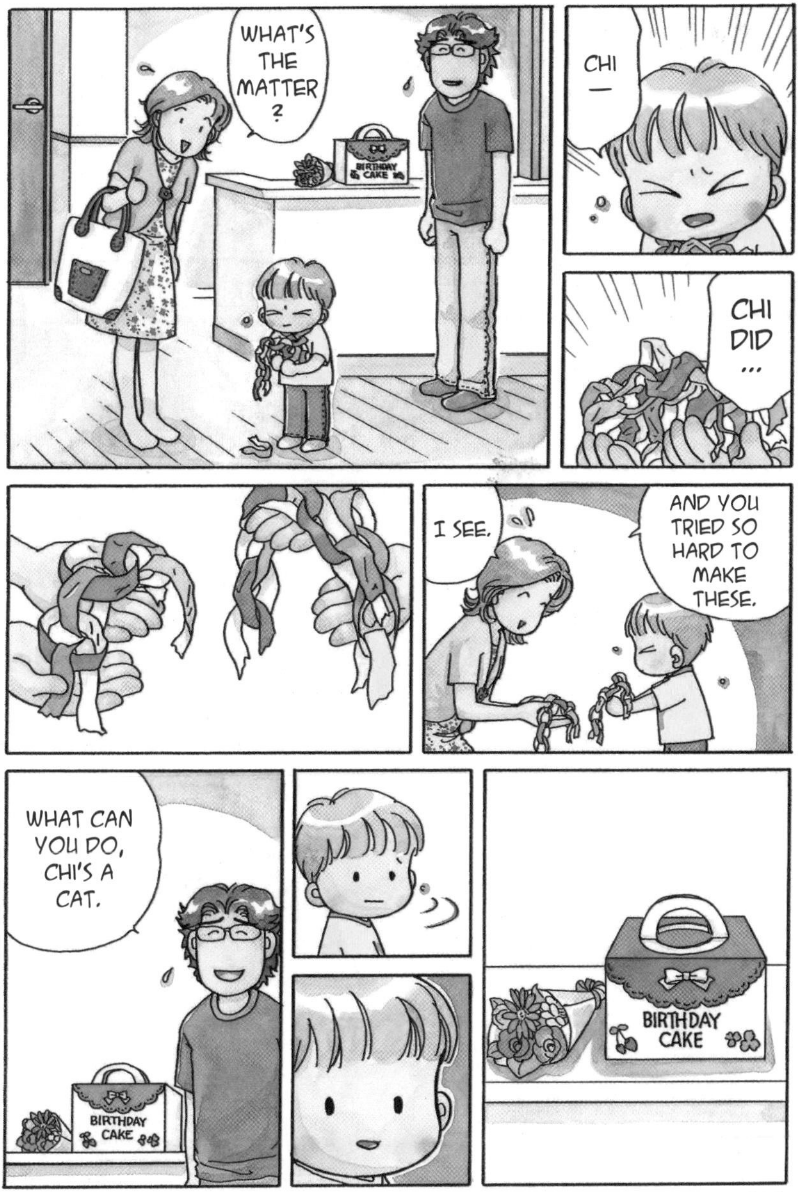
WHAT'S THE MATTER?
BIRTHDAY CAKE
CHI —
CHI DID ...
I SEE.
AND YOU TRIED SO HARD TO MAKE THESE.
WHAT CAN YOU DO, CHI'S A CAT.
BIRTHDAY CAKE
BIRTHDAY CAKE

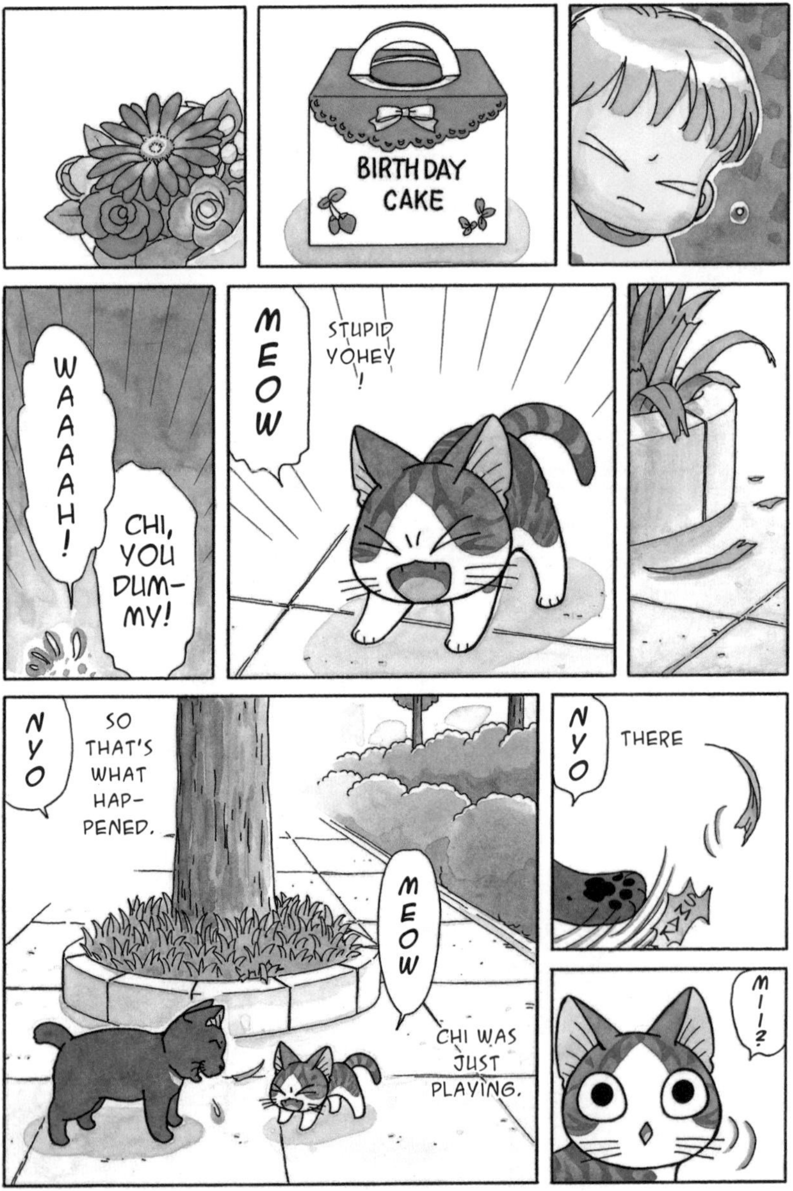
BIRTHDAY CAKE
WAAAAAAH!
CHI, YOU DUM-MY!
MEOW
STUPID YOHEY!
NYO
SO THAT'S WHAT HAP-PENED.
MEOW
CHI WAS JUST PLAYING.
NYO
THERE
MII?

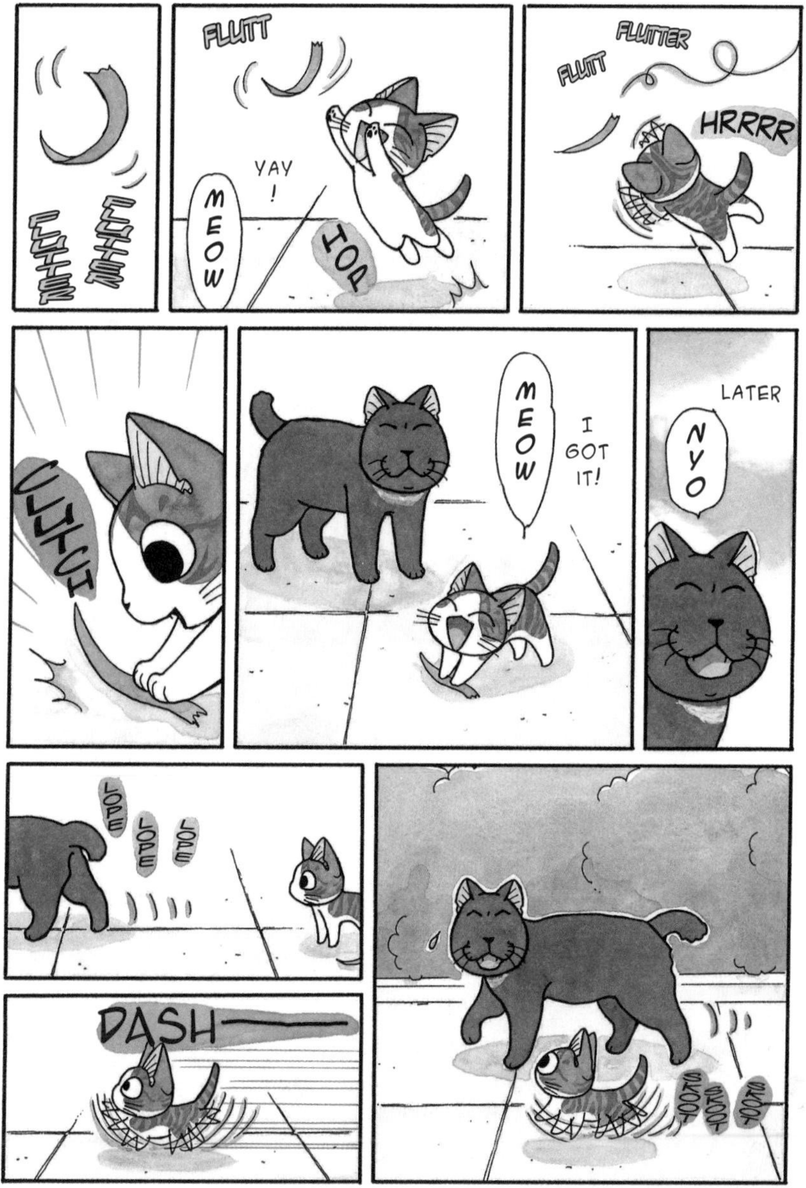
FLUTTER
FLUTTER
FLUTT
YAY!
MEOW
HOP
FLUTTER
FLUTT
HRRRR
CLUTCH
MEOW
I GOT IT!
LATER
NYO
LOPE
LOPE
LOPE
DASH
SKOOT
SKOOT
SKOOT

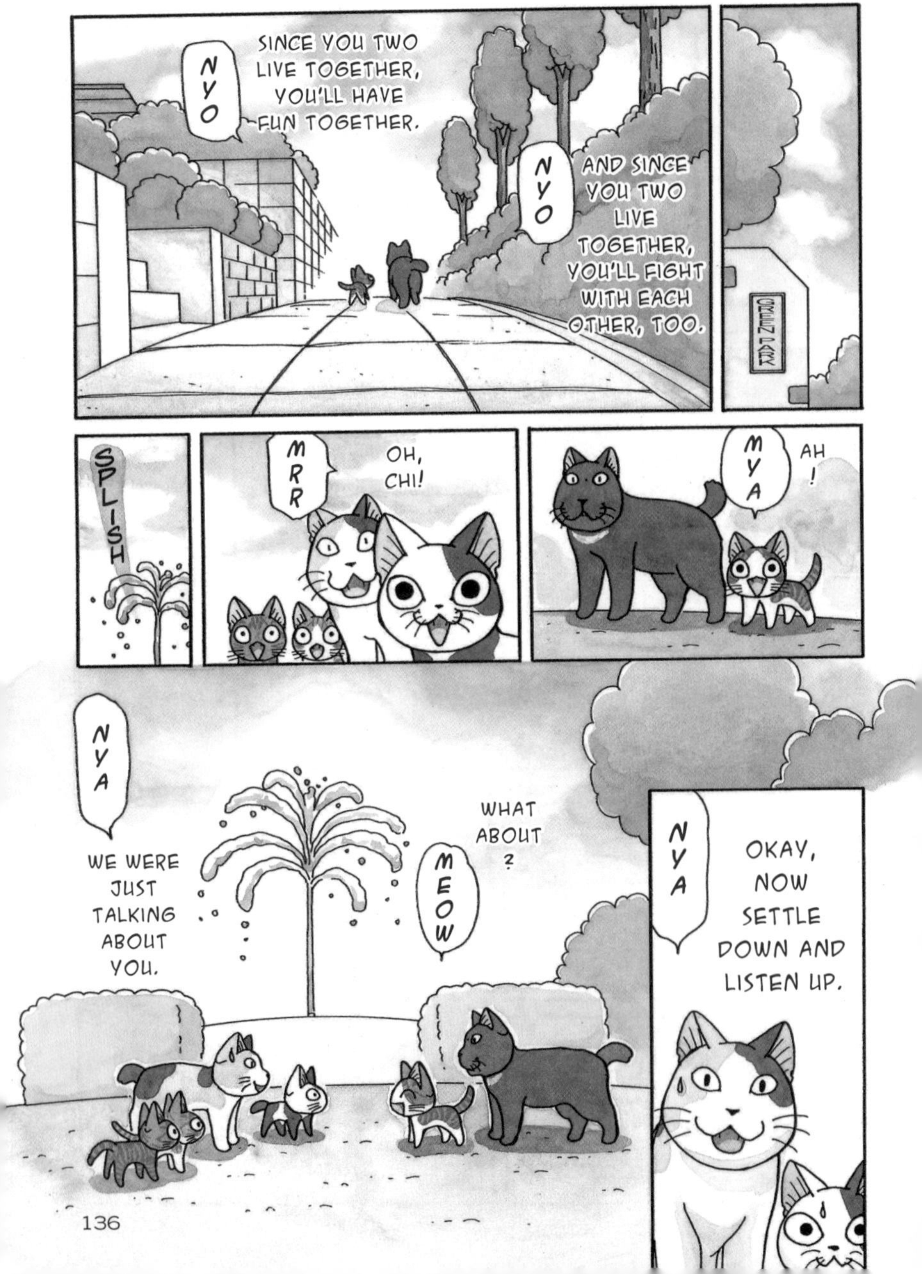
NYO
SINCE YOU TWO LIVE TOGETHER, YOU'LL HAVE FUN TOGETHER.
NYO
AND SINCE YOU TWO LIVE TOGETHER, YOU'LL FIGHT WITH EACH OTHER, TOO.
GREEN PARK
SPLISH
MRR
OH, CHI!
MYA
AH!
NYA
WE WERE JUST TALKING ABOUT YOU.
MEOW
WHAT ABOUT ?
NYA
OKAY, NOW SETTLE DOWN AND LISTEN UP.

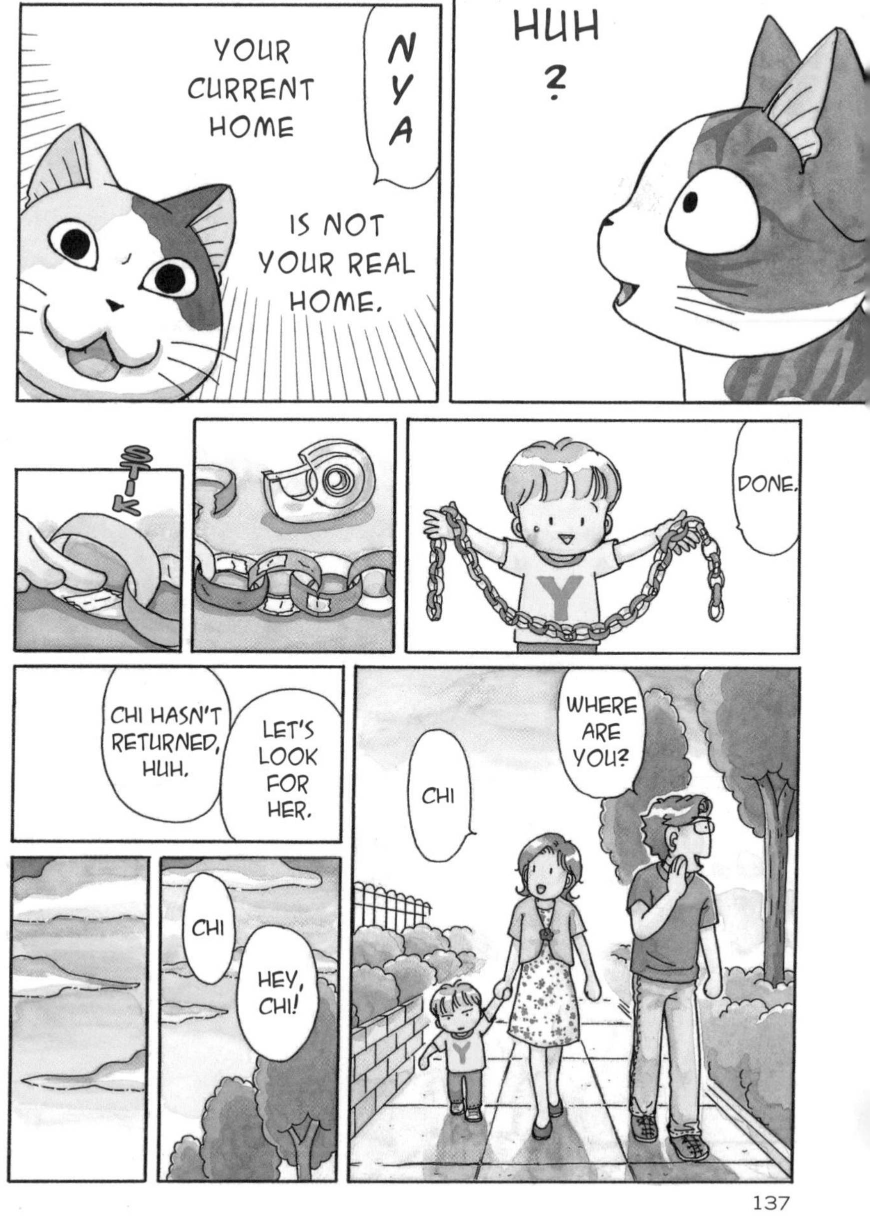
YOUR CURRENT HOME
NYA
IS NOT YOUR REAL HOME.
HUH ?
STIK
DONE.
CHI HASN'T RETURNED, HUH.
LET'S LOOK FOR HER.
CHI
HEY, CHI!
CHI
WHERE ARE YOU?

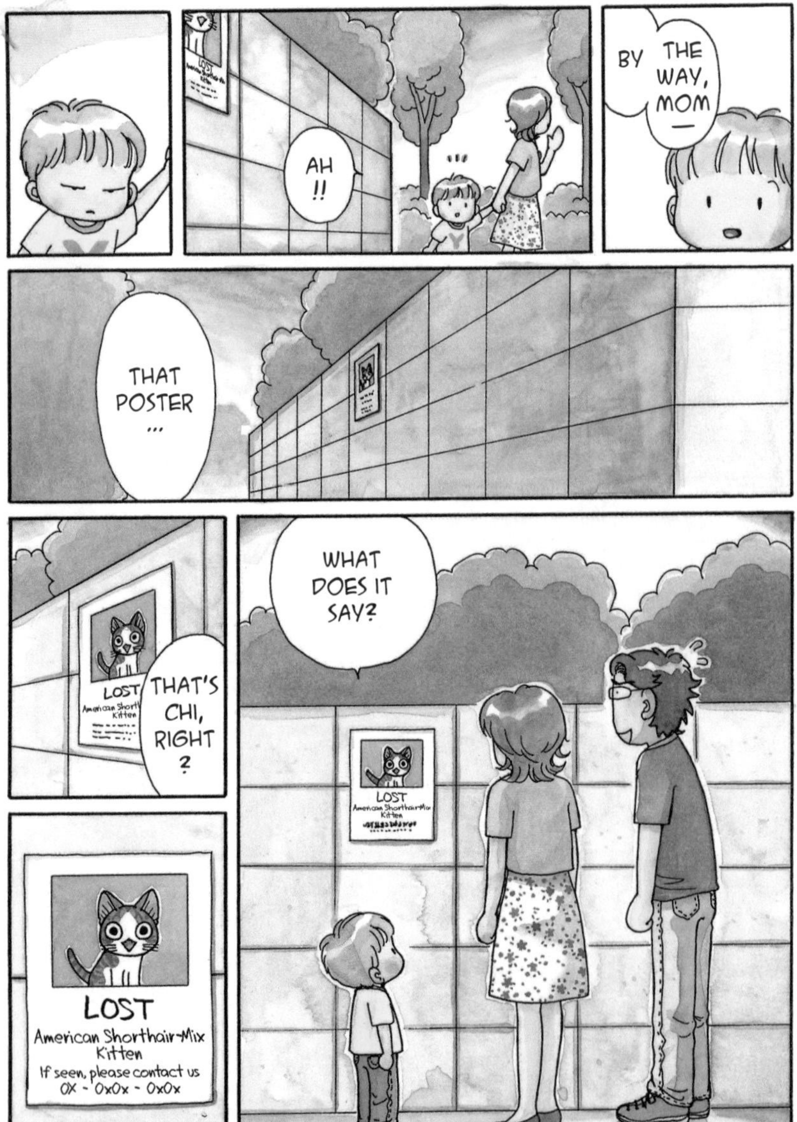
AH !!
BY THE WAY, MOM —
THAT POSTER ...
LOST
THAT'S CHI, RIGHT ?
LOST
American Shorthair-Mix Kitten
If seen, please contact us
0X - 0x0x - 0x0x
WHAT DOES IT SAY?
LOST
American Shorthair-Mix Kitten

the end

homemade 200: a cat has a chance meeting

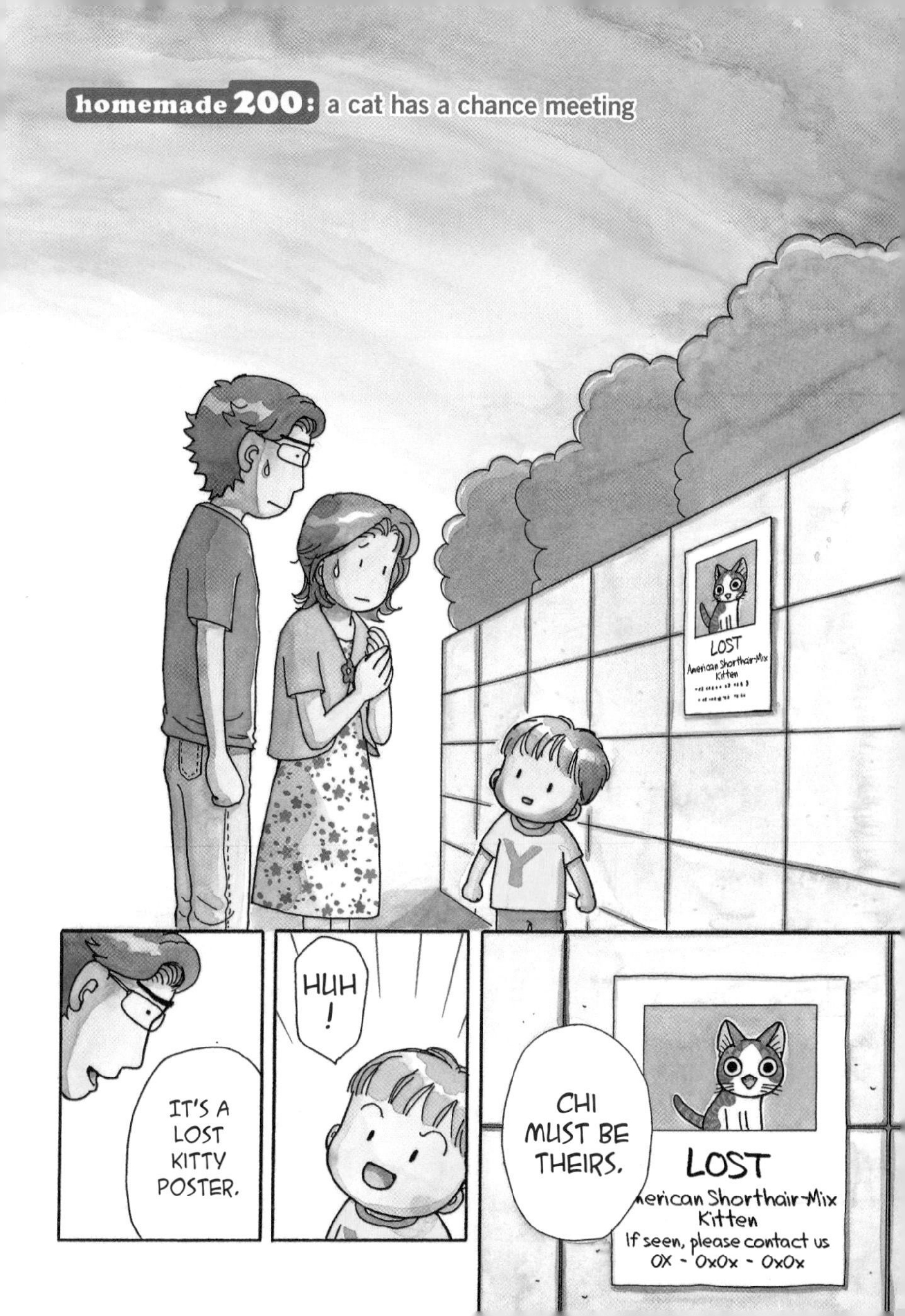
LOST
American Shorthair-Mix Kitten
IT'S A LOST KITTY POSTER.
HUH!
CHI MUST BE THEIRS.
LOST
merican Shorthair-Mix Kitten
If seen, please contact us
OX - OxOx - OxOx

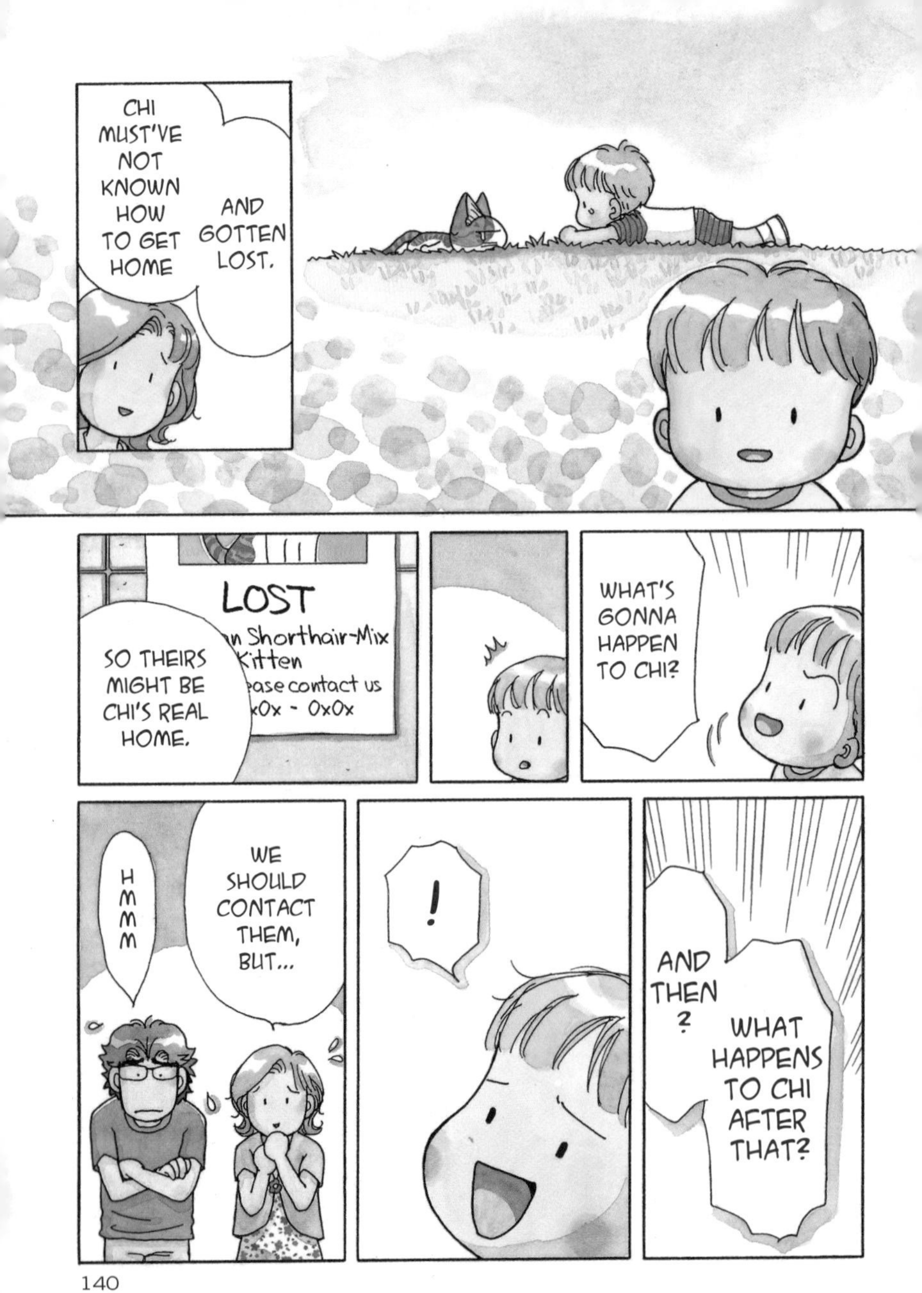
CHI MUST'VE NOT KNOWN HOW TO GET HOME
AND GOTTEN LOST.
LOST
Shorthair-Mix
Kitten
contact us
SO THEIRS MIGHT BE CHI'S REAL HOME.
WHAT'S GONNA HAPPEN TO CHI?
HMMM
WE SHOULD CONTACT THEM, BUT...
!
AND THEN?
WHAT HAPPENS TO CHI AFTER THAT?

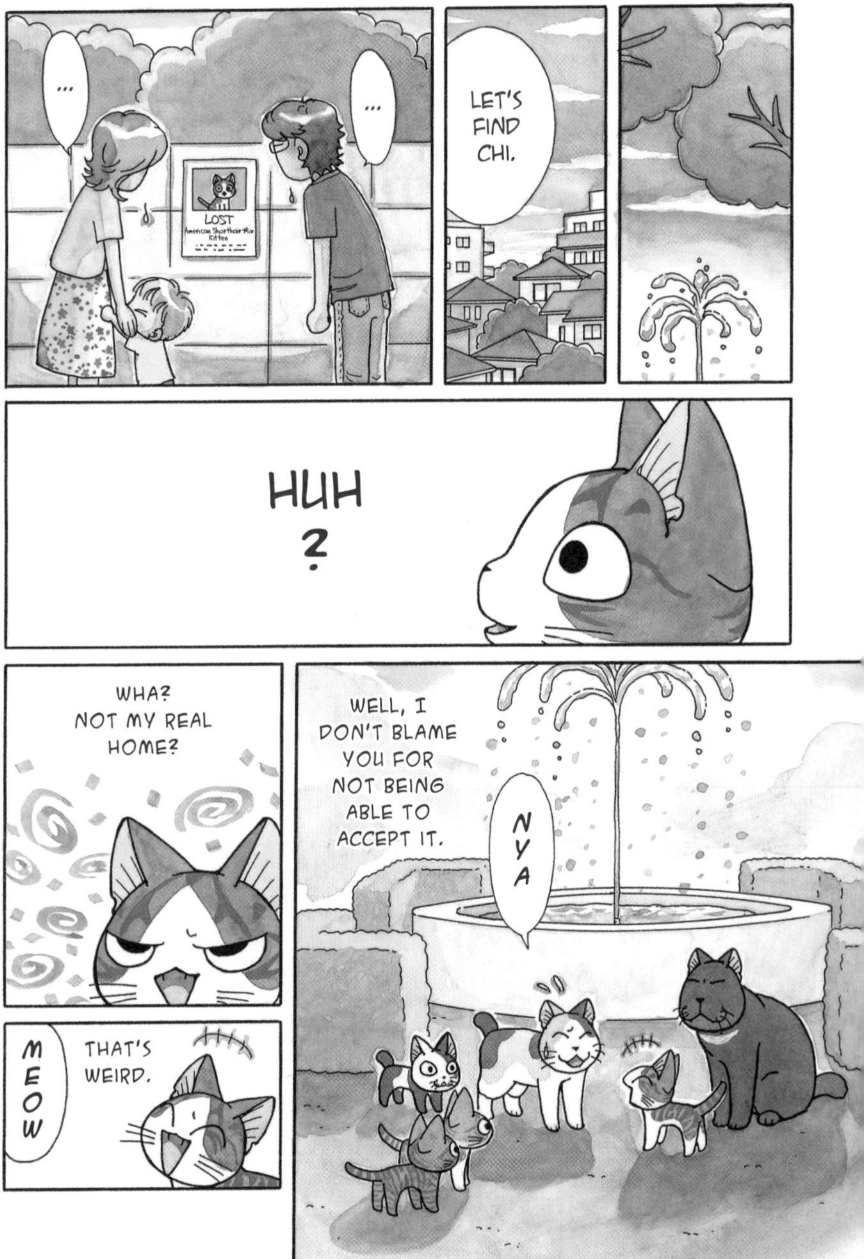
...
LOST
American Shorthair Mix Kitten
...
LET'S FIND CHI.
HUH?
WHA? NOT MY REAL HOME?
MEOW
THAT'S WEIRD.
WELL, I DON'T BLAME YOU FOR NOT BEING ABLE TO ACCEPT IT.
NYA

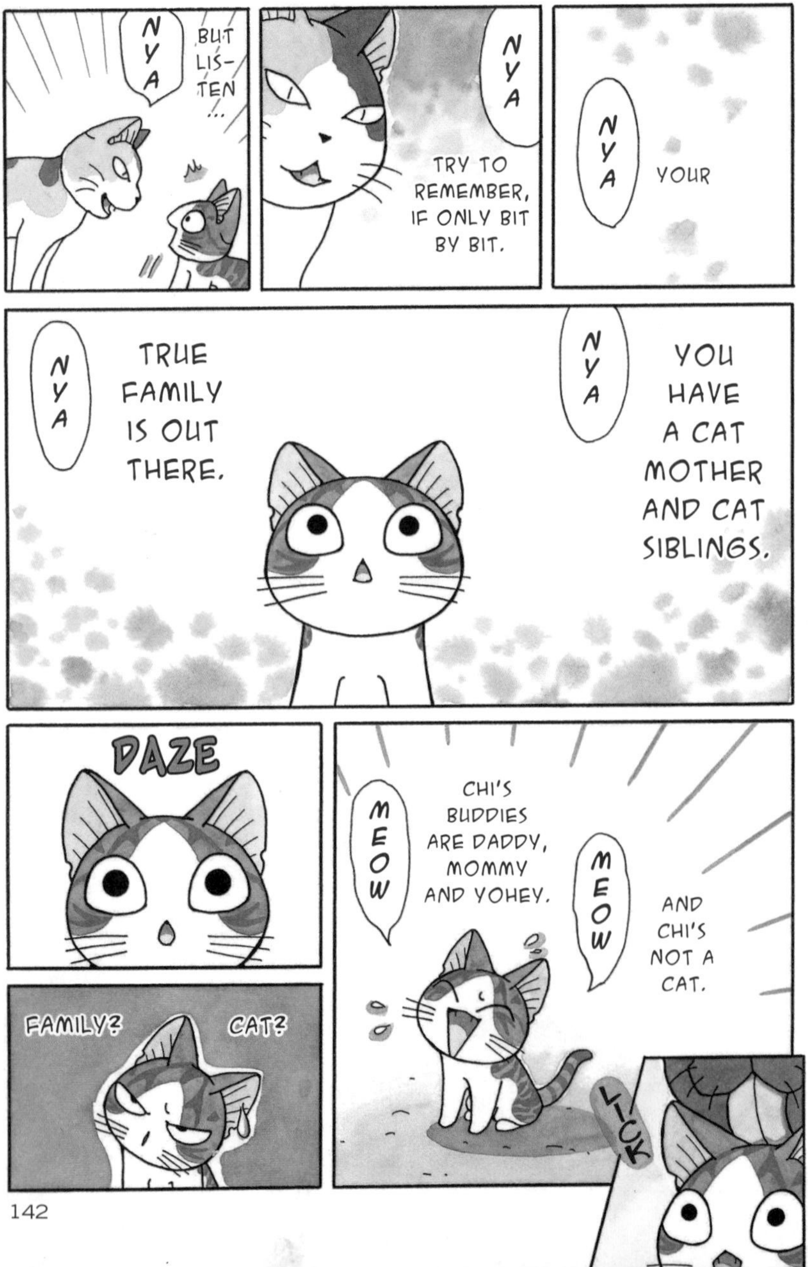
NYA
BUT LIS-TEN ...
NYA
TRY TO REMEMBER, IF ONLY BIT BY BIT.
NYA
YOUR
NYA
TRUE FAMILY IS OUT THERE.
NYA
YOU HAVE A CAT MOTHER AND CAT SIBLINGS.
DAZE
FAMILY?
CAT?
MEOW
CHI'S BUDDIES ARE DADDY, MOMMY AND YOHEY.
MEOW
AND CHI'S NOT A CAT.
LICK

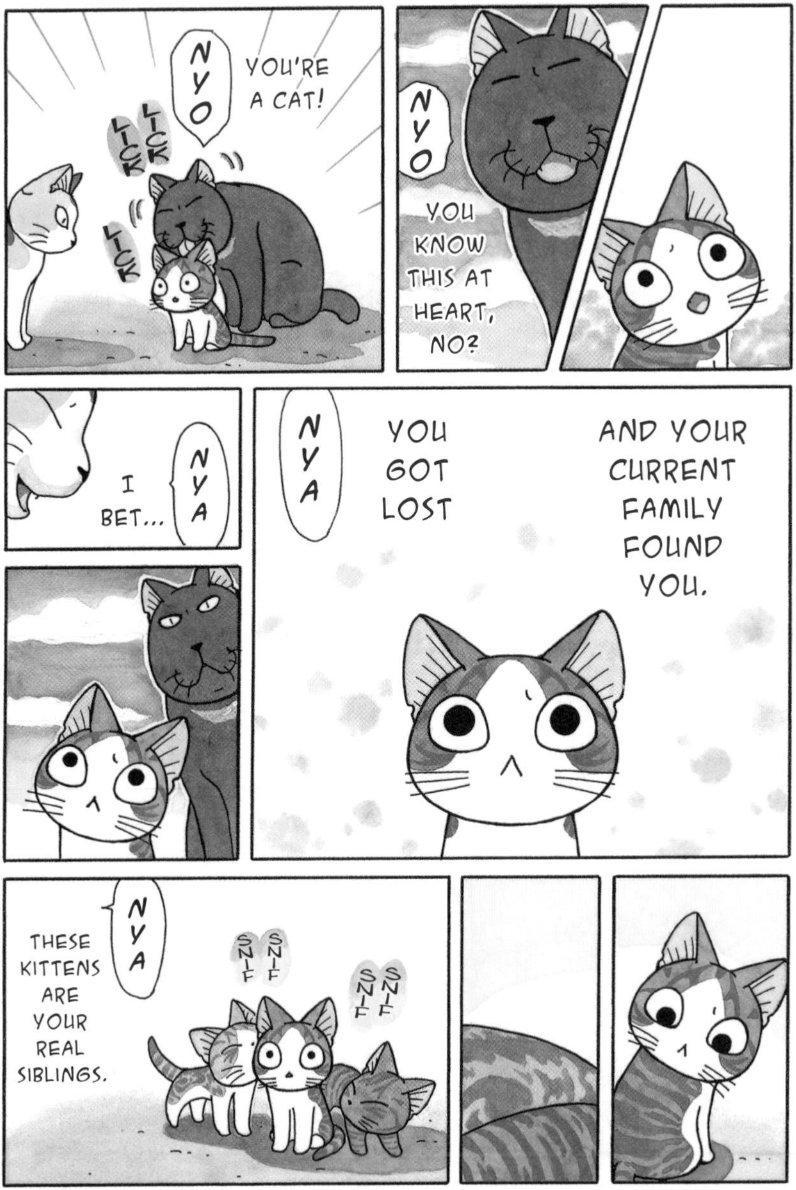
NYO
YOU'RE A CAT!
LICK LICK
LICK
NYO
YOU KNOW THIS AT HEART, NO?
I BET...
NYA
NYA
YOU GOT LOST
AND YOUR CURRENT FAMILY FOUND YOU.
NYA
THESE KITTENS ARE YOUR REAL SIBLINGS.
SNIF SNIF
SNIF SNIF

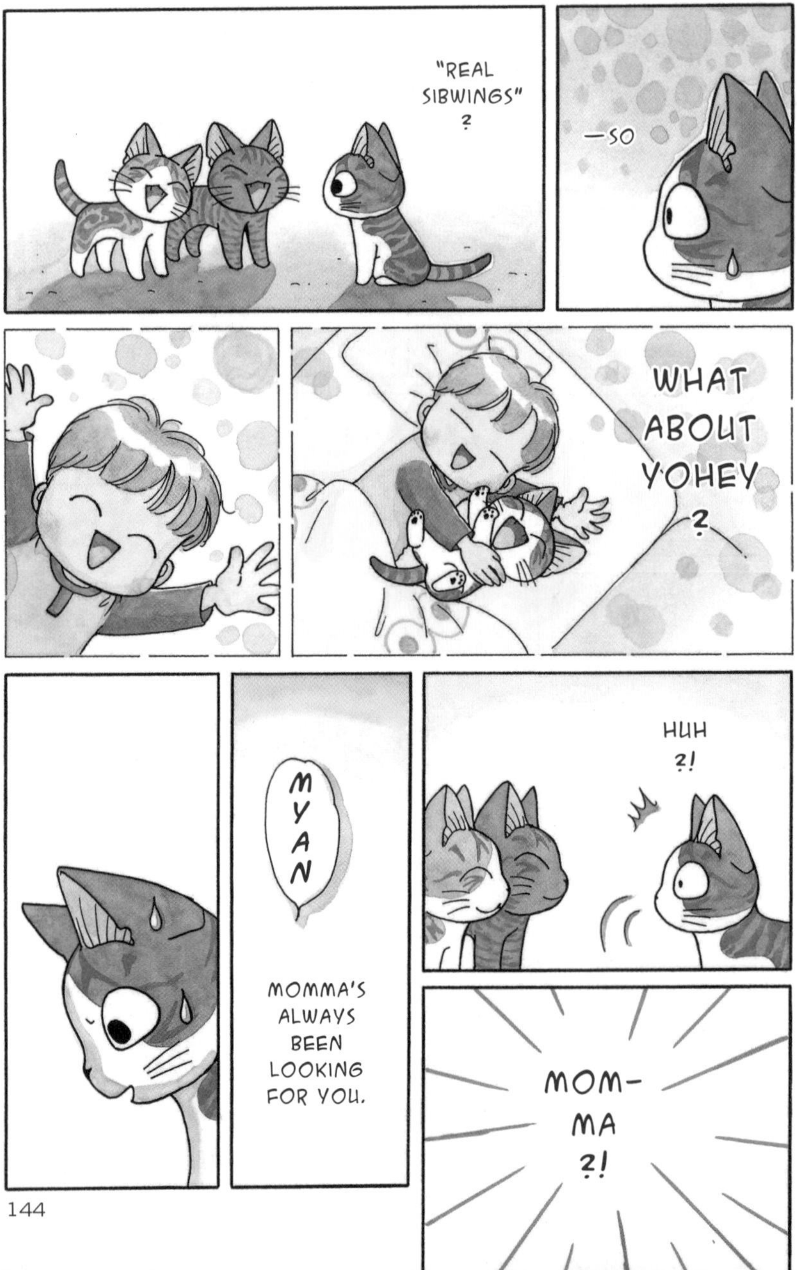
"REAL SIBWINGS" ?
—SO
WHAT ABOUT YOHEY ?
MYAN
MOMMA'S ALWAYS BEEN LOOKING FOR YOU.
HUH ?!
MOM-MA ?!

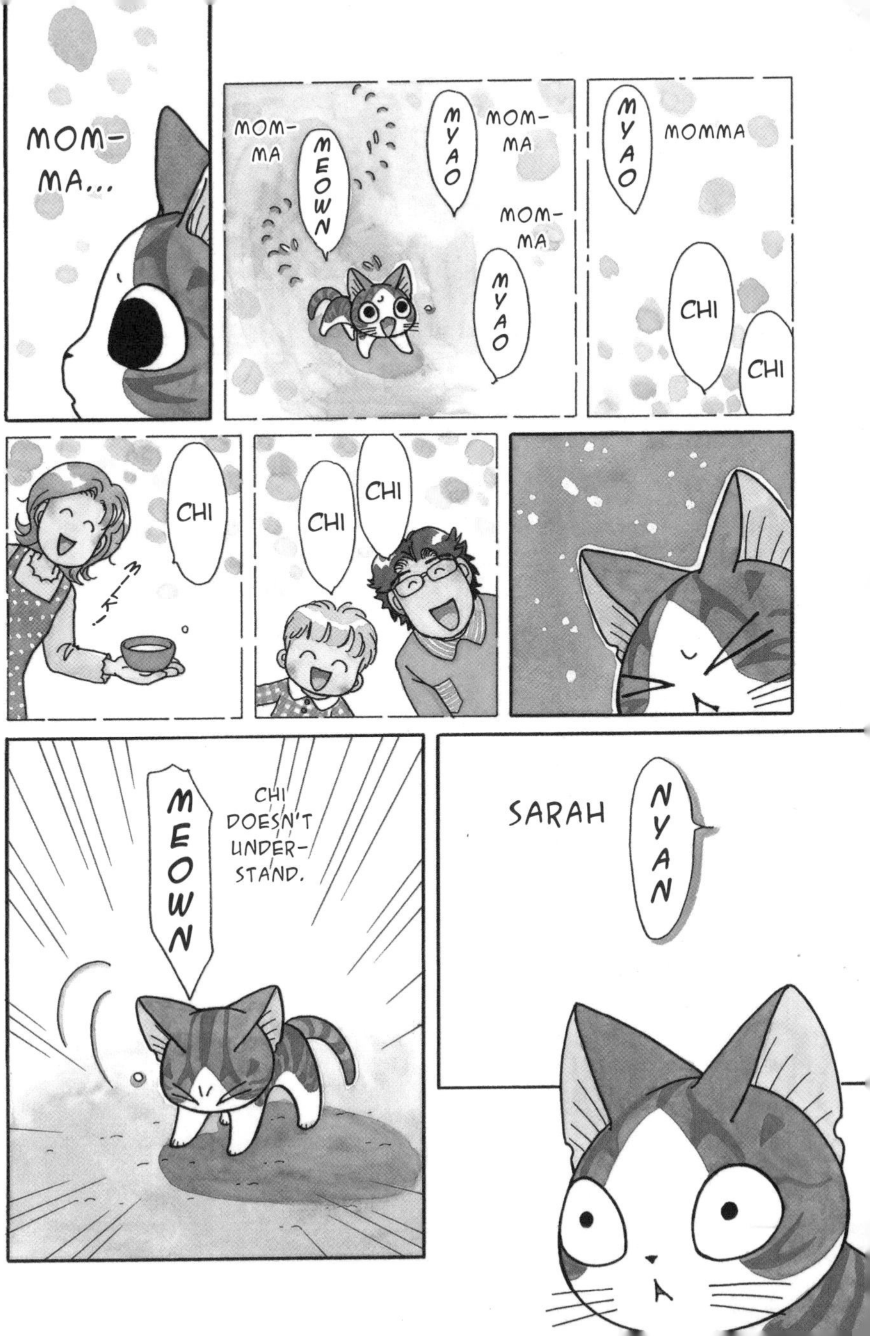
MOM-MA...
MOM-MA
MEOWN
MYAO
MOM-MA
MOM-MA
MYAO
MYAO
MOMMA
CHI
CHI
CHI
CHI
CHI
MEOWN
CHI DOESN'T UNDER-STAND.
SARAH
NYAN

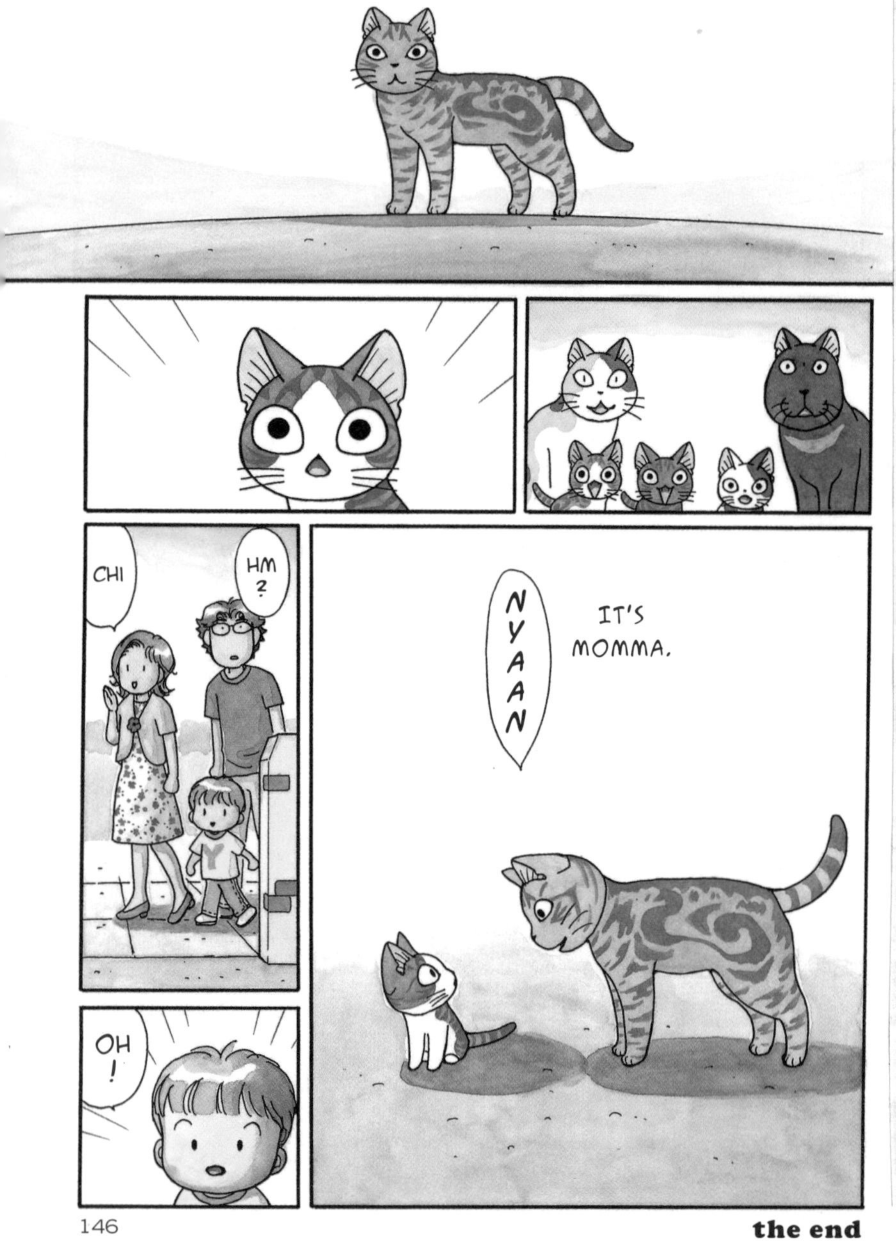
CHI
HM?
OH!
NYAAN
IT'S MOMMA.

the end

Chi's Sweet Home, volume 11

Translation - Ed Chavez
Production - Grace Lu
Hiroko Mizuno
Anthony Quintessenza

First published in Japan in 2014 by Kodansha, Ltd., Tokyo
Publication for this English edition arranged through Kodansha, Ltd., Tokyo
English language version produced by Vertical, Inc.

Translation provided by Vertical, Inc., 2014
Published by Vertical, Inc., New York

Originally published in Japanese as *Chiizu Suiito Houmu* by Kodansha, Ltd., 2012-2013
Chiizu Suiito Houmu first serialized in *Morning*, Kodansha, Ltd., 2004-

This is a work of fiction.

ISBN: 978-1-939130-51-8

Manufactured in the United States of America

First Edition

Vertical, Inc.
451 Park Avenue South, 7th Floor
New York, NY 10016
www.vertical-inc.com

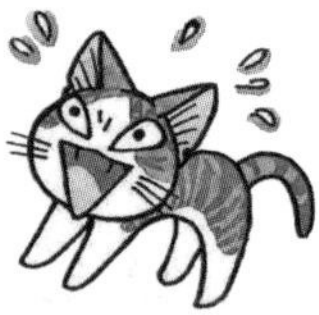

Special thanks to: K. Kitamoto

Chi finally meeting Momma,

who calls her "Sarah"...

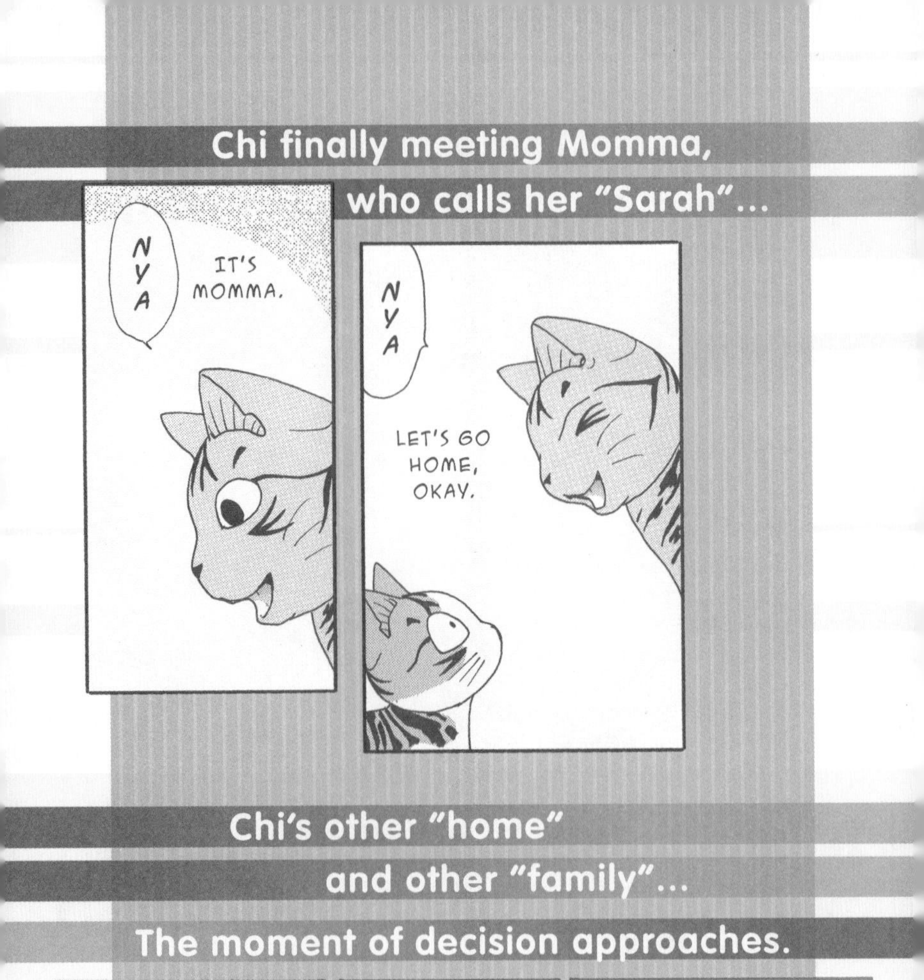
NYA
IT'S MOMMA.
NYA
LET'S GO HOME, OKAY.

Chi's other "home"

and other "family"...

The moment of decision approaches.

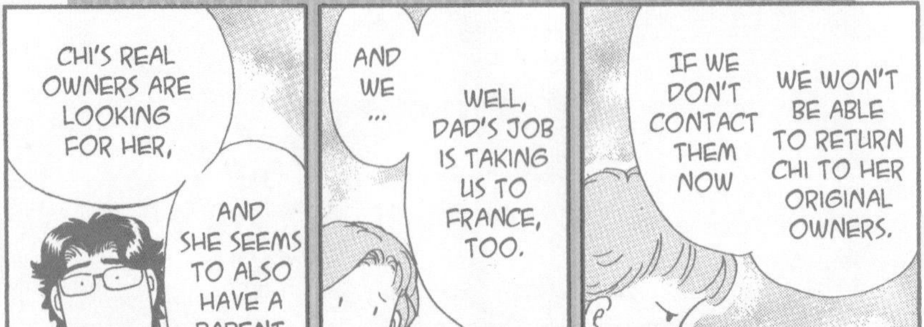
CHI'S REAL OWNERS ARE LOOKING FOR HER,
AND SHE SEEMS TO ALSO HAVE A PARENT.
AND WE ...
WELL, DAD'S JOB IS TAKING US TO FRANCE, TOO.
IF WE DON'T CONTACT THEM NOW
WE WON'T BE ABLE TO RETURN CHI TO HER ORIGINAL OWNERS.

Where can Chi feel at home?

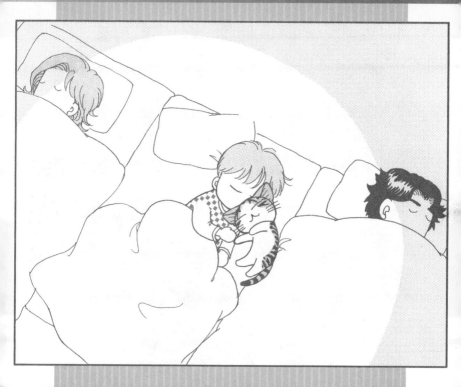

**Find out in Volume 12 of
Chi's Sweet Home on sale
SUMMER 2015!!**

Chi's Sweet Extras

Coasters: Cut out and prevent water rings!

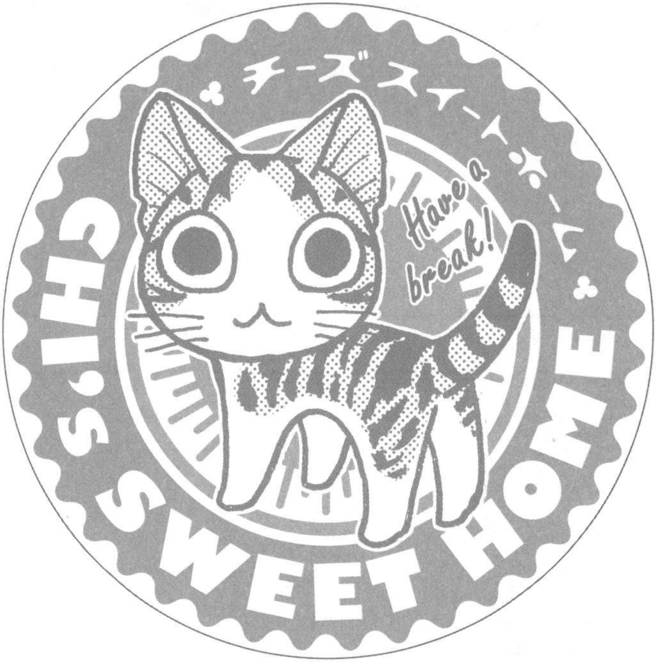

チーズスイートホーム
Have a break!
CHI'S SWEET HOME

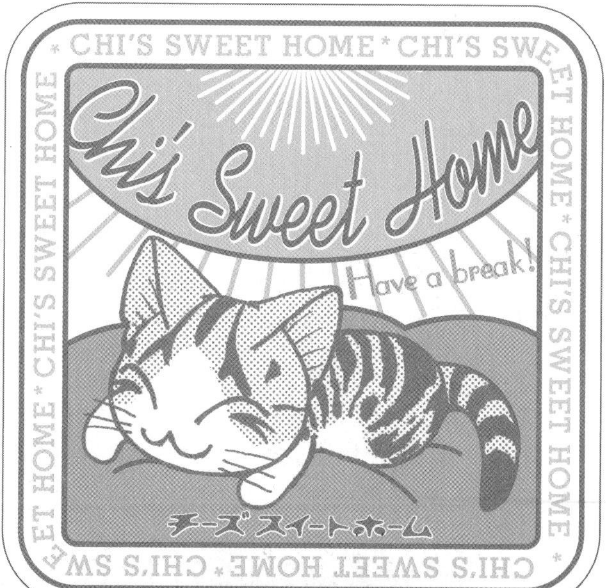

* CHI'S SWEET HOME * CHI'S SWEET HOME * CHI'S SWEET HOME * CHI'S SWEET HOME * CHI'S SWEET HOME * CHI'S SWEET HOME
Chi's Sweet Home
Have a break!
チーズスイートホーム